A VICTORIAN QUAKER

To ANN
Originally of York, England

I thank her for the original idea, for promoting the book's prosecution, and for much assistance. I thank her, too, for (at times) remarkable patience, in the face of hundreds of previously unknown Quaker relations and their and my thoughts.

FOR
Our family

Sarah Catherine Dilworth
Joanna Louise Peile
and
Jonathan Paul Dilworth

QUAKERS' ROOT, HOTHERSALL Near Longridge

This farm built by George Abbatt, was licenced on 18th July 1717, in George's name, for the holding of an 'Assembly of Quakers' i.e. Meetings for Workship – see page 9. The end of the building was a barn and the original house is behind the tree.

THE MARKET PLACE, PRESTON c.1814

The 'Legs of Man' is on the S. side of Fishergate behind the coach. The 'Old Shambles' was the street down which the coach is approaching and Robert Abbatt the Elder's new shop was on the left opposite Hamiltons – see page 9.

A VICTORIAN QUAKER COURTSHIP

Lancashire Love Letters
of the 1850s

John Dilworth Abbatt

William Sessions Ltd., York, England
in association with
Friends United Press, Richmond, Indiana, USA

Copyright John D. Abbatt
Victoria
British Columbia, Canada V8R 3L6

© 1988

ISBN 1 85072 043 6

Library of Congress Cataloging-in-Publication Data

Abbatt, Jonathan, b. 1832.
    A Victorian Quaker courtship: Lancashire love letters of the 1850s / edited by John Dilworth Abbatt.
        p. cm.
    Contains 166 letters exchanged between Jonathan Abbatt and Mary Dilworth between Jan. 1853 and June 1855.
    Bibliography: p.
    Includes index.
    ISBN 1-85072-043-6
    1. Abbatt, Jonathan, b. 1832—Correspondence. 2. Abbatt, Mary, b. 1825—Correspondence. 3. Quakers—England—Correspondence. I. Abbat, John Dilworth. II. Abbatt, Mary, b. 1825. III. Title.
BX7791.A35   1989
942.7'6081'0922—dc19
[B]
                                            89–1376
                                              CIP

Produced from text generated
by the Author in British Columbia.
Books lithographed and bound by
William Sessions Limited
The Ebor Press, York, England

CONTENTS

CONTENTS	v
ILLUSTRATIONS	vi
INTRODUCTION	viii
DATES - ONE HUNDRED YEARS	ix
THE ABBATTS OF ALSTON AND HOTHERSALL	x
THE DILWORTHS OF THORNLEY AND WYRESDALE	xii
JONATHAN ABBATT'S FIRST LETTER TO MARY DILWORTH	xiv
MARY DILWORTH'S FIRST LETTER TO JONATHAN ABBATT	xv
JONATHAN AND MARY ABBATT AGED 34 AND 35	xvi
Chapter I WHERE THEY CAME FROM - THE ABBATTS	1
Chapter II WHERE THEY CAME FROM - THE DILWORTHS	15
Chapter III GROWING UP AND ACKWORTH	29
Chapter IV THE APPROACH	48
Chapter V GETTING TO KNOW YOU	114
Chapter VI GLOVES AND BONNETS	185
Chapter VII MARRIAGE AND HEAVEN	241
EPILOGUE	266
APPENDICES	
i Jonathan Abbatt's Apprenticeship Indenture.	268
ii Pennsylvania Dilworths of Thornley, Lancashire.	270
iii Lancashire Origins of the United States Waln Family.	273
iv The Jacksons of Wyresdale.	274
v The Life of Timothy Cragg.	277
vi Lord Derby and the Quaker.	282
Bibliography	283
Index	284
MAP - After Index	292

ILLUSTRATIONS

QUAKERS' ROOT, HOTHERSALL.	ii
THE MARKET PLACE, PRESTON c. 1814.	ii
PENDLE HILL - As seen from Quaker's Root.	vii
JONATHAN ABBATT'S first letter to MARY DILWORTH.	xiv
MARY DILWORTH'S first letter to JONATHAN ABBATT.	xv
JONATHAN and MARY ABBATT AGED 34 and 35.	xvi
WYRESDALE MEETING HOUSE AND CHAPEL HOUSE.	10
BURIAL GROUND BEHIND WYRESDALE MEETING HOUSE.	10
ROWTON BROOK FARM.	26
LOW PLEASANT FARM, QUERNMORE, LANCASTER.	26
ORTNER in WYRESDALE c. 1895 - MARY'S BIRTHPLACE.	31
CALDER HOUSE - at CALDER BRIDGE 1987.	31
LANE FROM CALDER HOUSE TO CALDER BRIDGE F.M.H. 1987.	32
CALDER BRIDGE FRIENDS MEETING HOUSE 1987.	32
SAMPLER WORKED IN 1838 by MARY DILWORTH.	43
THE GIRLS WING ACKWORTH SCHOOL c. 1838-42.	43
JOHN AND MARY (BROWN) FLETCHER.	44
HENRY FLETCHER (1816-1876)	44
JANE (ABBATT) 1833-1901 and WILLIAM ADAIR 1831-1886.	74
AMELIA (SENNALS) and ISAAC WILCOCKSON Senr.	74
FRIENDS BURIAL GROUND COLTHOUSE - HAWKSHEAD.	75
JOHN JACKSON and ANN (WILCOCKSON) DILWORTH.	75
MARY (NICHOL) and SAMUEL PICKARD.	95
BENJAMIN and ELIZABETH (BROWN) ABBATT of BOLTON.	95
JAMES ABBATT 1796-1868.	96
PAUL BESWICK of BOLTON.	96
LOG CABIN, DILWORTHTOWN, PENNSYLVANIA.	96
OAKENCLOUGH (CALDER BANK).	129
JAMES JACKSON 1832-1890 of OAKENCLOUGH.	129
DAVID & EMMA (GOODALL) DILWORTH.	130
QUAKER DRESS.	130
THOMAS and JANE (HAWORTH) ABBATT and FAMILY.	156
ANNIE JACKSON M.D. 1863-1933.	156
MARY (WILCOCKSON) HARDING 1771-1859.	157
DIMPLES.	157
THE MANCHESTER PHOTOGRAPH.	219
THE OLD FRIEND'S MEETING HOUSE, FRIARGATE, PRESTON.	219
JONATHAN AND MARY'S 'AT HOME' WEDDING CARD.	220
A 1903 JACKSON WEDDING at WOODLANDS, GARSTANG.	220
THE POPLARS - 1 ALBERT ROAD, FULWOOD, PRESTON 1987.	245
JONATHAN and MARY ABBATT AND FAMILY c. 1871.	245
THE GOLDEN BOOT, 154 FRIARGATE, PRESTON c. 1930.	246
A REASONABLE BILL of 1871.	246
CRAKE MILLS FIVE GUINEA BANKNOTE.	246

ILLUSTRATIONS

ACKWORTH COUSINS.	255
ANNIE ABBATT c. 1898 - In Quaker dress.	255
THREE GENERATIONS IN THE POPLARS GARDEN c. 1900.	256
CONEY GROVE, WHITMORE, STAFFORDSHIRE.	256
DAVID and EMMA DILWORTH and FAMILY c. 1873.	258
DAVID DILWORTH'S WYRESDALE HOME - LOW ABBEY, ELLEL.	258
STARTING OUT FOR A VISIT FROM LOW ABBEY c. 1890.	259
MARY (NICHOL) PICKARD and her son CLEMENT 1900.	259
THE THREE MARYS c. 1884.	261
TENNIS PARTY AT OAKENCLOUGH 1891.	261
WEDDING of FLORENCE (D) & FRED JACKSON 1892.	262
JONATHAN and MARY c. 1893.	262
IN THE NON-CONFORMIST SECTION OF PRESTON CEMETERY.	265
MAP - After Index	292

PENDLE HILL
As seen from Quaker's Root.

INTRODUCTION

Over twenty years ago during a snowy Ottawa January dinner conversation, my wife suggested I write a book around my great grandparents' love letters and that it be called "Quaker Grey". Though the title has changed this book is the result. It is the love story of my great grandparents, Jonathan Abbatt and Mary Dilworth. Born in the late eighteen twenties, they lived all of the years of their lives in Lancashire, and both lived to see the twentieth century. Jonathan and Mary fell in love, courted - primarily by letter - married in 1855 and lived 'happily ever after'. They tell their own story of falling in love in one hundred and sixty-six letters exchanged between January 1853 and June 1855.

'The Letters' are written on thick vellum paper and are still preserved in a green, cloth covered, shoe box, which probably came from Jonathan's Preston shop - 'The Golden Boot'. They are nearly all in their original envelopes complete with penny brown stamps many of which are imperforate. The handwriting is clear, and the letters are expressive and at times amusing. The spelling, punctuation and paragraphing is unchanged and is the work of their authors.

To help the reader understand 'who is related to whom and how', a number of family trees have been included. Neither the family trees nor the background chapters are essential reading for appreciation of 'The Letters'. The material, information and my own memories are all from Lancashire and from my childhood in Lancashire.

A number of people have provided invaluable assistance. In particular I wish to record my indebtedness and grateful thanks to my great-uncle, the late Dilworth Abbatt, of Preston who spent much time - 'when I was young' - instructing me in 'The Families'; my brother, James Michael Peile Abbatt, of Bowness-on-Windermere, for material, field support and general assistance; Charles Ashton, of Preston, for invaluable work, finding and searching records in the Lancashire Record Office and elsewhere; M. Ian Crichton of Mortimer, Berkshire (Jonathan and Mary Abbatt's great great nephew) for Emma (Goodall) Dilworth's diary; and to Harry Kirby-Parkinson and his wife Frances (Leighton) (Jackson) of Heversham for some modern photographs.

                                          John Dilworth Abbatt

2805 Dufferin Avenue
Victoria B.C.   Canada

DATES - ONE HUNDRED YEARS

1815 Battle of Waterloo.
1819 'Peterloo' - Manchester.
1819 Birth of Queen Victoria.
1828 Birth of Mary Dilworth.
1828-9 Repeal of Test, & Roman Catholic Relief Acts.
1829 Birth of Jonathan Abbatt.
1829 Sir Robert Peel's Police force begins in London.
1830 Manchester and Liverpool Railway opened.
1834 Tolpuddle Martyrs.
1837 Queen Victoria ascends throne.
1840 'Penny Post' in Britain. (First adhesive stamp).
1840 British convict transportation to Australia ends.
1842 Repeal of Corn Laws and 1846.
1844 Death of John Dalton. (Chemist/Physicist).
1845 Irish Potato Crop fails.
1850 Death of William Wordsworth. Born 1770.
1851 Great Exhibition - Opening of Crystal Palace.
1854-56 Crimean War and Florence Nightingale.
1855 Jonathan and Mary (Dilworth) Abbatt married.
1857-58 Indian Mutiny.
1859 Darwin publishes: 'On the Origin of Species --- .'
1861-65 American Civil War.
1865 Death of Richard Cobden. Born 1804.
1865 Birth of Rudyard Kipling. Died 1936.
1867 British North America (Canada) Act.
1867 Death of Michael Faraday (Physicist).
1870 Death of Charles Dickens. Born 1812.
1870 English Education Act. (Local boards - primary edn).
1870 Franco-Prussian War.
1875 Death of Charles Kingsley. Born 1819.
1878 Congress of Berlin. (claim of 'Peace with honour').
1880 English Public Education Compulsory - but not free.
1881 Death of Disraeli, Born 1804.
1882 Death of Ralph Waldo Emerson. Writer/Poet. B. 1803.
1887 Birth of Rupert Brooke. Poet. Died 1915.
1889 Death of John Bright. Born 1811.
1895 William Roentgen discovers X rays.
1897 Queen Victoria's Diamond Jubilee.
1898 Death of Gladstone. Born 1809.
1899-1902 Boer War - British and Boers.
1901 Death of Mary Abbatt.
1901 Death of Queen Victoria.
1902 Marie Curie isolates first decigramme of Radium.
1904 Franco-British Entente Cordiale.
1905 Death of Jonathan Abbatt
1905 Ten Provinces in Canadian Confederation.
1908 Rutherford (1871-1937) Nobel Prize in Chemistry.
1914 First World War begins.

THE ABBATTS OF ALSTON and HOTHERSALL

ROBERT ABBAT (-1587) ⊤ ISABEL (_____)
Hothersall

- George Abote (1631)
- AND
  JOHN ABOTE (-   ) ⊤ Wife (-1616)
  Alston
  - Henry Abbatt = Wife (-1656)   Petitioner to Parliament.
  - Elizabeth   = 1628 William Walmsley. Both of Alston.
  - Galfred (1601-1602)
  - AND
    JOHN ABBOOT ⊤ 1626 MARGARET (TURNER)
    Alston
    - James "The Weaver".
    - Isabel (-1655)
    - Thomas "The Dyer" whose son: Thomas (1652-1742) = 1689 Mary (HADWEN).
    - Ellen (-1629)
    - AND
      GEORGE ABBOTTE (1635-1662) ⊤ ANNE (   ) (-1669)
      A Cloathier of Alston
      - William = 1685 Janet Harrison.
      - AND
        THOMAS ABBATT (1660-1714) ⊤ MARGARET (   ) (-1726)
        Alston
        - Mary (-1712) b. Newton in Bowland.
        - **GEORGE ABBATT (c.1685-1761)**
        - Robert "The Elder" (1687-1763) = 1723 Ann (CARTMELL) (1687-1755) of Liscoe.
          Robert and Ann progenitors of U.S branch.

GEORGE ABBATT ⊤ 1714 RUTH (FELL) (1685-1764)
George of Alston and Longridge, Ruth of Langtree.

- Thomas   (1715-1792) of Cockermouth.
- Joseph   (1717-   ) died young.
- Mary   (1719-1802)
- Benjamin (1722-1800)
- Elizabeth (1725-1783)
- George   (1727-   )
- John   (1730-   )
- **JAMES   (1735-1770)**

JAMES ABBATT (1735-1770) ⊤ 1760 ANN (LONSDALE) (1734-1788)
Both of Alston.

- Elizabeth (1761-1804)
- James   (1762-   ) died young.
- George   (1764-1770)
- Ruth   (1765-1767)
- THOMAS   (1767-1836)
- William   (1769-1771)
- George   (1771-1773)

THOMAS ABBATT = 1793 ALICE (SMITH) (1772-1825)
T. of Alston and Bolton-le-Moors, A. of Longridge.

- Jane   (1794-1798)
- James   (1796-1868) to U.S.A.
- **BENJAMIN (1799-1853)**
- Ann   (1801-1869)

- Thomas (1803-1844)
- Jane   (1806-1845)
- Paul   (1809-1810)
- Isaac   (1813-1839)

BENJAMIN = 1824 ELIZABETH (BROWN) (1800-1873)
B. of Bolton and E. of Standish.

- William   (1825-1901)
- Thomas   (1827-1897)
- James   (1831-1895)
- **JONATHAN (1829-1905)**

- Jane   (1833-1901)
- Robert   (1835-1835)
- Alice Ann (1838-1914)
- Elizabeth (1840-1886)

JONATHAN ABBATT = 27/6/1855 MARY (DILWORTH) (1829-1901)
J. of Bolton and Preston, M. of Ortner, Wyresdale and Calder Bridge.

- Annie   (1856-1927)
- Caroline (1857-1925)
- Dilworth (1861-1943)
- AND   Frank ABBATT (1866-1941) = 1893 SARAH MARIA (PEILE) (1868-1949)
  F. of Preston and Calder Bridge, Sally of Rogerscale, Cumberland.

- **GEOFFREY PEILE ABBATT**   (1895-1978)
- Philip Dilworth Abbatt   (1899-   )

GEOFFREY PEILE ABBATT (1895-1978) = 1921 MILLICENT JACKSON (1893-1968)
GPA of Poulton-le-Fylde and Bowness-on-Windermere,
M. of Woodlands, Calder Bridge.

- **JOHN DILWORTH**   (1923-   )
- James Michael Peile   (1931-   )

JOHN DILWORTH ABBATT = 1955 AINSLIE ANN GOER FERGUSON (1924-   )
Ann of York, JDA of Poulton-le-Fylde, Sawrey,
Ottawa and Victoria, Canada.

- Sarah Catherine Dilworth   (1957-)
- Joanna Louise Peile   (1959-)
- **JONATHAN PAUL DILWORTH** (1963-)

THE DILWORTHS of THORNLEY and WYRESDALE

                    JAMES DILWORTH = Wife
                    Chipping.

         JAMES DILLWORTH(E) (1577-   ) = ISABEL (   )
    Christened 15/07/1577 Chipping as were his family. Isabel's will 1649.

```
┌ John    (1609-    )              ┌ Jane     (1617-     )
├ Isabel  (1611-1655)              ├ Aveline  (1620-     )
├ Alice   (1613-    )              └ James    (1623-1678)*
└ Thomas  (1615-1669)

  AND
```

            WILLIAM DILWORTH* (1618-1689) = ALICE (-29/1/1683)
    Yeoman of Thornley; children all Christened at Chipping. A. a Friend?

```
┌ John    (1651-1690) = i   1675 Ellin (HADWEN) m. Ed. Cummings Ho. Arnside.
│                    = ii  1689 Jennet (RAINGILL) m. in John D.'s own House.
├ Ellin   (1653-    ) =          Richard BRACEWELL of Settle Monthly Mtg.
├ James   (1654-1699) =     1680 Ann (WALN) (1654-1710) m. 9 May in Nicholas
│                                Waln's ho. 'Chapel Croft', Newton-by-Bowland,
│                                Emigrated to Pennsylvania 1682.
├ Isabel  (1655-    )
└ Alice   (1656-1659)

  AND
```

                    THOMAS DIL(L)WORTH (1660-1726)
    Carrier of Thornley, Bradley Hall, Chipping & Farmer Moorhead, Wyresdale.

                = i   1680 Sarah (PEARSON)(1660-1687) A Cumbrian.
                            m. John Read's House, Langthwaite, Wigton.
                            Issue: Two females died young.
                = ii   1689 Mary (TOWNSON)(1664-1699) of Moorehead.
                            Sister to Jennet Cragg. m. Jennet Bond's
                            House, Woodacre, Wyrsdl. Issue: Dillworths
                            of Lancaster and Yealand Conyers.
                = iii 1705 ANN (CORLESS)(DRIVER)(-1/11/1759)
                            m. John Bond's Ho. Dunnishaw, Wyresdale.

```
┌ William Dillworth     (1705-1760)    ┌ Thomas Dilworth    (1713-1793)
├ Hannah Dillworth      (1707-1773)    ├ JAMES DILLWORTH    (1717-1789)
├ Jennet Dillworth      (1708-1773)    ├ Ann Dilworth       (1719-1775)
└ Elizabeth Dilworth    (1710-1712)    └ Lydia Dilworth     (1720-     )
```

    * Where possible all entries spelt as originally recorded.

```
JAMES DILLWORTH/DILWORTH (1717-1789) ᵼ c.1739 ELIZABETH (____)(1719-1794)
     James Hatmaker of Wray & Husbandman died at Quernmore.
```

```
├ Thomas Dilworth         (1740-1803) Feltmaker of Wray. 3 Issue to Ackworth.
├ Ann   Dilworth          (1743-1759) Of Wray.
├ James Dilworth          (1746-    )   "    "
├ James Dilworth          (1747-1826) Hatter of Wray, Ellel & Preston. Issue
├ Elizabeth Dilworth      (1750-    ) Of Wray.
├ William Dilworth        (1753-    )   "    "
├ Lidia  Dilworth         (1756-    )   "    "
├ WILLIAM DILLWORTH       (1761-1833)
│   and = twins:
└ Sarah Dilworth          (1761-    )
```

```
     WILLIAM DILLWORTH/DILWORTH ᵼ 8/3/1785 MARY (JACKSON) (1768-1858)
     W. Farmer of Chapel House and Greeenbank, Wyresdale. M. of Quernmore.
```

```
├ JOHN JACKSON DILLWORTH (1786-1870)
├ James Dilworth          (1788-1792)
├ Jane (Dilworth)         (1793-    ) = 3/6/1818 John WILCOCKSON (1792-    )
└ William Dilworth        (1798-    )   Emigrated to America.
```

```
     JOHN JACKSON DILLWORTH ᵼ 26/7/1821 ANN (WILCOCKSON) (1788-1874)
     John J.D. of Caton Green and  Ortner, Wyresdale
        and of Calder Bridge (House). Ann of Preston.
```

```
├ William Dilworth (1822-190 ) = Alice (BIBBY) (   -1892) Wm. d. Ortner.
│  Issue:  Mary Ann, John Jackson, Elizabeth, Alice and Jane.
├ DAVID DILWORTH (1824-1902) = 19/4/1855 EMMA (GOODALL) (1830-1894)
│  Issue:  Ann, Chas. Edw., Frederic, Ada, Lillian Emma, Florence and
│                                                         John Jackson.
│       AND
│
├ MARY (DILWORTH) (1828-1901) ᵼ 27/6/1855 JONATHAN ABBATT (1829-1905)
└ Mary of Ortner, Wyresdale and Calder Bridge. J.A. of Bolton and Preston.
```

```
├ Annie Abbatt         (1856-1927)
├ Caroline Abbatt      (1857-1927)
├ Dilworth Abbatt      (1861-1943)
└ Frank Abbatt         (1866-1941)
```

* William (1618-1689) and James (1623-1678) Dilworth have been confused because both had sons called John, James and Thomas. William was christened and buried at Chipping Church. But ALL his children are in the registers of the Society of Friends in London, as is Alice his wife who would have been an early Friend - burial place unknown.

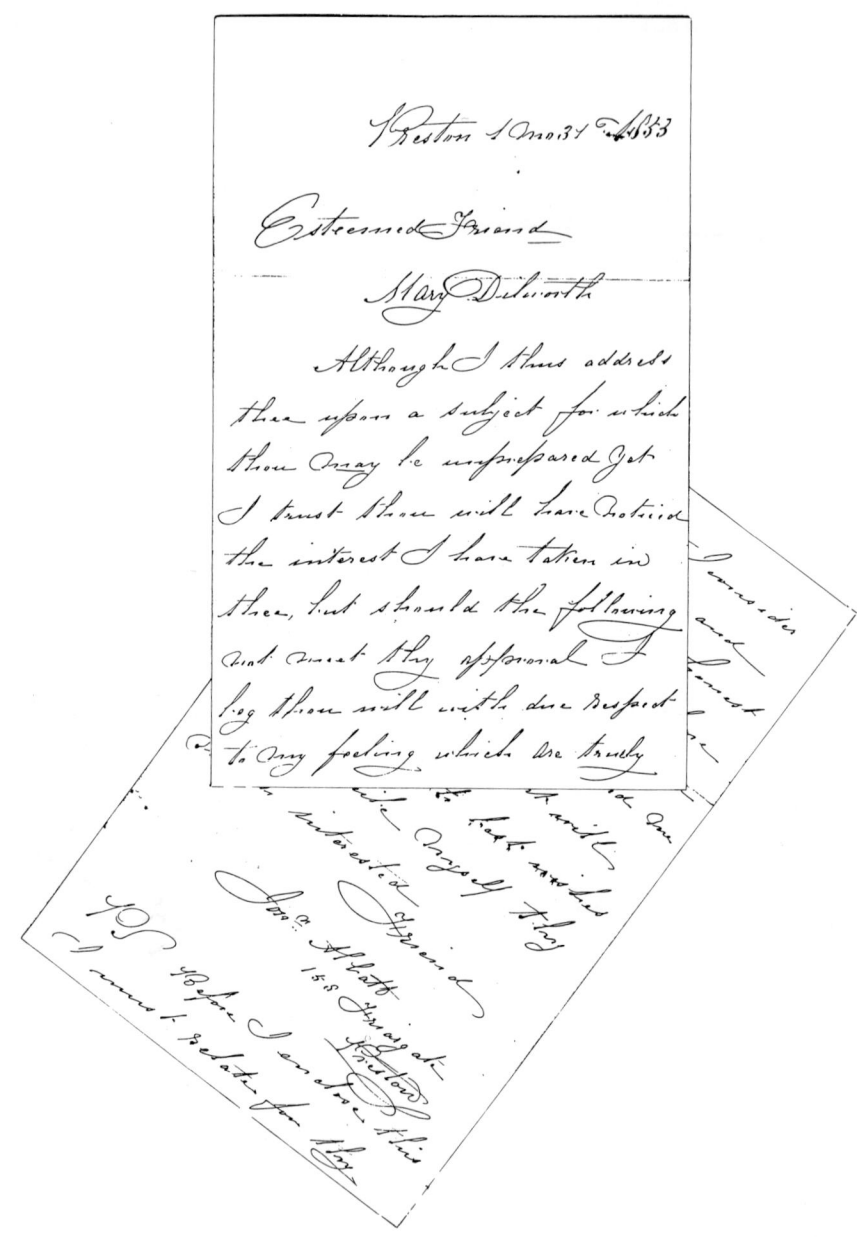

JONATHAN ABBATT's first letter to MARY DILWORTH 31st first month 1853 – (31st January).

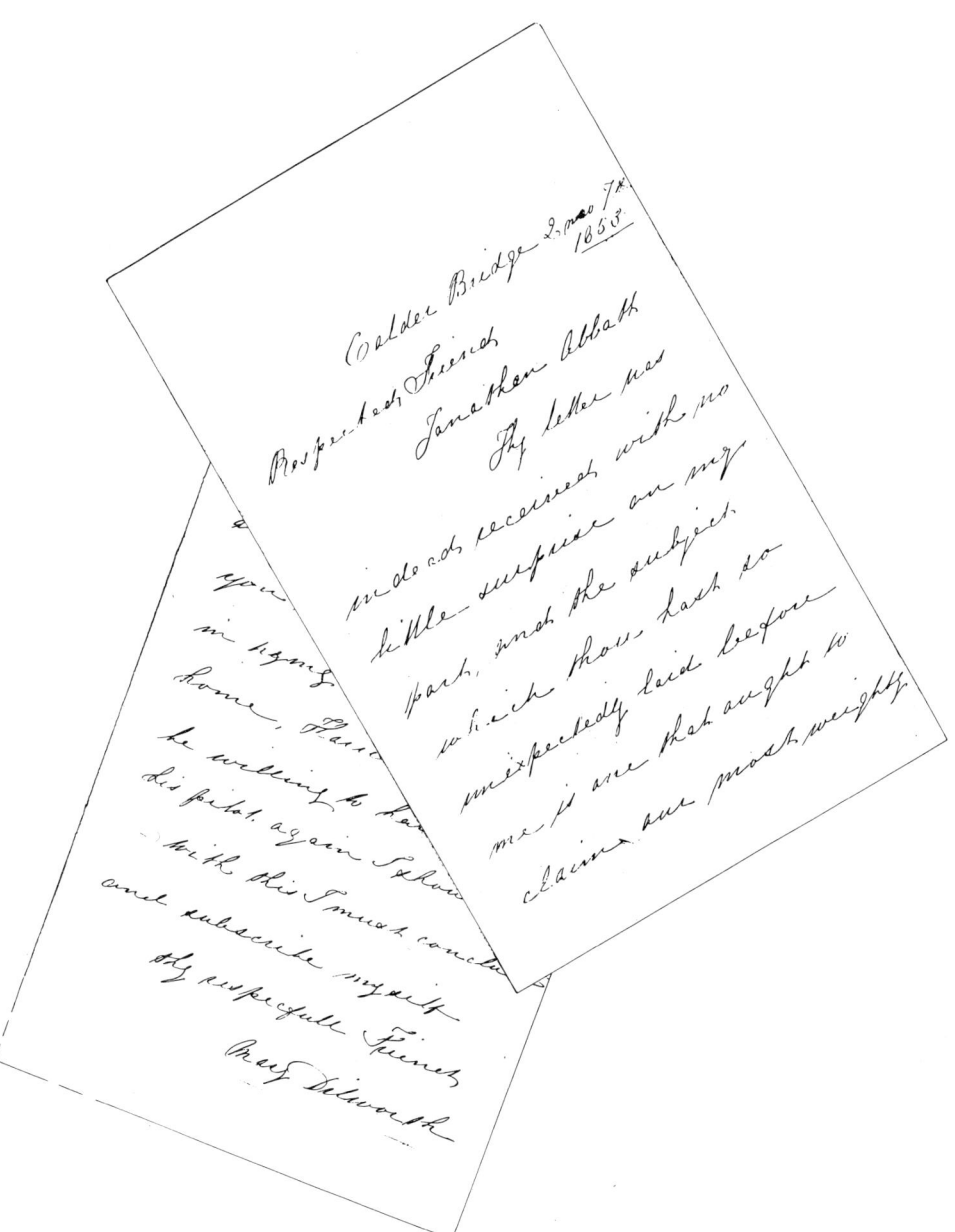

MARY DILWORTH's reply – being her first letter to JONATHAN ABBATT 7th second month 1853 – (7th February).

JONATHAN ABBATT 1829-1905 aged 34
and
MARY DILWORTH ABBATT 1828-1901 aged 35.

I WHERE THEY CAME FROM

THE ABBATTS

Spelling of names - Abbatt and Dilworth origins - Robert Abbat of Hothersall 1587 - North Western Everyman - early NW history of Friends - Seekers and Pendle Hill - Henry Abbatt 1659 petitioner to Parliament - 'The Obstinate Quakers' James 'The Weaver' and Thomas 'The Dyer' in Preston - Dilworth/Abbatt relationship - Early Friends - Poor but Worthy Thomas Abbatt's will - George and Robert Abbatt the Elder - Founder of U.S. branch of family - Longridge store - Preston's first water works - Every day shall be Good Friday - George A's licence for Meetings - 'Quakers Root' an ancestral home - Robert moves shop and sells alcohol cheap - Robert the Younger and Colthouse wedding - Fylde MM clerkships - A disastrous generation - Thomas and an C.18 move from Alston to Bolton - James first Abbatt to attend Ackworth 'The Hereditary School'.

This book is a love story and describes the lives and background of two mid-Victorians - Jonathan Abbatt and Mary Dilworth - who courted, fell in love, married and lived happily 'ever afterwards'.

On 30th January 1853, Jonathan of Preston was aged twenty four when he first wrote to Mary at Calder Bridge near Garstang. He had just completed his apprenticeship and was in the process of embarking in business on his own. Mary was the only daughter and youngest child of a retired farmer - John Jackson and his wife Ann (Wilcockson) Dilworth of Calder Bridge, Nr. Garstang. The courtship was conducted largely by letters exchanged at approximately ten day intervals from 1853 until their marriage in June 1855. Married life was, in great part, a fulfilment of their early hopes, plans and aspirations; and they remained deeply in love with one another to the end of their lives.

Jonathan Abbatt and Mary Dilworth were members of two old Lancashire Quaker families, who had been close geographic neighbours for at least two hundred and fifty years, before this courtship in the eighteen fifties.

The Abbatts under a variety of spellings - Abbat, Abote, Abboott and since 1714 (and occasionally before) as Abbatt - came from Alston and Hothersall near Ribchester. The name first appears in the later fifteen hundreds in Ribchester parish registers under christenings, marriages and deaths. The first 'detailed' record is that of Robert Abbat, a husbandman - farmer of Hothersall in the parish of Ribchester, who made his will on 21st April, 1587. In addition to desiring burial in Ribchester churchyard, by this will he left his 'estate' in three parts to his wife, Isabel, and his sons, George and John. To John he specifically bequeathed 'all the implements of smith craft', suggesting that he had been a farmer-blacksmith. Many of his descendants were nail makers or 'nailers' and it is probable that Robert began - or perhaps continued - that family craft.

Halley in 'Lancashire its Puritanism and Nonconformity' comments pointedly on the erratic spelling of names:

> Almost every family of the seventeenth century had two or three ways of spelling its own name and place of abode. Even signatures are not decisive for they vary considerably: in my vexation I have been ready to conclude that --- nobody in Lancashire knew how to spell the name of anybody else and few people their own.

This uncertainty continued to some extent into nineteenth century Wyresdale when Mary's own brothers initially oscillated between one and two ls.

The Di(l)lworths, apart from some continuing uncertainty about the number of ls, were more consistent in their spelling and, like the Abbatts, first appear in the middle of the sixteenth century, in the Chipping and later Longridge parish registers. They too, were, and remained, small farmers, and by the end of the century were living in and around Longridge - within a few miles of the Abbatts. There is no evidence that the two families knew each other in these early days. However, in the religious ferment prevailing before, during and after the Civil War and the Commonwealth, when some members of both families became Friends (Quakers), they became distantly related.

As well as being a love story this is the story of Everyman over three and a half centuries in rural North West Lancashire. Because so many Abbatts and Dilworths were Friends this necessitates the following brief and incomplete account of early Quaker history in North West England. This book is not a formal history but it is close to being a social history of a regional Everyman.

Quakers, or to give them their correct title, Friends, are a non-conformist sect whose specific origins lie in England in the teachings of George Fox (1624-1691). The

Society of Friends (Fox's 'shadow') came into being during the Commonwealth, and its formative years are, to a large extent, a cameo of the struggle, persecution and search for new beginnings during the seventeenth century.

The North West of England was, except for the aristocracy, relatively remote from high politics, but became caught up in the dissatisfaction with the times of the mid sixteen hundreds. In this period the population was small and relatively, was minute; its wealth, such as it was, was in agriculture. Travel was difficult and the Pennines and Lake District hills were formidable barriers to both mind and body.

With the execution of Charles I and the establishment of the Commonwealth, protestants of all complexions and flavours were supreme and the Anglicans and Roman Catholics were both equally discredited. This state of affairs, following years of verbal and then physical struggle, did not bring harmony with the nominal peace. In particular, the 'ruling' puritan sects while sharing high ideals did not practice worldly toleration. As a result many groups of people - frequently inchoate, sought spiritual rebirth, some finding it in established sects. But many more such as 'The Children of the Light' and 'The Seekers' were groups, often of very different views, all seeking a new spiritual authority to replace the existing churches, movements and sects.

In 1646 Oliver Cromwell wrote: ' -- and thus to be a Seeker is to be of the next best sect to a Finder, and thus shall every faithful humble Seeker be at the end.' The Seeker movements were very much movements of humble country people who were small farmers, chapmen, shoemakers and small tradesmen. They tended to be concentrated in remote rural areas such as Yorkshire, Lancashire, Cumberland and Westmorland.

In 1651 George Fox went North to Yorkshire from the Midlands, probably as a result of a Seeker's invitation, to explore the truth. At this time Fox was twenty-seven and had a growing reputation from his work in Nottinghamshire as a convinced and convincing preacher of the teachings of the 'Inner Light'. This journey followed an emerging pattern of discussion and preaching, in houses, market places and often in church. One of his specialities was to use existing churches as both his medium and his congregation. (It was not then an offence for members of the congregation to speak in church at the end of the service though interruption of the sermon was another matter). This practice was an undoubted irritant for the clergy, many of whom from very early days, violently opposed Friends.

Fox travelled through East Yorkshire, York, and then westward through the Dales, over the Pennines and, in the May of 1652, to Pendle Hill near Clitheroe - and Longridge, Chipping, Alston and Hothersall. On the summit of Pendle, George Fox had a partial vision of the future and looking North and West came to believe that there the Lord 'had a great people to be gathered.' These people did in fact exist - to a large extent in the 'Westmorland Seekers' but also close at hand in the immediate vicinity of Pendle.

Pendle Hill is on the Lancashire/Yorkshire border immediately south of the River Ribble. To the west it overlooks Ribchester, Longridge and Chipping. From its summit looking north west, one can see in the foreground, the Trough of Bowland and Bowland Forest and then a little beyond are the valleys of the rivers Wyre and Lune. (See map)

Fox then moved north into Westmorland, and in effect, on into history. On this occasion there is no record of the immediate local impact, if any, of his passing. It may be there was none, but (among others) the Abbatt and Dilworth families were exactly the type of seed he was seeking and found elsewhere. In all probability the very first Quaker Dilworths and Abbatts and their method of convincement will never be known but it would be easy to believe that the early words and activities of Fox in their immediate neighbourhood were somehow involved.

Henry Abbatt (whose wife died in 1656) was the first member of his family to become a Friend and in 1659 was one of 164 Quaker signatory petitioners to Parliament. The petitioners requested that they might: 'person for person and body for body lie in prison instead of such of their brethren as might be in danger of their lives through extreme duress' (from Joseph Besse 1733). Henry, a grandson of Robert Abbat the husbandman/smith and by this time a widower, is known to have 'travelled in the south' but the date and place of his death is not known.

Two other early Abbatt Friends were James and Thomas Abbott, brothers of Jonathan's direct ancestor George. They were respectively a 'Woollen Weaver' and a 'Dyer'; came from Ribchester, and seem to have been in partnership with George who was a 'Smith and Cloathier'. In 1653 as a result of what would now be called 'Unfair Trading Practices' they achieved local notoriety in the Court Leet Records. It is recorded from an Inquisition held in December 1653 in the Moot Hall, Preston that:

> Whereas it iss presented to this Jury that Thomas Abbott, dyer, doth constantlie frequent this Markett and receaves White cloth and after hee hath dyed ye same delivereth itt dyed in this Markett, to ye prejuidice of the ffree Burgesses of this Towne whofe livelyhood and maintenance wholelie depends upon the saide Trade; And fforeasmucheas wee doo conceave itt verie priudiciall that ye said Abbott should take ye beneffit of Tradeing in this Towne and bear noe parte of ye burden of assessments dues and services imposed on thiss Towne. Wee doe therefore thinke fitt that Mr. Maior and his brethren call ye said Thomas Abbott before them and proceede and take such course as in theire discretion shall seem meete.

A subsequent court four months later decided that:

> ---- nether Thomas Abbott nor his brother should have the libertie to bring in cloathe dyed, or receave white cloathe to dye, upon a Setterday, it beinge a mystery or trade and paying neither scott nor lott.

The matter is raised again in a lawyer's letter of 1745:

> ----- as there is scarce Precedents of such a Wilful and resolute Attempte heretofore, we have not many footesteps of proceedings on such occasions - only in the late instance of an obstinate Quaker who after some litigation was at last brought to submit.

The problem of 'rank foreigners' from Alston/Ribchester attempting to trade in Preston Market was common. Two hundred years later David Wilcockson, the Hatter, had similar problems which he solved by setting up his stall outside the town boundary. (See Chapter IV.)

It is not known whether George Abbotte (1635-1662), was a Friend. This is not unlikely as his two brothers, his uncle and his son (Thomas of Alston), were all Friends. George himself, described as a 'Cloathier', died at the age of twenty seven leaving a young widow and an infant son (Thomas) aged two. His brother James, spelling his name Abbott, was granted administration of his effects valued at three pounds and five shillings.

As somewhat of a postscript to this generation, it is interesting to note that Thomas 'The Dyer's son - another Thomas, but now spelling his name Abbat, - married Mary Hadwen of Arnside at Agnes Waithman's House in 1689. Mary was a sister of Ellin, and Thomas who, like John

Dilworth, was a Cordwainer became brother-in-law to John Dilworth i.e. Ellin's husband. Thomas and Mary Abbat became the ancestors of the present Kendal branch of the Abbatt family.

Among the witnesses at the wedding were a number of early Friends and in addition to John Abbat - the groom's brother - were:

- Richard Burrow or Burrough mentioned in George Fox's Journal as having been brutally attacked at Yealand by Sir Geo. Middleton's men of Leighton Hall.
- Chris Bissbrowne an associate of Richard Hubberthorn.
- Thomas Dockray who collected and arranged Fox's papers for publication.
- Thomas Wither or Widders, was a close associate of George Fox, and he wrote a 'Testimony against Tythes'.

The genealogy of the next, and of subsequent generations of the Abbatt family, is clear and unequivocal being derived from vital statistics and supported by a surprising amount of additional family documentation. If inaccuracies exist in data prior to 1660 they are unlikely to be appreciable because surprisingly little information is not cross referenced in its origins.

Thomas of Alston and his wife Margaret had three children, Mary dying in infancy and the two boys, George and Robert who are the ancestors respectively of 'our' Lancashire family and of the American Abbatt branch.

In 1708 Thomas' house in Alston was licensed for the holding of Quaker Meetings (as later were those of his sons). From the Records of the Quarter Sessions at Preston Sessions Hall:

> 1708 Preston October 7
> Petition of Thomas Abbot of Alston-in-Hothersall and Robert his son that the dwelling house of the Petitioners be recorded as a Meeting Place for Quakers
>
>   Recorded   Thomas Abbatt.

Thomas had financial problems and a Monthly Meeting minute for 1704 reads:

> Min 2. Care is to be taken to rase a collection towards the relief of Thomas Abbot against the next month meeting.

After Thomas' death in 1714 the Bond for Administration of his goods reads:

Thomas Abbatt of Alston husbandman.

Bond (22nd August 1714) By Margaret Abbott of Alston, co. Lancaster, widow and William Walne of Whittingham in the said county, yeoman on grant of admon of goods of the said Thomas to his said widow Margaret.
   The widow signs by her mark.

Inventory of the goods of the abovesaid Thomas, 10 June 1714.
by James Morton and William Walne.

The goods consist of household furniture and one cow.
Total value   £9.12s.3d.

Dilworth A. described Thomas as 'a Poor but Worthy Ancestor'. He was clearly not over-endowed with this world's goods.

Much more is known of his two sons George (1685-1761) and Robert The Elder (1687-1763).

George, was a "Nailer" by trade, and unlike his brother Robert 'stayed close to his roots' initially in Alston/Hothersall, and then in Longridge. Here, in addition to making nails he kept a shop - the Longridge General Store. Walkden's Diary published 1866 (Dobson & Preston Chronicle) mentions the shop a number of times:

> Sept 22 1729 - Thomas Seed o'th Little town being ill and fearing a fever, he sent for my love to come and blood him, which she did. Then went to Cousin Throops who is ill, and sat with him and got two pints of Ale 4d. Then we went to George Abbott's shop and bought a pair of shoes for John 3/6, a pair for my love 2/4; and a pair for myself 4/-, but mine we had not a silver on us to do it with, and therefore left it to pay; and a shower falling caused us to call at Cousin Throops again and get another pint of Ale.
>
>   -- and again in November:
>
> My love having an errand to George Abbott's shop I went with her and son Thomas having a sythe to pay for he gave me 2/2   --- and he demanded 2/4 for the sythe and 2d for the pole.

(Walkden was a dissenting Minister, half farmer and half

clergyman with two chapels at Hesketh Nr. Chipping and at Newton in Bowland).

In 1714 George had married Ruth Fell of Langtree near Standish, daughter of Heskin Fell. The latter was a weaver and second cousin of Judge Fell of Swarthmoor; he was an early Friend and had been a religious prisoner in Lancaster Castle for three years (as well as in other places). The marriage took place in Bogburn Hall, Coppul, home of John Haydock who was later to die a prisoner in Lancaster Castle at the age of 79 years. Among those who were witnesses at the wedding was Agnes Tomlinson, whose father was married while in Lancaster Castle, and who herself made many religious journeys throughout Britain. A Fylde Monthly Meeting minute records the provision of : " -- a hors, saddlebagges and Pocket money for Agnes Tomlinson --- " for one of her journeys.

George himself was a useful Friend who often served with his brother Robert to further their Meeting's concerns. An interesting Minute of Disownment (for marrying out of the Society) signed by the two brothers reads:

> Whereas Richd. Eccles of Brindle hath been educated among the people called Quakers and made profeffion with them of the Light and teachings of the grace of God but for want of living up to the Guidance and teaching thereof and observing the good order and advice of his friends hath let out his mind to a woman of another perfsuafion and joined with her in marriage by a Priest for which doing or practice we can do no less than disown him to be of our Society or Communion until by Repentance and amendment of Life he may thought worthy of Admittance.
>
> | Given forth at our Mo. | Robt. Abbatt |
> | Meeting held at Freckleton | John Barrow |
> | ye 1st | Geo. Abbatt |
> | of 1st mo 1742 | James Hall |
> | and signed in and by order thereby | |

On another occasion in the same minutes:

> 1739.5.3. Min. 10. Robert Abbatt and George Abbatt are appointed to visit Sarah and Ruth Sharples and advise them to refrain from keeping company with persons of other persuasions.

The above eighteenth century minutes, in addition to their intrinsic interest give a clear idea of Friends' views and practices with regard to 'marrying out' - a subject of much relevance in later years and to 'our' Mary Dilworth's own brothers, William and David.

George applied to Quarter Sessions for permission to hold Meetings in his own house both in Hothersall and later in Longridge, at which time he was an Elder of the Chipping Meeting. The Hothersall application reads:

> 1717 Preston Sessions July 18 1717
> George Abbot of Hothersall petitions that a dwelling house and barne therunto, belonging to your Petitioner is intended for an Assembly of Quakers.
> Recorded   George Abbatt

This house called 'Quakers Root' still exists in excellent condition and is the counterpart 'ancestral home' to the Dilworth's Bradley Hall, four or five miles away. Its situation is picturesque and from the mullioned front windows Pendle Hill is clearly visible a little to the East. It was George's home - and probably place of work. It may too, have been that of his penurious father Thomas but this is not certain. (In the author's youth it was still a house and barn, the barn has now been taken into the house, though without major external changes.)

George's younger brother, Robert, became something of a public figure in Preston and is the founder of the first American Abbatt family. Robert was, initially at least, a Chapman and moved to Preston with his widowed mother in 1722. (Note: In the 17th and early 18th centuries in Lancashire the term chapman referred to one dealing in textiles and other goods - no longer to a pedlar - and at this time the Chapmen of North and East Lancashire were a 'dignified and important' body of traders). In Preston, while conducting this business, he became in addition a wine and spirits merchant and the following appeared in 'The year of the '45' when Princes Charles passed through Preston on his ill starred venture:

Advertisement in the Preston Journal February 22nd 1745.

> Robert Abbatt, who lives next door to the 'Legs of Man', being to remove at May day next to the house and shop now in possession of John Cumbrall, Ironmonger in the Old Shambles in Preston; and the said Robert Abbatt now having considerable stocks of Wine, Brandy and several other sorts of Brandy, Rum, Holland Gin, Double Juniper, Double Wormwood and Double Aniseed, Daffy's Elixir and Godfreys Cordial, purposes in order to save the trouble and expense of removing the same to dispose of them where they are at very low prices.

WYRESDALE MEETING HOUSE and CHAPEL HOUSE
The Old Meeting House (and MARY's first School) are in the centre with Chapel House on the right. Tarnbrook Fell behind.

BURIAL GROUND BEHIND WYRESDALE MEETING HOUSE

At this time Preston was a town of 6,000 people and had no water supply beyond an assortment of wells and pumps. A little before Robert's time a narrow street leading from one of these pumps known as 'Petticoat Alley' was described:

> ----- by reason of the frequent carrying of water from the well by woemin, and milkmaids bringing daily their milk and butter to the town from beyond the River Rible.

To remedy this state of affairs, and to provide the means to fight fires, Robert, with one Woodcock, built the town's first water supply and waterworks. This was the subject of an agreement between the Corporation of Preston and Robert Abbatt. The construction involving wooden (hollowed trees) pipes and iron bound wooden cisterns (tanks), was not carried out without opposition and problems, and these have been well documented by Hewitson.

After the installation was complete and operating, Robert on one occasion, was fined by the Corporation for supplying water on a Good Friday. The strong minded Quaker responded with: ' --- then every Friday shall be Good Friday' - and no water ever passed through his wooden pipes on a Friday.

Robert married Ann Cartmell of Liscoe in 1723 at the Little Eccleston Meeting House. Ann was the daughter of a prominent Friend whose home was the local centre of Quakerism. There were many witnesses including George and Ruth (Fell) Abbatt.

After Robert's funeral, Samuel Fothergill (brother of John and Ann) wrote in his Journal:

> A messenger brought me an invitation to the funeral of Robert Abbatt the Elder of Preston; and I found upon looking at it, that duty required me to go. He was buried in that town in a piece of land he had lately contracted for as a burial place for the Society [he was the first to use it]. The Meeting was large, and the latter part of it solid, weighty and eminently favoured. I hope it was a Meeting of memorable use.

Much more could be said about both George and Robert, but this is not their story. They were worthy Friends who beginning with nothing had made their own way in the world. Robert was perhaps the more energetic, but both in his Meeting and in business, he was at times hasty and erratic. Nevertheless in the long run he was usually proven to have been be in the right.

It is unfair to include Robert the Younger (1725-1795) in a postscript but to do so will avoid confusion (and avoid his complete omission). He followed his father in business, in time becoming mainly a grocer. In 1752 he married Agnes Rigge of Swarthmoor at Colthouse, Hawkshead. Fylde Monthly Meeting (his own Meeting) in their Minute at his presentation stated: '--- we accept his first presentation. George Abbatt and Thomas Lonsdale are appointed to inquire into his clearness from all others in that respect --- .'

After his marriage Robert II - The Younger - became associated with his brother-in-law Thomas Rigge, Michael Satterthwaite and others in a Bank and in the Crake Corn Mills near Lowick (between Ulverston and Spark Bridge). Robert was a most useful, clerkly Friend and was for 39 years Clerk to the Fylde-Preston Monthly Meeting. At one time he also held the additional posts of Registrar and Treasurer.

Abbatts were Clerks to their Fylde/Preston Meeting for 65 of the 196 years between 1724 and 1920 when Dilworth Abbatt ended his stint. Jonathan's spell of three years pales into the normal beside that of Robert the Younger and the nineteen years of his son Dilworth.

James Abbatt (1735-1770) youngest son of George had a short, sad and probably unhappy life. He married Ann Lonsdale in 1760 at Preston and 47 witnesses signed the certificate including three Dilworths, one of whom was Lydia the youngest child of Thomas and Ann Dilworth (see Chapter II). Ann's father was a Yeoman and a very plain farmer from Chipping, and Ann, her mother and her sisters all signed the wedding certificate with their marks.

James of Longridge was a Nailer by trade and in 1768, eight years after his marriage, he failed in business. The case came before Monthly Meeting many times in a twelve month period and initially at least he did not face up to his problems and debts; indeed he was absent for some of the enquiries and the sifting of problems. In 1768 he was disowned by his Monthly Meeting:

> Whereas James Abbatt a member of this Meeting, having some time ago failed in payment of his just debts, to the great scandal of our profession, for which action, so inconsistant with our Known Principles of Truth and Justice, we can do no less than Testify against such. Therefore, this may

inform all whom it may Concern, that we do disown him from being any longer a Member in Fellowship with us, until something further appears in his favour, so as to convince Friends that he may be worthy to be united to the Society again; which is what we sincerely desire.

Given forth from Fylde Monthly Meeting held at Freckleton ye 2nd of ye 2nd Month 1768 and signed in and on our behalf behalf by:	Joseph Lancaster Robert Butler George Brown Robert Abbatt

Two years after his disownment James died, and his son George aged six, having died the day before, was buried with him.

James' brothers and sisters fared no better and were members of an ill starred generation:

- John was disowned in 1766 for intemperance, loose living and repeated singing in public houses.
- Elizabeth was disowned for loose living and flightiness in public houses.
- Thomas married twice, was a 'Nailor' and also failed in business. He was not disowned but: " --- was prohibited from attending Meetings for discipline and from contributing to collections." Despite this he was later described by Joseph Adair as a 'kindly and respectful old man'.
- Benjamin described by Dilworth Abbatt as 'rather a failure', his wife Ann Crampton of Hartshaw was disowned for immoral conduct.
- George, the only other member of the family, married out of the Society but was later reinstated and his wife became a Member.

It is tempting to omit the story of James and his siblings for it is difficult to imagine a more disastrous family or generation! A very partial explanation may perhaps be that their story coincided with the state of the country and of society in general. It was the age of Fielding, Smollet and Hogarth and their outrage at the excesses of the times is well known. The Society of Friends, in addition to the problems of these years, was also beginning to be seriously changed by the increasing wealth of some Friends and by the fact that it was not being appreciably persecuted.

However, it seems unfair to blame all of this Abbatt generation's problems on the times and their social environment, and though this may have been relatively sheltered they were perhaps more exposed to 'The World' than were the Dilworths in Wyresdale. Not all Dilworths followed the paths of rectitude and there are examples of individuals 'going off the rails' and forsaking Friends, (which need not have been the same thing); but at no time did a whole Dilworth generation 'go wrong'.

Thomas Abbatt (1767-1836) was Jonathan's grandfather and is therefore almost a modern. He was a fifth child and the last member of the family to come from Alston, having moved to Bolton on completing his apprenticeship as a tailor. It was an old Friends' custom for sons to be 'placed', i.e. apprenticed, with other Quakers to learn their trades. An old Query regularly read at Monthly Meeting was:

> What apprentices are put forth, and are there any offers for Masters of Apprentices? and if in their apprenticeshipp they be duly instructed, and kept in good order, and if none be put Apprentices to the World?

This was an area of life that Thomas' grandson Jonathan understood only too well, - as a prospective apprentice he was not consulted at all. It is not known whether Thomas was consulted about the choice of trade or Master; the latter was T. Cragg (a member of the Wyresdale Cragg family, see Chapter II) a Lancaster tailor Friend. On completing his 'time' and after moving back to his own Meeting as a journeyman Thomas moved to Ridgway Gates, Bolton in March 1791. In 1793 he married Alice Smith, daughter of Paul Smith, Nailer of Longridge. At the wedding in Preston 48 people signed the certificate as witnesses. The bride's sisters rejoiced in wonderful names including Dinah, Miriam, Abigail and Zipporah.

Thomas died at the age of 68, but of his seven brothers and sisters only Elizabeth (1761-1804) survived childhood. James Abbatt of Preston and Peoria, Illinois, described his father as: " --- a quiet, steady going man who dressed in the Quaker costume of the day in knee-breeches, collarless coat and broad brimmed hat." He and Alice had seven children including James the eldest - a tailor and a family historian - who emigrated to the U. S. A. from Preston at the age of 45, where he became a successful farmer in Peoria, Illinois. Thomas was clearly interested in education and his eldest son James (though not Jonathan's father Benjamin) was sent to Ackworth in 1808.

II WHERE THEY CAME FROM

THE DILWORTHS

James Dilworth of Chipping 1577 - Publishers of Truth in Bowland 1653 - Dilworth Quaker origins - Alexander and Clement Parker - Thomas Bond - Bradley Hall and Dilworths - Thomas D. and his three wives and families - John Moone and Jennet Cragg become his 'in-laws' - Thomas D. migrates to Wyresdale - William Dilworth Clerk to Yearly Meeting is kinsman to Robert Abbatt the Elder - James and Ann (Waln) Dilworth married 1680 - Migration to Philadelphia 1682 - Death of James D. and Nicholas Waln's letter from Philadelphia - Dilworths throughout N. America - Jennet Cragg's famous ride to London and back - Dilworth wills.

James Dilworth of Chipping, whose wife had a son named James in 1577, is the first of his family for whom we have a record. James, of Thornley near Chipping died first and his widow, in a quaintly worded Will mentions all of their children:

> Abstracts of Wills of Archdeaconry Richmond.
>
> Isabell Dilworth of Thornley, in Coun. Lanc. widdow makes her will the 8th October 1649. She gives unto Jane her daughter one cowe. She gives to James her son one mare, she gives unto Avelline her daughter 20$\underline{s}$, she gives to William her son, one Ark. And after her funeral expenses discharged, she gives all the rest of her goods unto William, James, Alice, Thomas, Isabell, Avelline and Jane, her children, and to the children of John Dillworth her late son equally amongst them. And she makes William and James her sons, executors.
>
> The Estate Inventory amounts to £18.13.3.

William (1618-1689) is Mary's direct ancestor and he and his brother James appear to have farmed as Yeomen in partnership, one at 'Rosagreave' and one at 'Whittakers' farm, both in Thornley. Williams wife Alice was probably a Quaker, as was the eldest brother John who died in middle life. However whether the first Quaker Dilworth was Alice or John, all three of William and Alices' sons and at least one daughter (John, James, Ellin and Thomas) were very certainly early Friends. (See Dilworth tree).

Within a few months of George Fox's vision on Pendle Hill some of his followers were travelling the country, and particularly the North West, proclaiming the 'truth' they had accepted. In 1653 two of these 'Publishers' arrived in the Bowland district and a number of the country people from Newton, Slaidburn, Chipping and Whitewell became Friends. One of these Publishers, who became a close friend of George Fox, was Alexander Parker of Lees in Bowland on the River Hodder (three miles from Chipping) who was himself convinced during Fox's imbroglio in Lancaster in September 1852.

A partial description of this visit by a contemporary Friend reads:

"In ye yeare 1653 and about ye 6th month, there came two Friends our of ye North, whose names were Thomas Vears and Christopher Atkinson to a Little Town called Newton, not far from Slaidburn-in-Bowland on a 7th day at night, and were received by James Bond, a Poor man, who had a meeting the day following where John Dillworth, Ann Thown and severall people were convinced. -----

And y^e 2nd day of ye^e week had another meeting att Cuthburt Hayhurst's in Essington where they were well received. And a little after came $Will^m$ Dewsbury to y^e house of John Croasdale, and had some meetings thereabouts and soe came down to y^e house of Richard Leigh and stayd there three days and after some illnesse came to Essington to Cuthburt Hayhurst's house, and had a meeting at Slaidburn and was Pulled down and y^e Towne was all on an Uproar, but there was some who were convinced by him.

Not long after John Audland came, and had a meeting at Richard Leigh's; and Alexander Parker being come to his his fathers's house fro. Lancaster, where he was convinced, and Cuthburt Hayhurst alsoe being convinced and both of them called to ye Ministry with those who were convinced by ye ffriends aforesaid, and began to keep a meeting neare unto Newton ---- and is called Bolland Meeting.
Note: ye said Cuthbert Hayhurst, afterwards travelled in ye service of ye Gospell and became an able minister of Divers Parts of this nation and in some parts of y^eSeas, as Jamaica; and afterwards with ye unity and consent of his Brethren removed himself and his family into Pennsylvania where he died in full unity with his ffriends." *

*Extracts from mss received from Dilworth Abbatt.

The John Dillworth referred to above was probably 'that' John christened at Chipping 13th December, 1609 who was an elder brother of William and James D. and hence uncle of John, James, Ellin and Thomas who were all early Members of the Society of Friends.

Thomas Bond married Ann Parker, sister of Alexander, referred to above. Their early Friends' wedding record reads as follows:

> 'Thomas Bond of Chipin*, and Ann Parker*, daughter of Robert Parker of Bowlands, was joyned in marriage the 22nd day of 3rd mo. 1656 in the presence of Cuthbart Harst, John Driver*, William Harst and others, Richard Walne*, Jane Walne*, William Crosdall, John Crosdall, Eliz. Waddington, Robert Crosdall, William Harst, Christopher Porter, Mary Crosdall.'

(Richard and Jane Walne were the parents of Nicholas W. and they and others marked * are referred to later.)

After Ann's death Thomas Bond married Janet Laithes of Chaigley and removed to Hawkshead Monthly Meeting. Thomas was a 'first publisher of the truth' (i.e. one of Fox's earliest disciples and Quaker propagandists) and there has in the past been some confusion of identity. His 'sufferings' are documented by Besse. He died in Felixstowe and it has been suggested that there were two men of the same name. However, Dilworth Abbatt was of the firm opinion - and has left documentary evidence - that Thomas Bond of Chipping and Hawkshead and the Thomas of the 'Sufferings' and Felixstowe were the same man.

Early Meetings were held in Thomas' house in Chipping and in 1674 Clement Parker (Alexander's nephew) of Lees in Bowland and Susanna Salsbury of Lagram were married there, among the witnesses being Ann Bond and Alex. and John Dilworth. In 1686 Clement and Susanna went to live in part of Bradley Hall, one mile south of Chipping near Longridge, the other part then being the home of Thomas and his first wife, Sarah (Pearson) Dilworth. Prior to this Thomas and Sarah, James and wife Ann (Waln) together with Clement Parker had each been fined 5/- (five shillings), together with thirty five others, for participating in an unlawful Quaker Meeting. (Lancashire Quarter Sessions: QSP 529/15 1680)

Thomas Dilworth, by his third wife, was Mary's direct ancestor. He was the youngest of four staunch early Quaker siblings - James, John and Ellin being his seniors. Initially, he is described as being a 'carrier' though at his death in Wyresdale in 1726 he had prospered as a farmer, as shown by his Will and the inventory of his goods. Both James (see later) and Thomas once lived at Bradley Hall which had its first Quaker Meeting licence in 1689 in Thomas' name.

The original Bradley Hall, once the home of the Bradley family, (see map) was leased in the sixteen hundreds. In Thomas and Sarahs' time in the sixteen eighties, when they shared the roof with the Parkers, (and before that briefly with James and Ann (Waln)) it had clearly been subdivided and was rented by them. Bradley Hall, 'Rosagreave' and 'Whittakers' at Thornley, are the earliest of the identifiable 'ancestral' Dilworth homes.

Thomas married three times - see family tree - his first wife was Sarah Pearson of Tiffenthwaite, Nr. Wigton, Cumberland; they were married in John Read's house Langthwaite. Sarah was the daughter of William and Jane Pearson who were early adherents of George Fox being mentioned in his Journal. At this time Thomas was a 'Carryer' no doubt using a string of pack horses (the roads were then too rough for wheeled vehicles) and this trade no doubt took him to his first wife. By Sarah Thomas had two girls, both of whom died without issue.

After Sarah's death in 1689 Thomas removed to Wyresdale and remarried; his second wife being Mary Townson, daughter of John Townson of Chapel House, Wyresdale. The wedding took place in Jennet Bond's house - also in Wyresdale. Jennet (Janet) (Laithes) Bond was the widowed second wife of Thomas - see earlier - who after his death in Felixstowe had returned to Lancashire and Wyresdale.

Mary D's two Townson sisters were Margaret and Jennet. On the death of her first husband, Thomas Harrison of Carr House, Garstang, Margaret married John Moone the ardent Quaker propagandist and 'Publisher'. (Margaret was John Moone's second wife). Carr House is believed to be the site of George Fox's 1657 General Meeting 'between that (Preston) and Lancaster' on his way back to Swarthmoor.

By his second marriage Thomas Dilworth acquired formidable 'in-laws' and established the first 'in-law' family relationship with Jennet (Townson) Cragg 'the heroic Quakeress', (see later), who was his wife Mary's other sister. A blood relationship between 'our' Mary and Jennet, the heroine, was to come later through Jennet's great-grandchildren.

Thomas' family by Mary (T.) of Moorhead became the Lancaster and Yealand Dil(l)worths. Many were active Friends and were influential Lancaster citizens, being engaged in shipping and banking and having a major part in the Lancaster/Kendal canal. (The Dilworth bank, like so many others of its time, failed in February 1826.)

One semi-notable, William Dillworth (1716-1789), son of John Dilworth of Lancaster and a grandson of Thomas, was Clerk to Meeting for Sufferings and also Clerk to London Yearly Meeting in 1753 and 1773. On one occasion in sending a notice to Robert Abbatt junior (who was, for nearly forty years, Clerk to Preston M.M.) he attached the following postscript:

    Robert Abbatt   Lancaster 18th 8th mo. 1778

        Having recd. copy of a Minute of the Meeting Sufferings who are desirous the same may be dispersed as speedily as may be I send the above copy for you Mo. Meeting
            and remain with due esteem thy
                Affecttn. Kinsman

                      William Dillworth

This kinsman relationship is unclear but would not be imaginery and is probably evidence of another early interfamily relationship similar to the following. In 1675 John Dilworth (Thomas' elder brother) had married Ellin Hadwen, sister of Mary H. of Arnside and Mary, who married Thomas Abbatt, Cordwyner, son of 'Thomas the Dyer' (Chapter I). Whatever the connections the two families quite certainly knew each other - and probably could not have avoided so doing.

Part of the 'testimony' issued on William's death reads:

    --he kept his Habitation, in all lowliness of Mind, near to the Root of Life, and was preserved, fresh and green, and faithful in old age even to the conclusion of his days.

Both William and his brother Thomas (of Lancaster) had mainly female families. Their name died in 1830 with the death, aged 85, of John Dillworth of Yealand Conyers. They married Wilsons, Crewdsons and Wakefields of Kendal, Dockray and Jepson of Lancaster, Birkbeck of Settle, Arthington of Leeds and Satterthwaite of Colthouse.

In 1705, Thomas of Bradley Hall and Wyresdale, who obviously did not like living alone, married Ann (Corless) (Driver) at John Bond's house in Wyresdale. Ann, the widow of James, brother of John Driver (see earlier) came from Dolphinholme and was reputably a formidable woman; she not only gave her husband a family of eight but also outlived him by thirty-three years. Both were buried in Lancaster.

Thomas' will shows that he maintained contact with his origins in Chipping and Thornley as evidenced by Richard Dilworth of Chipping being an executor. The inventory of goods is valued at £61.07.04 and is signed by Robert Dunderdale of Thornley. Among his belongings, in addition to furniture, farm implements and livestock are included 'a Pinter of White Mettall' (silver) = £1.14.00, 'Turf (peat) and Cannel' (coal) = £1.00.00, standing crops, and dairy equipment.

Thomas's elder brother, John Dilworth (1651-1690) cordwainer (leather worker/shoemaker) lived in Goose Lane Chipping. His marriage to Ellen Hadwen of Arnside, Beetham took place in the house of Edward Cumming of Moss Side, Warton. Among the twelve witnesses - all men Friends from the Yealand district - were Thomas Abbatt of Newby Stones who was later to marry the bride's sister Mary, and eight others mentioned in George Fox's Journal including the latter's friend Thomas Dockwray of Silverdale. (See also note in Chapter I following 'Thomas the Dyers' wedding). John's second wife was Jenet Raingill of Chipping whom he married in his own house. He was buried at Newton-in-Bowland above the old Meeting House. It is not known if there were issue of the second marriage - those of the first died in infancy.

James Dilworth (1654-1699), the third Quaker brother, was a flaxman by trade of Thornley and Bradley Hall, near Chipping. In 1676 he had 'trouble' from the Conventicle Act under which Friends and others were heavily fined if five or more people met together for Worship. The first incident is mentioned by Joseph Besse:

> On the 13th of Dec. 1676 James Dilworth of Thornley for holding a meeting at his house had two Oxen taken from him value £9.

He married Ann Waln (1654-1710) daughter of Richard and Jane Walne of Burrholme near Whitewell - see earlier. The Walnes/Walns have been known in the Chipping area for over six hundred years with Nicholas Ws. as early as 1450! See appendix. The wedding in 1680 took place in Ann's brother Nicholas' house - Chapell Croft near Newton-in Bowland and the witnesses were:

Thomas Dilworth, Jane Birkett, James Harrison, Nicholas Waln*, Eliza Bedle, Clement Parker, Edward Wallis, Alice Salisbury, Thomas Walmsley*, Thomas Wig, Mary Hayhurst*.

All those marked * and the bride and groom sailed for Pennsylvania in 1682.

The following brief account of James and Ann's lives is taken from a Dilworth Abbatt account:

> Alexander Parker would be on intimate terms with William Penn, and it seems reasonable to believe that it was through that intimacy that a number of Settle (W. Yorkshire) Monthly Meeting Friends in the Bowland district, joined with other Quakers from Sussex who sailed in 1682 for Pennsylvania - some, including Nicholas Waln with his wife and children and families, sailing in the ship "Welcome" with William Penn on board --- immediately followed by the "Submission"

The Friends from Settle Monthly Meeting with a few from the Chipping district, --- seem early to have located themselves in the country district of Neshiminy, a score of miles to the north of Philadelphia. A note in Bowden's 'History' says: "there were many settlements of Indians in this district who were kind neighbours".

James and Ann whose first child was about a year old when they sailed, became Ministers of the Society and occasionally travelled long distances on religious service; thus in 1698, "James Dilworth visited Friends in Maryland and New England, a district previously traversed by his wife. In 1698 Ann Dilworth set out on a more extensive religious journey, this being a visit to her native land.

From the published 'Letters of William and Mary Ellis' (whose home was at Airton in Yorkshire) there is a postscript to one which he addressed to Friends of Settle Monthly meeting, 20 viii 1698, in which he says:

> "James Dilworth's wife, I suppose by this is gone to Barbadoes, and if she lives, she intends to come to England". and later in the same letter: "Nicholas Waln is well and hath many fine children".

While Ann Dilworth was on this visit to England, James Dilworth her husband, died from yellow fever†, during a terrible epidemic which attacked Philadelphia and the surrounding district.

Nicholas Waln, who would no doubt convey the intelligence

† James died at Bristol, Bucks. Pennsylvania; and Ann in 1710 in Philadelphia.

_{Note on William Penn's twenty three '1682' ships: The author has determined that James and Ann (Waln) Dilworth arrived in Pennsylvania 22nd October 1682 aboard 'The Lamb' from Liverpool. (The 'Welcome' with William Penn and Nicholas Waln arrived 28th October.) 'The Lamb' was chartered by the Settle Monthly Meeting who gave a Certificate of Removal for 30 people including seven families. These included Cuthburt Hayhurst pp. 16-17, James and Ann D., their infant son, their servant – Stephen Sands – and Mary's aunt – Mary Rudd – with their five children.}

to his sister direct, alluded to the sad event in a letter he wrote to William Ellis:

> Philadelphia 22 7 mo 1699.
>
> Since thou left, we have met with great exercises and a great mortality hath happened in the town of Philadelphia, and some in the country. But may we nothonestly say as Job said -- 'shall we receive good at the hand of the Lord? and shall we not receive evil?' -- So my dear friend, I am willing to give thee a short hint of things, and who they are who have laid down their bodies, and of those persons we had great love for ---- My dear brother-in-law James Dilworth is dead, and was buried the first-day before our Yearly Meeting.

--- Nicholas concludes:

> My dear love to my sister Ann Dilworth, if thou seest her, and let her know that her dear children are well.
>
> My son Richard desires to have his kind love to thee and thy wife, though unknown, and to his Aunt Ann Dilworth, and I desire thee to remember my love to all our relatives and Friends in Bolland.
>
> This from thy friend and brother
> Nicholas Waln

Note. Nicholas Waln was a man of individuality and education and his name appears frequently in the early history of Pennsylvania. He represented Bucks-County in the Assembly of 1693, and was a distinguished preacher in the Society, having taken up an extensive tract of land in the township on which the first Neshiminy Meeting House was built.

Nicholas, grandson, Nicholas III or tertius (1742-1813), was a distinguished lawyer and a religious described by Bowden the historian:
"As a great man, as a wise man, as a learned man, and as a rich man - I know of none possessed of as much childlike humility and simplicity as Nicholas Waln"

James and Ann Dilworth had seven children who survived infancy. Ann remarried and had a second family and there are today many Dilworths and Walns - some still Friends - throughout the United States and Canada - there is even a Dilworth Mountain in the City of Kelowna in British Columbia! See Appendix for U.S. Dilworth family tree.

A Quaker practice dating from the earliest days was for a Friend to have a concern (call) to 'minister' to a group or groups of people, who might be close at hand in their own Meeting or might equally be on another continent. In the latter case the Friend would, with a minute /introduction from their own Meeting, set out to minister to people in the places to which they had been called. Of course the vast majority of concerns to minister were satisfied in the individual's own Meeting, though extensive religious travel - as by James and Ann Dilworth and the Walns - was common, particularly in the earliest days of Quakerism.

These concerns were frequently felt and implemented by women who, as we have seen in the case of Ann (Waln) Dilworth, sometimes travelled far and often. For Friends this was not unusual, since from the days of the very first Friends, women have always been 'equal', or nearly so. (It has always seemed to the author that since men and women are different - and hence not equal - a better term and approach is one of 'Equal Terms' which does not imply an impossible equality. In any event 'Equal Terms' seems to have been the early Friends' general approach.)

Our own families do not have many notables, but of those there were, many were women. Margaret Abbatt, Sarah Ord, Elizabeth Abbatt, Jane (Adair) Abbatt, Dr. Annie Jackson and Ann (Waln) Dilworth, are examples of women with religious concerns many of whom travelled. Not all concerns were so obviously spiritual and Jennet Cragg of Wyresdale is an example of a simple welfare traveller.

Until the advent of the railway in the first half of the eighteen hundreds all travel was arduous and most of the time it was dangerous for women to travel alone. Travelling alone, which is exactly what so many Quaker women did, only added to the perils of their journeys. In 1698 when William Ellis says of Ann Dilworth, then in Barbados, 'and if she lives, she intends to come to England' he was not speaking of a remote but of a very real probability of her **not** surviving her journeys. Indeed many Friends perished while from home and John Woolman and his York death from smallpox is only one example of the health hazards of travel in times past.

'Our' Mary's grandmother - Mary (Jackson) Dilworth (1768-1858) - herself a ferocious Jackson woman - undoubtedly 'brought up' her grandchildren including 'our' Mary and her brothers on the story of her own great, great grandmother **Jennet Cragg.**

Jennet (Townson) Cragg, daughter of John Townson of

Chapel House, Wyresdale, was sister-in-law to Thomas Dilworth and through her grandson, Joseph, 'our' Mary Dilworth's direct ancestress. In 1687 Jennet rode alone from Rowton Brook, Quernmore near Lancaster, to London and back to 'rescue' her two orphaned grandsons. This feat has long been a piece of family, and at times, much embroidered, local history.

Jennet's daughter Elizabeth Cragg (1660-1685) and John Kelsall (1650-1684), of Kelsall in Cheshire, married on 2nd November 1682 and went to live in London where their two boys John and Joseph were born. John Kelsall, a Friend, and a prosperous merchant was imprisoned for persistent preaching. He was sentenced to transportation to the West Indies and later died on board ship. Jennet's daughter, Elizabeth, died soon after her husband's imprisonment and the orphans were left in the care of a Wyresdale girl - Ruth - who had been taken by the couple to London after their marriage.

On hearing of the family tragedy Jennet set out alone on horseback - reputedly riding a galloway called Midnight - and after many adventures with footpads and other unsavoury characters, returned safely to Quernmore with the two orphans in panniers. The servant girl, Ruth, later made her own way home to Wyresdale where the two boys were brought up by Jennet and her relations.

When Jennet made her journey she was aged 54 - a young grandmother - her husband, Thomas Cragg, having died three years earlier. She had then married Thomas Thompson described by his stepson Timothy Cragg (Elizabeth's brother) as 'a rough Quaker'. Timothy's 'Life' (Appendix v.) is similar in content and tone to many of the other Friends' Journals from this period. It deals with religion, politics, and provides a first hand glimpse of Wyresdale and of Jennet and Thomas Thompson.

The author as a small boy was much troubled by the then authorised version, which was as above but much embellished. He was frequently shown a warming pan and grandfather clock said to have come with Jennet and the twins. The little boy wondered (and still does) how they all fitted into Jennet's panniers. In all probability they came much later, perhaps with Ruth, after the estate had been wound up.

Many versions of the story have been told and perhaps the most appealing is the verse written in Mary's ms. album by Charles Holmes when he was staying at Calder Bridge in 1852. (Charles H. 1784-1858 and his wife Elinor Jackson were yet others of Mary's kinsmen and Cragg connections.)

The Journey to Town

I can write nought in this album, My dear Mary Dilworth
That will be worth thy perusal, much less can still be worth
The paper and ink I consume, the wear and tear of the pen
But, as I have written in others, I will make an attempt once again.

But what must I write about? I scarcely can tell,
Yet, hold! there's a subject on which I might dwell
As recounted to me in, in a late conversation
With a much valued friend, thy paternal relation.

It may interest thee, for thou art descended
From the friend about whom my story's intended;
In ardour she equalled the 'Maid of Orleans",
Though hers was displayed in far different scenes.

I think thy grandmother said, her Great-Grandmother Cragg
Rode to London, betwixt panniers, upon a stout nag.
'Twas a wonderful feat! for woman to ride,
Betwixt mane and tail with a child on each side!

Though drear the journey, and rough then the track,
These two little boys were in baskets brought back;
And were the first of the Kelsalls bearing the name
That tradition informs us to Wyresdale came.

A charming Victorian, redcovered, penny, paperback, in the Paternoster Series, was published in 1877 by Maria Wright (Charles Holmes. niece) titled "Jennet Cragg. A story of the time of the Plague". The author wrote to Mary Dilworth on publication saying that she had followed the verses above and "idealized your ancestor in my tale". This version of Jennet's story is colourful, telling of footpads and robbers, setting the London scene and attributing Elizabeth's death to the Plague.

Jennet's journey coincided with London Yearly meeting held in the third month - March - of 1687 and whether she really travelled alone all the time is not known. It was the custom to ride or drive to Y.M. in small groups and Lancaster Friends may well have convoyed her for some or all of the journey.

The author has been told that not all of the incidents are untrue. One particular aspect of Maria's story and other versions is the persistence of the Plague as a major peril for Jennet and as the cause of Elizabeth's death. This aspect has been discounted by many since the

ROWTON BROOK FARM
It was from here that Jennet Cragg rode alone to London and back on her black galloway 'Midnight'. She returned with her two orphaned Kelsall grandsons in panniers.

LOW PLEASANT FARM, QUERNMORE, LANCASTER
In MARY's day Low Pleasant was farmed by William Kelsall. (William's father Thomas was Mary (Jackson) Dilworth's uncle through his sister Ann Kelsall and William was a brother-in-law of 'our' MARY's brother William Dilworth.) This farm, well known to MARY, is immediately adjacent to Jennet Cragg's Rowton Brook (Rowton Brook Wood is at the top of the picture) and is a typical Wyresdale/Dilworth farm. In 1988 it is still in Kelsall occupation.

Plague of London proper was in 1665. However, endemic plague, with the same effects for individuals as epidemic plague, continued to be a London hazard for many years and this part of the story could well be founded on fact.

The two little boys were brought up by their grandparents and became worthy Friends. John, the elder, taught, preached and came to know well-known people including:
" --- my old acquaintance Mary Penn -- " (wife of William Penn junr.). He had a flair for writing verse and his Journal is another good example of a Quaker journal. Of Jennet he says: "She was one who loved Truth, and truly esteemed the faithful friends thereof."

In 1728 John took a farm near the Meeting House at Dolobran for £6 a year and kept two cows and the school. From 1729-34 he was Clerk to the Payton family at Dolobran furnace (N. Wales) at £30 p.a. overseeing workmen and teaching school in town. Later, he went to Cork in Ireland to find work - again teaching school - and had 25 pounds and his board. Here he was taken ill and on 4th December sailed for Bristol and his family at Dolgyn. In 1743 he went to Yearly Meeting in Wyresdale.

Joseph, the younger, married Margaret Winder, daughter of William Winder of Wyresdale (1700- 1782). Initially they farmed at Tarnbrook, but later removed to Rowton Brook, Quernmore. John and Margarets' descendants intermarried with virtually all the families of our story, and he himself never left Wyresdale. Kelsalls still farm at Low Pleasant the next door farm to Rowton Brook. Another family story of this period in Wyresdale is:

> 'At the time of the Scotch Rebellion in 1745, when a party of Scots went up there in quest of baggage carts and horses. Joseph Kelsall, very likely being aware of their coming took his horse up to an outbarn some distance from the house and left his wife and children to take their chances with the Scots. They (the Scots) behaved curtly, but wanted something to eat and were in a great hurry to get it cooked, there was a poor fire, so the officer who commanded the party ordered one of his men to help the woman to blow. I have heard it said they took a horse and cart and serving man with them and the family were very much afraid they would never come back, but they did come back again.'

Including the first Thomas, five generations of Dilworths lived without interruption in Wyresdale, in the more than two hundred year period from 1687. (William Dilworth died at Ortner in 1902). Thomas' third family moved less than the children of the second and throughout remained close to the soil. During these years they inevitably met and intermarried with the Craggs, Jacksons, Kelsalls, Swindlehursts, Simpsons, Wilcocksons, Winders and other families mentioned in 'the letters'.

Thomas' grandson, William Dillworth, (1756-1833), of Chapel House, illustrates the above very well. William had married Mary Jackson (1768-1858), daughter of John 'The Honest Miller' and Ann Kelsall of Wyresdale, in 1785 and by her had three children - John Jackson, Jane and William. By his will he appointed: "My Friends Richard Jackson of Calder House in Barnacre, --- Joshua Kelsall (his first cousin) of Over Wyresdale and my Son John Jackson Dilworth -- ". By this will his wife, Mary, received enough furniture --- of her own choosing to furnish two rooms and an annuity of £25 per annum. In addition: " -- to my Son William the annuity or yearly sum of six pounds --- ". The remainder of the estate was to be divided equally between his Son and Daughter John Jackson and Jane Wilcockson. These provisions are contingent upon " ---- in case my said son William Dilworth shall continue in the opinion of my said trustees - unreformed during the remainder of his life."

William, who was very handsome, was disowned by the Society for drunkenness and womanising. He emigrated to America and remained unreformed, with drink, gambling and women being his weaknesses.

Dilworth wills tended to be simple and straightforward, with few strings. Wives did not lose their inheritances if they remarried, few sons were 'cut off with a shilling (or six pounds)', and estates were equally divided. Trustees tended to be close relations and were usually Friends. These wills are in marked contrast to those of the Jackson family which, almost invariably, established long, complicated, unequal trusts, to deal with unequal divisions and contingencies such as William Dilworth's reformation. Whether Jackson wives and children merited conditions or whether it was a Jackson way of doing things will never be known. William was half Jackson and the son of Mary, one of the formidable Jackson women, - a family where women tended to be stronger than the men. One cannot argue or learn from single examples.

This sketch of Mary's Dilworth origins, with its mixed Wyresdale skeins of Kelsall, Jackson and Dilworth blood, is not 'a family history' but intended as background. The picture, despite the minor dramas of Jennet Cragg and James and Ann Dilworth, is one of unrelieved yeoman Quaker stock from a Wyresdale which is still unchanged.

III   GROWING UP AND ACKWORTH

Jonathan born Bolton - Ackworth 1838 - Mary born Ortner - Ackworth - to Calder House - Richard, John and Jonathan Jackson - Building of Calder Bridge Meeting Ho. - First Abbatt at Ackworth - Ackworth founded - John Fothergill - Wm.and Esther Tuke - For children of parents'not in affluence' - Bills of Admission - Early curriculum - Written examsfrom U.S.A.- Discipline and rules - Punishments- Pleasureand recreation - Garden plots- Societies- The Green - 'Eo ad Pontefractum- Thomas Frith - Hessle Common excursion & description by Wm. Howitt - Childrens dress - SchoolMenu - Rebecca Thursfield's letters - General Meeting - Joseph John Gurney - Not a closed society - Travel subsidy - The Family - The Flags - Travel to school in 1840 - Jonathan bound apprentice - John Fletcher - Apprentice tales - Wood cutting at Brock - Dilworth Family at Calder Bridge - Jno. in love with Mary - Henry Fletcher and John J.D.

Jonathan Abbatt was the third son of nine children born to Benjamin and Elizabeth Abbatt. According to his Mother's diary he was born at 8.10 am on the 'Eighth of the Third month 1829 and is a fine child'. The birth note, signed by Thomas Walker, surgeon and Susanna Mulliner, records Benjamin as a Basket Maker and the birth as occurring at Great Bolton in the Parish of Bolton-le-Moors. Nothing is known of his early childhood beyond the fact that he went for two years to 'the same dame [school] as his brother William' and that he assisted his Father in the cane business for 'some months before I went to Ackworth'. He was then aged nine and remained there without a break until the spring of 1843.

John Jackson and Ann (Wilcockson) Dilworth, at the time of Mary's birth, farmed at Ortner in Wyresdale. Mary, born 30th April 1828 the third child and only daughter of Ann and John Jackson, was a year older than Jonathan. Her early schooling was at Friends School, Wyresdale where she was taught by a 'cousin' Joshua Kelsall. Here she learnt to write using sand trays and at the age of twelve, following her brothers, William and David, she, too, went to Ackworth, remaining there until 1842.

In addition to Ann D. and her Wilcockson brothers and sisters,at least five Wyresdale Dilworths had been to Ackworth in the early days of the seventeen eighties and nineties. Therefore, going away to school was no novelty for Dilworth children. Nevertheless, the long horse drawn

29

road journey from Wyresdale, through the Trough of Bowland and Yorkshire, to Ackworth was a major adventure for young children travelling alone from home.

John Jackson and Ann (Wilcockson) Dilworth lived and farmed at Ortner in Wyresdale and it was here that David and Mary were born, spent their childhood and to Ortner that Mary's elder brother William later retired. In or about 1850, eight years after Mary left Ackworth, John Jackson D. and his family left Ortner and moved to Calder Bridge in Barnacre. Calder House is immediately in front of Calder Bridge Meeting House and about one mile south of Garstang and eight to nine miles from Wyresdale (see map). John's mother, (and Mary's grandmother) Mary (Jackson), who had lived at Greenbank, Wyresdale had been widowed in 1833 and at the time of the move was living with her son and daughter-in-law.

The move to Calder House was not a move into unknown territory since Mary (Jackson) Dilworth's three kinsmen had preceded the Dilworths in their move from Wyresdale. The three brothers, Richard, John and Jonathan Jackson of Spout House, had left Wyresdale in 1820 to 'make their way in the world'. They ultimately became cotton and paper manufacturers in Calder Vale and at Oakenclough, though Richard soon retired. In 1820, for his second wife, Richard had married Mary Wilcockson of Preston, Ann Dilworth's elder sister and 'our' Mary's Aunt. After his father's death, John Jackson D. and his uncle (and brother-in-law), Richard, had became close friends, when, over a long period as executors and trustees of William Dilworth's will, they had administered an onerous trust regarding John J. D.'s brother William, (see Chapter II).

Following Richard's retirement from 'cotton' he led a rural farming life and Hewitson writing in the eighteen sixties described Richard as:

> ---- a Friend after the right pattern, honest straight forward and unassuming; who delighted in the quiet life of a country yeoman. ------ there are many living who love to picture the good old man in his broad brimmed hat, drab clothes, knee breeches and clogs - to which he was very partial - and to recount the many deeds of kindness which he was continually extending to his neighbours.

After leaving Wyresdale, the Jackson brothers and their families had continued to attend their old Meeting for Worship in Wyresdale and from time to time in Richard's home at Calder House. This arrangement, in the days of the horse and of bad winters, was not a reasonable long

ORTNER in WYRESDALE c.1895 – MARY'S BIRTHPLACE
John Jackson and Ann Dilworth farmed here for 27 years, MARY (D) A. and her brother David were born at Ortner and MARY's elder brother William was born at Caton Green but later retired and died here in 1901.

CALDER HOUSE – at CALDER BRIDGE 1987
MARY's home from which she was married, whence she wrote and where she received 'The Letters'.

LANE from CALDER HOUSE to CALDER BRIDGE F.M.H. 1987
MARY's 'Sunday Go to Meeting' path.

CALDER BRIDGE FRIENDS MEETING HOUSE 1987
Built by Richard Jackson of Calder House in 1828 (the porch was added in 1890).

term proposition. Therefore in 1828 Richard, who lived at Calder House, - with a little assistance from his brothers - built the present Meeting House immediately behind his home. It is one of, if not, the most picturesque and peaceful places on this earth.

After Richard's death in 1846 what could have been more natural than for John J. and his family, including, of course, his mother, to move to his uncle and his friend's old home at Calder House when it eventually became vacant. Ann Dilworth favoured the move as both their sons had left Wyresdale and were now relatively close in her old hometown of Preston. Calder Bridge provided exactly the setting and life J.J.D. sought for his semi retirement. In 1853 the rent was a mere ten pounds a year, and here, he and Ann happily lived and died, cattle grazing and dealing from rented land at Little Calder.

It was at Calder Bridge that Mary grew up and it was at Calder House that Mary first consciously met Jonathan. From here she wrote and received her letters and it was at Calder Bridge Meeting that they were to be married. Throughout her life she remained, as did so many members of the families, deeply attached to Wyresdale and to the Calder Bridge area.

Ackworth is a Quaker school in the village of Ackworth about three miles south of Pontefract in Yorkshire. It has been described as the "ancestral school" by generations of Abbatts and Dilworths. The first member of the Abbatt family to go to the school in 1807 as no. 2870 was James (1796-1868), Jonathan's eldest uncle, who in 1843 emigrated to Peoria, Illinois in the U. S. A. Jonathan and his six brothers and sisters, as well as Mary Dilworth and her two brothers, all attended the school. It is certain that the school was regarded as an important influence for good in their lives, since all four of their children were sent there. Subsequently, all spoke favourably and with nostalgia of their schooldays.

Jonathan and Mary were at Ackworth together (Jonathan 1838-42 and Mary 1840-42) and it was a very potent 'extra- familial' influence of their formative years.

Ackworth was founded by the Yearly Meeting of the Society of Friends (Quakers) in 1779. John Fothergill M.D. who died in 1780, acquired the site and donated generously to the project where he was the catalyst (and a 'name'), in a continuing process with many leading actors prominent among whom were William and Esther Tuke of York. Fothergill, a leading Quaker physician and friend of Benjamin Franklin, had been enlisted by the latter together with David Barclay in 1774-5 in an attempt to resolve the British/American differences that led to the War of Independence. Education of the young was one of his lifelong concerns. Ackworth was a boarding school established for the children of Friends "whose parents are not in affluence". The original buildings were constructed for the London Foundling Hospital and operated from 1757-73 until closed by financial failure. From its foundation, Ackworth was a school for both sexes - two schools run in parallel but not co-educational. In a very real sense the school set a Quaker pattern, since in addition to surviving and flourishing it was to a very large extent the model for other later foundations. Friends schools at Sidcot 1808, Wigton 1823, Bootham 1823 and Leighton Park 1890 in England, were to an appreciable extent, influenced by Ackworth: in the U.S., Westown School in Philadelphia 1779 was, after much "thought and correspondence", patterned after Ackworth's model.

In the latter part of the eighteenth century educational facilities available to Quakers were unsatisfactory for two reasons. The first was material but much the more important reason was conscience. This arose from the fact that one line of Quaker thought throughout the eighteenth century mistrusted reason, intellect and intelligence and held that God could speak most clearly through the 'Inner Light' to a mind uncomplicated by thought. Carried to its logical end, which Friends usually did, this belief was not conducive to establishing and promoting a good educational system. It must be emphasised that this line of thought, belief and action, represented only one school of Quaker thought and was at odds with many of the beliefs and the teaching of George Fox and William Penn.

The material reasons for the educational differences were, in part, that many early Friends were yeomen, farmers, chapmen, nailers and the like; and as a result, while they were not poverty stricken, they were not yet in 'affluent cicrcumstances'. Relative material poverty and the inaccessibility of education were the problems. The limitation of access arose because most education was, and in England remained for many years, tied to and run by the established (Anglican)Church. Dissenters were thus automatically disbarred from access to the best schools and to all universities.

In a fund-raising effort prior to the opening of Ackworth 18th October 1779, four methods were proposed:
    a. Donations.
    b. Annuities paying 5% p.a. for life. Minimum 50 pounds sterling.
    c. Bills of admission* at eight guineas (eight

pounds and eight shillings) per year per child for tuition board and lodging.
d. Ordinary annual subscriptions.

----

*BILL of ADMISSION

No.   Ackworth School
"Received the ---- day of the ---- Month 17--. The sum of Eight Guineas, for the use of this Institution, for which a child, not under Seven nor exceeding Thirteen years of Age, being a Member of the Society called Quakers, is entitled to Education, Board, and Cloathing for One Year".   --- Day of the --- Month 17--

Admit   a Child aged --- Years and ---
Months, a Member of ------------ Monthly Meeting.

"To the Treasurer of Ackworth School, in Yorkshire. Before this Bill of Admission can be made use of the Order must be properly filled up and signed by an Agent to the School, in whose name the Child's account will be kept: it will be most agreeable to receive all future Payments and directions concerning the said Child thro' his Hands."

The first subscriptions invested in Navy Bonds were later sold at a considerable loss; to meet this the trustee successfully appealed to "the Committee of the American Fund" for a loan. This fund had been established for those Friends suffering religious persecution in America.

The initial curriculum consisted of the English language, writing and arithmetic for both sexes, and in addition a requirement ' --- that girls also be instructed in housewifery and useful needlework'. Geography was introduced for both sexes in the early eighteen hundreds (girls after boys) and formal religious instruction commenced in 1812, followed later by the systematic teaching of the classics and in 1820 by English history.

The expanded curriculum of the late eighteen thirties and forties included, geography and classics together with religious instruction and scripture.

Children were sent to Ackworth at seven, eight or nine years of age for three to four years. There were no holidays at Ackworth until Jonathan and Mary had left school (a first trial of holidays was begun in 1845). It seems that Jonathan, and probably Mary, were never visited by their parents when they were at the school.

All examinations, which were frequent, were oral and conducted by members of the School Committee. Women Friends examined the girls and men the boys. Written examinations were imported later in 1845 from the U.S.A. where they had attracted Friends' attention.

Discipline and rules were appreciable and though they were slightly different for girls and boys, they differed not at all in spirit.

RULES TO BE STRICTLY OBSERVED BY ALL BOYS AT ACKWORTH SCHOOL, AND TO BE READ TO THEM ONCE A MONTH

1st That they rise at 6 o'clock in the Summer and 7 o'clock in the Winter, and dress themselves quietly and orderly, endeavouring to begin the day in the Fear of the Lord, which is as a fountain of life preserving from the snares of death.

2nd That they wash their faces and hands, and at the ringing, of the bell, collect themselves in order and come decently into the school; that they take their seats in a becoming manner, without noise or hurry, and that they begin business when the Master shall direct.

3rd That they refrain from talking and whispering in the schools, and when repeating their lessons to the Master that they speak audibly and distinctly.

4th That they shall not be absent from school or go out of bounds without leave.

5th That when the bell rings for breakfast, dinner, or supper they collect themselves together in silence and due order, having their faces and hands washed, their hair combed etc., and so proceed quietly into the dining room.

6th That they observe a Solemn Silence, both before and after meals, that they eat their food decently and refrain from talking.

7th That they avoid quarrelling, throwing sticks, stones and dirt, striking and teazing one another, and they are enjoined not to complain about trifles, and when at play to observe moderation and decency.

8th That they neither borrow, lend, buy nor exchange without leave, and they strictly avoid gaming at all times; that they never tell a lie, use the Sacred Name irreverently, or mock the aged or deformed. That when strangers speak to them they give a modest, audible answer, standing up and with their faces turned toward them. That they shall not be possessed of nor have the use of more than one penny per week; that if any other money be found upon them it shall be taken away.

9th That they use a sober becoming behaviour when going to, and coming from religious meeting.

10th That their whole conduct and conversation be dutiful to their Masters and kind and affectionate to their schoolfellows, and that in all cases they observe the command of Christ "All things whatsoever ye would that men should do unto you do ye even so unto them".

11th That in the evening they collect themselves and take their seats in the dining room and, after answering their names when called over, and attending to such parts of the Holy Scriptures as may be read to them, they retire to their bedchambers and undress with as much stillness as possible, folding their clothes neatly and putting them into their proper places; and they are tenderly advised to close, as well as begin the day with remembering their Gracious Creator, "whose mercies are over all his works."

The rules were maintained by a variety of punishments, the most formidable of which (apart from **very** rare expulsion) was confinement in either "Light and Airy" rooms or in "The Fourth Room". Close confinement was normally for days or parts of days, but spells as long as six or more days are recorded. The boy was placed in "a light and airy" room which was about eight feet by eight feet and was alone with a wooden chair and no other furniture; he had a view of the sky only, through a louvred window. Prior to incarceration the boy's pockets were emptied and his diet for a serious offence was bread and water. "The Fourth room", used until the eighteen fifties, for troublesome disobedience, was never heated, was barely lit and had a wooden log for seating.

Another form of punishment, later abolished, related to the stomach, since it involved depriving the child of 'spice money'. In Mary and Jonathan's time at school 'spice money' consisted of the right to select from a school institution, a certain Mrs. Snowdon, a pennyworth of candies, whip cord, pocket combs or whatever. Pocket money was introduced later, at first in the form of 'penny notes' and then as coinage. Corporal punishment or caning was a disciplinary standby and employed relatively rarely. From the beginning there was acute awareness of the dangers of this punishment.

Extract from Rules:
   In order that punishments be inflicted with coolness and temper, and in proportion to the nature of the offence the following method is agreed upon, that the treasurer and each master keep a book and minute down offences committed within the day; that once a week or oftener they meet together and inspect these books and administer such punishments as may be agreed upon, useing their endeavours to convince the children that the only purpose of the correction is for their amendment, and to deter others from the commission of like offences.

For corporal punishment the master minuting an offence for which the cane was agreed to be appropriate, did not administer the punishment nor did retribution occur until a week after the offence. In this way punishments were inflicted with "coolness and temper".

Pleasures and recreation were few and simple. One of the more remarkable recreations was gardening; each boy was permitted to have a small plot of land and cultivate it mostly with flowers but also with vegetables, seeds for this activity being bought by the individual gardener to a limit of ten pence per year. This is a surprisingly large sum and indicates the perceived importance of this activity. A school custom arising from the gardening activities was for radish and nasturtium growers to eat their produce at the evening meal. The meal then consisted of radish, nasturtium leaves, bread and butter with water to drink; all considered it to be delicious!

Societies existed but did not abound. They included a Horticultural Society, a Society of Arts for drawing, mapping modelling and penmanship, and an 'Association for the Improvement of the Mind' which produced an internal periodical 'The Ackworth Review' which had three objectives:
   - to correct wrong opinions among members.
   - to teach them to think correctly.
   - to excite a love of knowledge and improvment.

During a school year there were two whole days designated as school holidays. One was of doubtful value since it was devoted to preparing the school premises for the Pontefract Friends' Monthly Meeting in the Fifth Month (May). For boys this preparation consisted of weeding a large area of pebbles known as "The Green". Two hundred small boys on hands and knees weeding! The girls at this time were similarly 'well occupied', but this was **not** a popular holiday. Despite the unpopularity of the 'preparation' holiday, Monthly Meeting and its attendant festivities were an 'event'; and at this time twenty of the older boys were chosen by lot and given an 'Eo ad Pontefractum' leave slip where they were entertained by Pontefract Friends. At this time Thomas Frith a Friend, was manufacturing Pontefract Cake (a liquorice based sweet or candy) behind his shop. It became a school child's dream to be entertained by the Friths and to eat unlimited sweets! Outings were rare and leisure and pleasures rationed, and whether happiness then was less than ours today will never be known, however in retrospect the children were not unhappy. For those boys who did not receive Pontefract invitations there was a popular alternative excursion to Hessle Common ("for those who did not dine on liquorice"). William Howitt describes this trip of the eighteen twenties which remained valid for the next twenty five years.

- The bell rang and they ran to collect in the shed, drew up in two lines facing each other perhaps two yards apart. Large wicker baskets were brought forth from the store room, piled with hats of all imaginable shapes and species; for they were such as had been left by the boys from the commencement of the Institution; they wear none except at these times: and there they were - broad brims, narrow brims, brown, black and white; pudding crowns, square crowns, and even sugar loaf crowns, such as Guy Faux himself wore. These without ceremony were popped on the boys at random - little ones were left sticking on the very summits of great round headed lads ready to fall off at the first move - and great ones dropping over the noses of little ones. Away they went, --- Oh the pleasant memories of these excursions! The along green and bowering lanes, cottages, gardens; past great waters, and woods and gentlemens houses, to a common - such a common!" (Hessle Common near Ackworth). It seems to me it was boundless, and full of all sorts of pleasant and wonderful things. There at the lifting of a hand, a shout broke out, like the shout of an army; and we dispersed in every direction. There too when it was time to return - a time alas that pounced on us too soon! - a handkerchief hoisted on a pole, upon some eminence; a shout raised by a little group, collected with some difficulty, became the signals of retreat; and every minute the group grew and grew, and every moment the shout swelled lounder and longer; and parties of 'hare and hounds' came panting up, all warmth and animation; and stragglers were seen toiling wearily from far distant nooks; till the last - some embryo poet very likely - roused at the last minute from some brook-side reverie, arriving we marched homeward.

The Hessle Common morning outing was the only occasion in the year when the boys (en masse) were allowed off their own premises. The afternoon of this day was spent in the playground - no school or lessons.

Clothing for the children at Ackworth was provided by the school as part of the board and lodging. Changes in style were made during the years - though sometimes rather later than the changes that had occurred in the outside world. In the early days (c.1790-1820) the dress has been described:

- the cocked hat, long tailed coat, the leather breeches and the buckled shoe were the dress even for boys. The girls figured in white caps, the hair turned back over them, and combed straight down the forehead, checked aprons with bibs and white neck handkerchiefs folded neatly over their stuff gowns in front. Their walking costume was a kind of hat, the pattern of which cannot be indicated, and a long cloth cloak with coloured mits reaching to the elbows. --- while Friend's-bonnets and long cloth cloaks forme the winter costume --- .

In 1820 the boys leather breeches were abandoned for trousers of velveteen or 'whistling corduroy'. One pair of leather trousers was retained for temporary punishment wear of boys who inked their trousers. By 1832 boy's nightshirts had appeared, washed every two weeks, also flannel waistcoats for winter wear. At this time, too, caps of dark brown worsted replaced the boys hats for wear in the playground. In 1837 the wearing of caps by girls in Meeting was discontinued, though their other dress was unchanged.

From this we have a remarkably clear sartorial picture of Jonathan A. and Mary Dilworth in their schooldays.

The quality of the school food was a constant preoccupation of the Friends County Committee responsible to Yearly meeting in London for the day to day running of Ackworth. The menu changed very little in the first fifty years of the school, but by Mary and Jonathans' time the menu probably contained a little more beef than is indicated below. Otherwise it was essentially unchanged. The beef was Scotch being bought on the hoof from drovers on the Great North Road (Edinburgh to London) as they passed through Wentbridge (four miles East). Wheat was bought in Pontefract and ground by windmill at Ackworth.

BILL of FARE
BREAKFASTS

EVERY DAY
- Milk Porridge poured on bread.

DINNERS

FIRST DAY [Sunday]
- Boiled sweet Puddings with Currants. Sometimes Apple Pies, and in Summer occasionally other Fruit Pies or Cheesecakes.

SECOND DAY [Monday]
- Beef or Mutton, dressed by steam, (sometimes a little Pork) with Turnips, Carrots, Greens, or Potatoes, and Bread; no Butter.
- Roast Meat may be substituted occasionally, but not often.

THIRD DAY [Tuesday]
- Boiled Suet Puddings, with Sweet Sauce.

FOURTH DAY [Wednesday]
- Meat Soup. In Summer this Dinner may be occasionally changed for Bacon, with Beans, Pease, Lettuce, Roots, or Greens and Bread; no Butter.

FIFTH DAY [Thursday]
- Baked Batter Puddings, with Sweet Sauce; (sometimes baked Rice Puddings) if Milk can be spared, if not, boiled Rice Puddings, with a few Eggs.

SIXTH DAY [Friday]
- Beef of Mutton, dressed with Steam, with Potatoes, Greens, or other Vegetables, and Bread; no Butter.

SEVENTH DAY [Saturday]
- Meat Soup.

The girls' side at Ackworth was very similar to that of the boys. even though it was virtually separate. One of the distinguishing features was needlework, both plain and 'fancy' - a once popular vogue was working samplers. Mary's sampler dated 1838 (in the authors possession) is plain, small but very neat - her mother Ann Wilcockson's worked in 1801 was bigger and more elaborate!

The following extracts from letters written in the eighteen seventies by Rebecca Thursfield of Evesham, deal with her time at the school in the late eighteen twenties about ten years before Mary Dilworth's time at Ackworth:

General Meeting for all Ackworth and for those associated with the school, was, from early days the 'Grand Festival' of the year. I found myself amidst this scene of interest and excitement, entering into it heartily, and looking out for the appearance on the "Green" of friends either known or unknown. From time to time as the day wore on, messenger after messenger arrived summoning one girl or another to some Friend who enquired for her. These were the privileged ones, whom some of the others regarded, perhaps, with a pardonable measure of envy. But there was **one** arrival anticipated, in which all share with equal interest, and when it was announced that Joseph John Gurney (a prominent Quaker reformer and brother of Elizabeth Fry) had reached the school, the girls gathered with one accord upon the "Green" to receive him, clustering around him like a swarm of bees. The scriptural examination he was to conduct was looked forward to as among the chief interests of the General Meeting.

Among the 'officers' told off for various little services during occasion, two of the older girls had been deputed to have charge of the tables placed on the "Green" with a small display of fancy work for sale - the occupation of girls in play hours. Conspicuous among this were the pincushions knit in two colours, either of silk or crewel, some having the words 'From Ackworth School' knit on one side.

Third Day (Tuesday) evening passed amid a variety of preparations for the much thought of morrow. We rose that morning later than usual, as there was no school before breakfast. There were no devotional or other meetings in those days in the early morning; no gathering of First Day (Sunday) school teachers, as yet such schools were unknown in the Society. But at ten o'clock the girls began to file out of the playroom, where they had collected, across the "Green" to the Meeting House - then occupying the end portion of the opposite wing. They were dressed in their usual dark stuff frocks, with white muslin caps and tippets, the short sleeves of the frocks being supplemented by long mittens as covering for the arms and hands. We had to sit closer than usual on our backless forms to make room for the large influx of visitors; and then, when all were assembled, the usual solemn silence of a Friends' Meeting gathered the worshiping company and much earnest prayer and preaching doubtless followed, which my memory has failed to retain.

--- How strange it seems, in these days of railways and penny postage, [written about 1870] to recall the

SAMPLER
WORKED IN
1838 BY MARY
DILWORTH
AGED TEN

THE GIRLS' WING, ACKWORTH SCHOOL c.1838–42
Note the costumes of MARY and JONATHAN's period and 'The Flags' (flagstone path).

JOHN FLETCHER 1802-1854 and MARY (BROWN) FLETCHER 1802-1874
John was JONATHAN's stern apprentice Master and Mary, his wife, was sister to JONATHAN's mother, Elizabetha (Brown) Abbatt.

HENRY FLETCHER 1816-1876
Henry, John's younger brother, supervised the Brock valley alder cutting expedition which was the occasion for the apprentice JONATHAN to meet MARY at Calder Bridge and for them to fall in love.

infrequency of visits from near relatives, and the
rarity of receiving letters from home. I remember,
after having been three or four months at school,
being seriously reproved for having said I had either
a letter or a parcel every time a certain teacher had
been on duty, which was once in four weeks; it was
thought a thing incredible that I should have been so
favoured beyond the most - for alas! some poor
children had very little from their homes. A letter
from my home, by post, cost elevenpence by the time it
reached the school. Only four times in the the year
had we the liberty to write a letter; and that was a
careful school production revised and corrected in due
form and order. Sometimes, in order to save postage,
two girls residing in the same town wrote on one sheet
of post paper - the prescribed quantity in those days,
for one postage.

In 1825, one fourth of the girls - those sitting at
the First Table in the dining room - wore small thick
muslin caps. All had their hair cut short and just
parted on the forehead. Before I left in 1829, the
caps had almost disappeared. Only a few of the biggest
girls continued to wear them, except that the parlour
waiters were always expected to wear them ----- .
They were retained however for going to Meeting in,
during the summer; while Friends' bonnets and long
cloth coats formed the winter costume on those
occasions. A variety of beaver and straw bonnets etc.
did service when we went all together for our monthly
walk in procession.

That Ackworth had a religious background and a strong one
is beyond doubt; attendance at Meeting for Worship was a
part of the way of life and certainly compulsory. There
is no question, however, of the school - or the Society -
having shut out the outside world, or of having a closed
order. The evidence of being 'open' is early, frequent
and clear. The first non-Friend was admitted to the
school in 1787 and in 1816 a clergyman from Ferrybridge
was engaged to teach classics and scripture.

An interesting and illustrative feature of Ackworth's
perspective, practicality and intent was the early
existence of a travel 'subsidy'. The school allowed a
deduction of two pence per mile in excess of fifty miles
to aid the parents of children living an appreciable
distance from the school. This 'subsidy' was available
only for children at the school for two years or more.
The average length of stay at Ackworth during its first
century (1779-1879) was three years and eight months.

Since so many of the children were Friends, they were often related, and the numbers of sisters, brothers and cousins was appreciable. Jonathan 'overlapped' with two of his brothers - as did Mary Dilworth. Since Ackworth was not coeducational, it was best described as two schools in one community and the whole was referred to as "The Family". Boys and girls lived, ate, and were taught separately; though they attended meeting together and together they shared the very few high days and holidays. Brothers and sisters and cousins (who might be fairly distant but whose relationship had to be genuine) were recognised and were permitted to meet frequently and to walk and promenade on "The Flags", a simple path of flag stones below "The Green" situated between the boys' and girls' wings. That "The Flags" were important is certain, and it is equally certain that many of the children who walked "The Flags" subsequently married.

From the time the school began in the late eighteenth century until the advent of the universal train in the middle of the nineteenth, travel was slow, difficult and in the early days dangerous, as there was an abundance of highwaymen and footpads. A brief description of the journey from Bolton in Lancashire to Ackworth has been provided by Jonathan's younger brother and partial school contemporary - James (1831-1895). This account is interesting in that it illustrates very well the tedium and length, in 1840, of a simple journey of perhaps fifty five miles. Mary's journey five years earlier was even slower and more arduous from Wyresdale and through the Trough of Bowland.

> In 1840 the only bit of railway on the route to Ackworth was that between Bolton and Manchester. We stayed in Manchester all night, leaving by coach at six o'clock the following morning via Oldham. At Huddersfield a private carriage was engaged, a number of Friends sharing the expense; we then arrived at Ackworth at three p.m. a nine hours journey from Manchester.

In Jonathan's time it was customary for boys to 'be educated'at Ackworth, often after a 'Dame' school, from the age of eight or nine and then from the age of twelve or thirteen to be apprenticed to a trade for the customary seven years. It was then quite common to "set out on one's own account" (i.e. in business) at about the age of twenty-five. Marriage often followed.

Jonathan followed this pattern. After leaving school he was at home for a little under a year during which time he worked in his stern father's cane business, while his future was being decided for him. The cane business had been considered for Jonathan, but was rejected and he was apprenticed to his maternal aunt Mary (Brown's) husband, John Fletcher of Leigh near Bolton. Jonathan was not at any stage consulted and 'never fancied' the trade to which he was apprenticed. Later he frequently recalled to his children how 'he wept bitterly after signing his indentures for seven long years'. For the poor little boy of just fourteen it must indeed have been a depressing prospect, not only was he to leave home (which he hardly knew), but he had to live in Leigh apprenticed to a particularly stern and unyielding Quaker uncle and Master. The indenture (see appendix i.), is a fascinating document and an unspoken commentary on a thought process and way of life long gone.

In later life Jonathan told his children many stories of his life and exploits as a 'prentice'. Much the happiest of these were of wood cutting expeditions to Ruabon in North Wales and to Snape Rake in the Brock Valley immediately south of Calder Bridge. Henry Fletcher, the younger brother of Jonathan's Master, was in charge of two chosen apprentices who slept in the woods for spells of three weeks or more. While there, they selected, felled and rough trimmed Alder trees prior to cutting clog soles from the resulting lumber. On Sundays they went to the nearest Meeting and at Calder Bridge the two old Ackworth scholars consciously met for the first time. (They had not known each other at school). Ann Dilworth's kitchen had a famous reputation and since the Meeting House and Calder House are adjacent to one another John Jackson or Ann D. frequently asked the party from the the woods to eat with the Dilworth family. It was at this time and in her own home that Jonathan met and fell in love with Mary. It was at this time, too, that Henry and John Jackson D. formed an enduring friendship.

If Jonathan's preparation for life is compared with present practices the net result and the timing has changed little. It should be remembered when making comparisons, that a university education, until quite late in the present century, was only related rather distantly to earning one's living. In the nineteenth century - apart from the religious barriers - it was available only to those "above the middle walks of life". However, Mary's life - as opposed to her education - prior to courtship and marriage was very different from that of a modern girl. The main differences, as will be seen in the next chapters, lay in a virtually 'permanent' home and a busy and stimulating way of life in a country society of friends and relations. This no longer exists.

IV THE APPROACH - 1853

Jonathan's formal Esteemed Friend letter and Mary's reply - Seeking and gaining Parental Approval - Jane (Abbatt) /Adair - A misunderstanding - Concern for Secrecy - Travel to and from Garstang by rail and foot - Wilcocksons and Satterthwaites - Quaker cousins - Gilbert and the Adairs - John Jackson and Ann Wilcockson/Dilworth - The Wyresdale Cradle - White Blue Bells - Quaker Relations - Jacksons - The Information Grapevine - Mary stays with Relations - Liverpool/Birkenhead etc. - Jno. and Mary's station in Life - A Quaker Answer - Death and funeral of Benjamin Abbatt - Jane A. stays at Calder - Mary D. and Mary Nichol to Preston and Fleetwood - Jno. is Unsettled - Buys his own Business - John Fletcher - House Rental and other costs in 1853 - More Grapevine - The year End.

Jonathan's first letter to Mary is dated 1 mo 31st 1853. From the earliest days Friends had used neither names of months nor named days of the week, feeling that such usage was pagan and close to blasphemy. Both months and days were referred to numerically with January and Sunday thus being 1st month and first day respectively.

To: Mary Dilworth
    Calder Bridge   Nr. Garstang

Preston
1 mo 31st 1853 [Monday]

Esteemed Friend
    Mary Dilworth

Although I thus address thee on a subject for which thou may be unprepared yet I trust thou will have noticed the interest I have taken in thee, but should the following not meet with thy approval I beg thou will with due respect to my feelings which are truly sincere preserve entire silence. Having now known thee for a longer time than thou art perhaps aware at least to a limited extent and being more pleased each time I have seen thee I have been induced though not without thinking it well over to pen these lines. Having but few opportunites of seeing thee I am obliged to adopt this course though would rather of asked thee personally if I may reasonably expect to form a more intimate acquaintance or may I ask am I preceded by some one more fortunate than myself in obtaining a share of thy affections.

Do not take this question as the result of inquisitiveness but from motives purely sincere.

Knowing this to be an important step where our future is concerned I thought I would write now that I am going from home tomorrow to stop till next first or 2nd day when perhaps by that time thou would have had time to weigh the matter and I hope thou then could return me a favourable answer but if not do please let me have an answer it is so unpleasant to be kept in suspense. I have thought much of thee this long time past a[nd] trust I may be allowed to esteem thee as something more than a friend. Thou will perceive I have used no high flown or extravagant expressions of admiration as is frequently the case on occasions like this which I consider much out of place and prefer the simple honest truth ungarnished. I have now said sufficient for thee I think to understand me and for the present will conclude with best wishes and subscribe myself thy much interested
        Friend
          Jon.n Abbatt
            158 Friargate
              Preston

P.S. Before I enclose this I must relate for thy edification an adventure we had after leaving you caused by my own carelessness for professing to know the way to the station I acted as pilot and it being so dark we kept too much to our left hand and found our mistake out too late for the train and as we were both wishful to be home and Harrison being rather delicate and not fit to walk so far we walked to Brockholes Arms and enquired for a conveyance and got one from a farmer close by named Topping and arrived home about 1/4 past 10 no worse for our disappointment but received shuch a lesson that will make me think on it - reminds me of the man coming from America and as the song says instead of Old England landed in France. I dont know when I committed shuch a foolish blunder but think it will not occur again, but once more I say farewell
              J.A.

Jonathan's letter is business like and speaks for itself, he makes clear that he is enamoured of Mary, asks if this is in any way reciprocated and whether he has been 'preceded by some one more fortunate'. He then asks for a prompt reply and concludes with a slightly humorous postscript telling of his blunder in losing his way to the station.

Mary's replies one week later.

    To: Jonathan Abbatt
            158 Friargate   Preston

Calder Bridge
2 mo 7th 1853

Respected Friend,
           Jonathan Abbatt

Thy letter was indeed received with no little surprise on my part and the subject which thou has so unexpectedly laid before me is one that aught to receive our most weighty and serious reflection, though often one that is lightly and carelessly conversed upon but when it is in reality brought home to ones own feelings, and we are called upon to act, it is then indeed, an important matter.

Little have I imagined that I was held in such high esteem by thee and that the interest which thou has taken in me and which thou trusts has been noticed by me was anything more than the promptings of common friendship.

I feel bound to tender my sincere thanks for the favour thou has extended in thus addressing me, and if I have read my heart and feelings aright thy message has not found altogether an unwelcome reception, yet while I make this delicate confession I would have thee remember that we are almost entire strangers to each other, and that in bestowing our affections we may not do it without careful consideration and above all may we seek for divine direction in this important step.

Perhaps it may be rather out of place but I must say that I was not a little amused in the blunder you made the other night in trying to find your way home, Harrison will not be willing to have thee as his pilot again I should fancy.
With this I must conclude and subscribe myself
                thy respectful Friend
                      Mary Dilworth

This letter is as formal as is Jonathan's, but leaves him in no doubt as to her feelings, 'thy message has not found altogether an unwelcome reception'. However she retains him at some distance by saying 'I would have thee remember that we are almost complete strangers to each other'. Jonathan's blunder in getting lost is gently noted and she concludes - 'thy respectful Friend'.

In the first letter Mary is addressed as 'Esteemed Friend' and as: Mary Dilworth, Calder Bridge, Nr. Garstang on the envelope. This mode of address without style and title (Mr. Mrs. Miss etc.) is another Friends' convention which is maintained throughout the correspondence - and which Friends continue today. 'Esteemed Friend', is a formal, perhaps slightly distant, Friends address since 'Friend' is a normal Quaker address to another member of the Society.

It is possible to judge the ripening relationship through the letters, by their tone and content and more directly by the manner in which the address and salutation change, at times, and with time, almost imperceptibly. After two years Jonathan talks at times to his 'Dearest Polly' a far cry indeed from his Esteemed Friend.

The next five letters, three from Jonathan and two from Mary, deal with the next step which it is agreed should be a personal approach by Jonathan to Mary's parents. This approach is intended to obtain their approval for Jonathan to court their daughter. Approval of this nature by mid-nineteenth century Quakers was of enormous importance since in addition to the danger of 'marrying out' of the Society a number of other factors were likely to be considered. When Jonathan asks his own father for approval at the end of March, Benjamin responds in a very provisional manner and with many questions and this despite knowing that Mary was a Friend.

At this time a Friend was supposed to inform his own and the girl's parents of his intention to court before any formal courting and certainly before emotional involvement. Parents had the right to consent to their children's courtships, but once they had consented were no longer free to withhold or withdraw their subsequent permission to marry for any reason of the world. At times Mary, found some of the more public of the formal practices to be very irksome.

In a letter on 9th February Jonathan raises the question of parental consent, suggesting that he appear in person a course of action approved by Mary on the 12th February. Jonathan then suggests that he will call on 'the day called Good Friday' - six weeks hence. Six weeks hence may seem a long time today and it probably was in the mid-nineteenth century but the reasons for delay were a desire for privacy since Jonathan feels that an earlier visit might 'give rise to some suspicion'. This particular exchange is concluded by Jonathan saying that, though he would like to, will not write more, until the consent of John Jackson and Ann Dilworth is obtained.

Mary's letter of 7th March written immediately before the meeting with her parents suggests that if anyone else calls at the Dilworth household on the appointed day - then Jonathan should seek 'some future opportunity might perhaps answer thy purpose as well.' She concludes:

> It is I think needless for me to ask thee to make thy visit as private as possible. In the mean time I remain thy respected Friend
> Mary Dilworth

In reply Jonathan reassures Mary that he and she are the only ones 'acquainted with my intentions':

> To: Mary Dilworth
> Calder Bridge Garstang

Preston
3 mo 23rd 1853 [Wednesday]

Esteemed Friend
Mary Dilworth

Thy last came to hand in due course for which I am much obliged. Hoping it will still be convenient I intend being over with you on sixth day and thinking thou would like to know at what time I shall arrive I may say about three o'clock for I intend to open shop in the morning and to leave here about half past twelve, for the trains running as on first day, I shall have to walk it so calculating it to be 2 1/2 hours walk I shall arrive at three or soon after. I think the evening train returns about 8 o'clock and feel pretty certain from 'dear' bought experience I shall not so foolishly lose my way again.

I am looking forward if successful with thy Parents to a more frequent correspondence with thee which I much long for, and am sure should much enjoy, hitherto with not having yet obtained their consent I have felt so much restriction in addressing thee

that when I do obtain it I shall feel almost as though I had escaped from bondage, but I must not, say more at present so in hopes of finding you all well I will conclude and remain
                    Thy sincere Friend
                    Jon.n Abbatt

P.S. Thou may depend on my visit being as private as possible so far as I know thee and I are the only persons acquainted with my intentions.
                    J.A.

This crucial visit was successful and in his letter the following Monday, Jonathan not only expresses his pleasure in a satisfactory outcome but concludes his letter with a little mild frivolity from a favourite source - Chambers Journal. In this letter too there is the first of many mentions of friends and relations in the shape of Joseph and Lucy (Holmes) Jackson and Jonathan's eldest sister Jane Abbatt. Joseph J. was the son of Jonathan Jackson of Vale House, Calder Vale and was a nephew of Mary's grandmother - Mary (Jackson) Dilworth - and first cousin to her father. It is possible to identify nearly everyone who is mentioned in the letters because so many of them are related, if not to Jonathan or Mary, then to each other - or by marriage in the future!

    To: Mary Dilworth
            Calder Bridge Nr. Garstang

Preston
3 mo 28th 1853 [Monday]

My Dear Friend
                Mary Dilworth
I was very much pleased with my sojurn amongst you on sixth day and my previous impression of thyself and thy dear parents were so much strengthened that I feel unable to express the satisfaction I feel, for from my first visit to your house which perhaps thou may not remember I was <u>struck</u> with the evident comfort and happiness that reigned amongst you and am now led to think on the importance of the step I am now taking for though I may be the means of taking thee from such a home of happiness yet I do hope with divine assistance so to do, as to render the change to thee agreeable for though our acquaintance so far is but short, yet I feel shuch that in thy company I could entirely devote myself to the promotion of thy happiness and comfort.

By no means let me discourage thee by speaking of thy leaving shuch [such] a home for I mean to make full reparation for shuch doing yet it is very proper one should think on these things beforehand.

After leaving you I had only proceeded a short way up the meeting house lane when I met Joseph and Lucy Jackson returning from the Vale but I dont know whether they recognised me or not but doubtless it has become known through Jon.n Jackson.

Since I saw thee I have been to Bolton and was very agreeably surprised to see such a remarkable change in my sister Jane for when here thou may remember how thin she was and now she is getting quite stout and is looking better than ever I knew her. I will now bring my note to a close though not without requesting I may hear from thee again soon as it will always afford me so much pleasure to receive from thee an acknowledgement of mine, indeed I must consider this correspondence the opening of a creditor and debtor account and shall so contrive to have thee frequently in my debt and shall now take great interest in seeing our postman. Thou must excuse this bit of nonsense though it is true but I am sometimes so light hearted and full of frolic that a little nonsense is acceptable. I am much in the same opinion of Chambers Journal I read some time ago which is
        A little nonsense now and then
        Is relished by the wisest man
In hopes this may find thee well I will conclude and remain
        Thy sincerely attached friend

        Jon.n Abbatt

JANE (ABBATT) ADAIR 1833-1901

Jane, Jonathan's oldest sister, was the fourth child of Benjamin and Elizabeth; she was at Ackworth from 1843-1847 and became the second wife of William Adair of Cockermouth, Maryport and Keswick. William's first wife was Mary Ann Peile who died in 1858.

On leaving Ackworth Jane lived at home in Bolton and after Benjamin's death, in Preston. In March 1858 she went into partnership with Catherine E. Quilliam in a Baby Linen business at 109 Fishergate Preston. The partnership agreement lists assets of £586.1.7. and reads: --- each giving their services, to enjoy equal profits and to share equal risks --- .' Later in 1868 the youngest Abbatt girl, Alice Ann, took Catherine Q.'s place and two years later, on Jane's marriage to William Adair she was replaced by Eleanor Jesper. Alice Ann and Eleanor traded for many years as "Abbatt and Jesper".

William was the son of Joseph Adair of Cockermouth, and at the time of their marriage he was a clerk working for the Peases of Darlington; he then went into business as a draper in Maryport. William's health was never good and he retired to Keswick aged 54. At this time there was no Meeting House in Keswick and Meeting was held in their own house Eskin Lodge which William had built. William had strong reformist views which he openly advocated until his death aged 66 in 1897 and this, though Jane shared these views, often made life difficult for her.

Jane, never strong, was tall and good looking, and in later years was much limited by rheumatism. At her death she was described as possessing a 'quiet unostentatious spirit, being very interested in every good work, but particularly in the cause of Temperance'. For many years she was President of the local B.W.T.A. She died in 1901 aged 68 years. Her death depressed Jonathan, who lost Mary in the same year, - she was always the sister to whom he was the most attached.

By the beginning of April the courtship had been formally accepted by John Jackson and Ann Dilworth, though not yet by Benjamin and Elizabeth Abbatt who were probably the 'stricter' and certainly the more rigid of the two sets of parents. As a result Jonathan, because he says so, and Mary, from her more relaxed way of writing, were happy and felt that their lifetime course had been permanently set. Jonathan's last high spirited letter shows that he was under no illusions about the need to provide a comfortable home, and writing of it so soon illustrates his worldly 'reality'. Later letters clearly show that both he and Mary were genuinely religious. In reply Mary is almost skittish with an 'early' letter:

    To: Jonathan Abbatt
           158 Friargate   Preston

    Calder Bridge
    4th of 4mo 1853 [Monday]

    Esteemed Friend   Jonathan Abbatt

Perhaps thou will have been looking for a letter ere this as thou expressed a wish to hear from me <u>soon</u> -

pray what time does thou consider soon: may I take the liberty of telling thee that I think the present quite soon enough for me - at least to answer thine, not that it was unfavourably received but that I still feel such a stranger to thee.

I am glad that I am not by myself in thinking of the great importance of this correspondence; and I must say that I sometimes almost wonder why I have given thee the encouragement that I have done, not that I am beginning to doubt thy sincerity but from a feeling that, how far thy acquaintance with me may be agreeable to the different members of thy family to whom I am an entire stranger; doubts and feelings such as these will sometimes arise however I may wish to look on the bright side, but I will say no more on that subject now.

It was rather unfortunate thou should meet Joseph and Lucy Jackson on they return home the other evening; both have been here several times since and had they recognised thee, I am almost sure they would have said something about thee; as yet I have not heard a single whisper from any quarter. It was pleasant to hear so good an account of thy sister Jane, we have a nice time of the year coming and with that her health will I hope be quite restored.

With thanks for thine I must conclude this and remain -- Thy sincere Friend
                                        Mary Dilworth

Poor Mary has overestimated her new fiance's lightness and her light hearted letter produces a misunderstanding. So too do her misgivings about her acceptability by the Abbatt family. There is an immediate reply:

    To: Mary Dilworth
           Calder Bridge Nr. Garstang

Preston
4 mo 6th 1853

Dear Friend Mary Dilworth

I have received thine yesterday for which I tender thee sincere thanks and from the tenor therof must confess that I was not a little induced to think (considering our short acquaintance) that thou has thought me rather too forward not only in the expression of my feelings but also in requesting thee to favour me with an early reply without giving thee a definition of my meaning in so doing which was that thou would comply with my request only at thy convenience, but perhaps thou willt excuse me, and remember that out of the abundance of the heart and mouth speaketh, trusting this may be sufficient explanation for my apparent impatience and forwardness, I will leave the matter to thy own good sense to deal with me as I deserve.

But in coming to the latter part of thy letter where thou expresses thyself glad that I consider that I consider the importance of the steps we are taking as well as thyself, I was struck by the expression that thou was almost induced to <u>wonder</u> <u>why</u> thou had given me the encouragement thou has. Now my dear friend expressions such as these are calculated to produce in me a state of mind not very enviable, for I have felt myself ready to bestow on thee my best feelings and affections and doubts like these tend more to induce feelings of despondency such as I do not wish to entertain.

But as thou was saying these feelings arose from the reflection of how far the members of my own family might approve of our acquaintance, I can I think satisfy thee on this point for I have already mentioned the subject to my dear Mother who seems to have full confidence in my discretion and believes I shall do according to what she may desire. My Father I have not spoken to on the subject though I am intending to do so and have not the slightest doubt of his concurrence of which I can let thee know in my next.

Thou mentioned too the feeling of my being such a stranger to thee and as it is desirable that no such feelings should exist may I suggest for thy consideration the propriety of my coming to see thee once in three weeks or a month at the extent that we may thus have a little more of each others society and thereby be more intimately acquainted.

And as it is desirable that my visits may be still as private as possible would it be convenient if I should come over on first day afternoons whilst friends are in meeting, perhaps thou will say in thy next.

In conclusion permit me to say that I was well pleased with the general sensibility of thy letter yet the expressions I have named gave me some pain

though I myself was the cause, but since I have endeavoured to correct and excuse myself perhaps thou will look over it and allow me once more to to subscribe myself
    Thy sincerely interested and attached Friend

                                    Jon.n Abbatt

Jonathan has misinterpreted or 'got hold of the wrong end of the stick'. In a long letter written almost by reply he endeavours to reassure Mary both about her genuine concerns and the ones he has imagined, 'that thou has thought me rather too forward --- ' and also about his parent's acceptance of their future daughter-in-law. He has already discussed his 'project' with his mother Elizabeth A. - with a view to 'softening up' Benjamin.

He proposes somewhat ponderously to deal with the problem of strangeness by making his visits to Calder Bridge more frequent, every three or four weeks, and with the problem of being observed by calling on: 'first day (Sunday) afternoons whilst friends are in meeting'!

This is not the reply that was expected by Mary who, after expressing surprise at the letter's contents says: 'but on solid reflection since thine was received I have been led to see the error I have commited and of which I am now ashamed ever to have been guilty'.

    To: Jonathan Abbatt
           15b Friargate.   Preston

Calder Bridge
11th of 4 mo 1853 [Monday]

Esteemed Friend
        Jonathan Abbatt

In acknowledging thine for which I am obliged, I must say I was at first surprised at the tone in which it was written, little did I think (or perhaps would not) when I wrote my last that it would call forth such a reply; but on solid reflection since thine was received I have been led to see the error I have committed and of which I am now ashamed ever to have been guilty.

I find I have been expecting too much from affections it has been my good fortune to win, and moreover I have addressed thee in a selfish and independant spirit; but I now must tell thee I do at times find it exceeding hard work to keep that <u>much loved</u> self of mine in its proper place and that it is very apt to assume a spirit of independance.

Nevertheless I am not without hope that thy influence and sometimes gentle chiding may have in some degree the desirable effect of bringing me nearer to Him who alone can subdue all things to Himself.

The plan thou proposed of seeing me at times has met with my approval and I think might tend to the advantage and happiness of both.

Thou says thou was not a little induced to think, I had thought thee too forward; permit me to take the present opportunity although it is earlier than I otherwise should have done had not an explanation appeared needfull, of commending thee for the upright and sensible manner in which thou has proceeded to make known thy affections to me.

In concluding this allow me to ask if I have now performed the pleasing duty of healing the wound my last so wantonly caused, in hopes that it m<u>ay</u> be the case I remain thy sincere Friend

Mary Dilworth

Her conclusion could be Palmerston or Disraeli: ' -- ask if I have now performed the pleasing duty of healing the wound my last so wantonly caused --- .' On the proposed visit plan: 'the plan thou proposed ---- has met with my approval --- .' This letter is a good example of Mary's clarity and real sensitivity. One often wonders if Mary did not at times write with her tongue in her cheek, as it is known from her sons that, though shy, she had a keen if rather dry sense of humour. Certainly if she was gently mocking Jonathan it was undetected since he writes on Thursday 14th and 'expresses great satisfaction' in the 'full and candid manner in which thou acknowledges --- .' He tells her that he expects to hear from his Father 'in the morning' and that he will will call on Mary at 2.30 because 'if I remember thy meeting begins at 2 o'clock.' He concludes: 'I hope to make my visit without the knowledge of other friends though if it cannot well be avoided I dont mind much about it.'

The concern for privacy and desire to avoid 'being seen' was a continuing concern though it begins to abate somewhat towards the end of 1854. Both Mary and Jonathan were always shy, private, people, Mary more than Jonathan. Jonathan was not a 'forward man' and though he was a staunch Friend and an Elder of his own Meeting for many years, he was well into his sixties before he began to speak regularly in Meetings for Worship.

Meantime Jonathan had been corresponding with his formidable father to seek formal approval and blessing.

    To: Jonathan Abbatt
            Thomas Mulliner, Shoe Warehouse
            Friargate   Preston

Bolton
7 of 4 mo 1853 [Thursday]

Dear Jonathan

Thou judges correctly when thou states that we always feel much interested in thy welfare, and on the present occasion I can assure thee most particularly so.

Thou solicits our approval of the steps thou has taken in a very important matter yet thy information is very meagre indeed, and in consequence thou will not of course require an immediate opinion from us upon such a slite acquaintance with the subject of thy letter. We should like to have more particulars such as who is this female friend and what is she, what age, and what is her qualifications for making a poor mans wife, can she wash thy shirt and do all such like work, who are her Father and Mother, what are they, are they a healthy and sound family, what number of family are they, these and other particulars which thou may be acquainted with respecting them would interest us, and which we aught to know before we can chime in with all that thou wishes from us on this to thee. I can say for myself that I shall never object to my children being married if they go about it in a right and proper manner, and do the thing respectably and of course marry in the Society, which I suppose in thy case as for her being a member will be all right. Such an engagement should also by all means be made in the fear of the Lord, if you expect his blessings to attend and rest upon you. Thou will of course at thy leisure write and give us all particulars, meanwhile I am
                      Thy Affectionate Father
                            Benjamin Abbatt

To: Jonathan Abbatt
        Thos. Mulliner
        Friargate   Preston

Bolton
19 of 4 mo 1853 [Tuesday]

Dear Jonathan

I scarcely know what to say to thee about thy new and most important engagement I have consulted with thy Mother about it and I dont see that we can raise any reasonable objection to thy proposition, therefore I may shortly say that thou has our approbation in the matter, and may thou be abundantly blessed in thy new undertaking is the prayer of thy Affectionate
                              Benjamin Abbatt

As planned Jonathan visited Mary at Calder Bridge on Sunday 17th and all we know is that it rained and he was drenched, producing 'such an uncomfortable slovenly feeling'. We have only brief but informative glimpses of these courting visits: 'pleasant walks together --- on a bright summers day to walk in company with one in whom our affections are centred to enjoy pleasant chat --- '. They were courting and said so.

The Lancaster and Preston Railway (later the London and North Western (L.N.W.R.) and later still the London Midland and Scottish (L.M.S.) had been completed in 1840 and among other Stations stopped at Garstang and Catterall for Woodlands, The Dimples, Calder Bridge, Oakenclough etc. and at Bay Horse for Wyresdale and Dolphinholme. The service was good and exceptionally reliable though - to Jonathan's occasional irritation - it did not always provide him with suitable Sunday and holiday trains. When there was no train he walked - both ways from Preston to Garstang and back - and thought nothing of it. The return journey took about five hours brisk walking - in addition to his 'strolls' with Mary.

Following this visit to Calder Bridge on 17th April (and Benjamin's letter of approval and blessing) there is a longer gap than usual in the letters due to Mary's cancellation of a planned visit to Preston because of a sudden, apparently serious, illness of her Mother. Ann's illness was pneumonia from which she rapidly recovered.

In replying on May 3rd to a 'lost' letter Jonathan is pleased and reassured by his fiancee's increasing affection for him, he comments on her Mother's satisfactory convalescence and half apologises for his own plainness of expression. He concludes by telling of his brother Thomas's fiancee, Jane Haworth, who has just been convinced and admitted a Member of the Society. This letter is followed by a visit and the next letter on Wednesday 11th May when Jonathan's salutation becomes 'Dear Mary' marking another step in their relationship. This letter mentions a visit by Jno.'s sister, Jane, to Calder Bridge and of an encounter with Richard Jackson: 'When just getting on the train on first day night R. Jackson seized hold of my hand and enquired how I was just as though he meant me to know he saw me.' He ends by enquiring about the wedding of Ellen Kelsall (Mary's cousin of Chapel Cottage, Wyresdale) and George Glover:

> Thou will by this no doubt be some <u>little</u> acquainted with George Glover, what does thou think of him?? and how did he and Ellen get through their business.
>
> What inquisitive questions!! thou may say, yet we young folks like to enquire in matters of this sort when we may ourselves be in the same scrape sometime or other.

The next letter on Friday 13th Jno. encloses his sister's letter (lost) to M. explaining her inability to visit Mary and goes on to say that he will himself walk over on second day - the day arranged for Jane, arriving at 2 o'clock or a little after. He supposes she has heard of the death of her cousin, Isaac Wilcocksons's, baby.

We now have letters 'crossing' and Jonathan's apologises for being late with his 'love letter - being busy preparing to leave the shop for a day, and joining my brother and friends yesterday at Fleetwood'; he also asks for details of Mary's pending stay in Wyresdale - this has been mentioned before. On the same day, 21st May, Mary writes hand/delivered from Isaac Wilcockson's in Friargate where she is staying to keep her cousin Isaac company prior to the funeral of his baby the following Monday. She tells Jonathan that she will be going to Meeting the next day and says she 'may perhaps get a sight of thy sister.' [Jane A.]

Ann Dilworth's family, the Wilcocksons, were a north Lancashire Quaker family who, with the Satterthwaites, intermarried with the Dilworths and Jacksons. The family trees give an idea by * of the number of relations in Marys life and hence in the letters.

```
                    J. WILCOCKSON = MARY (GILPIN)(    -24/4/1728)
         I. of Wray nr. Lancaster.  M. d. of James and Jane (Holme) GILPIN.
        |
─ JAMES     (4/3/1754-    )  = Mary (MASON)
─ JANE      (24/12/1758-  )  = Thomas DEWHURST
─ ANN       (1/10/1763-   )  = Robert HALL
─ MARGARET  (14/6/1760-   )  = Charles HARRISON
─ ISAAC     (29/11/1768-  )  = Martha (SMITHSON)
─ MARY      (3/7/1771-    )  = James HARDING                         ***
          and
─ DAVID WILCOCKSON (1/5/1752-  ) = ESTHER (SATTERTHWAITE)(1756-1814) **
  |
─ MARY (1780-1853) = Richard JACKSON (29/11/1783-1846)   No issue.  **
  R. of Spout Ho. & Calder Ho. Elizabeth (Labrey) = i. & M. = ii. wife.

─ SARAH     (1780-     )   = i.  Cuthbert MEADOWS       No issue.
                           = ii. Thomas BROWN           Issue.      *

─ ISAAC     (1783-     )   = Amelia (SENNALS)           No issue.   ***

─ ANN   (9/19/1788-1874)   = 1821 JOHN JACKSON DILWORTH (1786-1870) ***

─ JANE      (1790-     )   = James NICHOL               Issue.      *

─ JOHN      (1792-     )   = 1818 Jane (DILWORTH)(1793-    )        **
                                                        Issue.

─ JAMES     (1794-     )     Unmarried.

─ ELIZABETH (1796-     )   = Samuel PICKARD             Issue.      *

─ WILLIAM   (1798-     )     Unmarried.

─ JANE and EDWARD died in infancy.
                    --------------------

                 JOHN WILCOCKSON = 1818 JANE (DILWORTH)             **
         J. of Preston brother of Ann (W) D. and Jane sister to John J. D.
        |
─ DAVID    = Ann (SIMPSON)                              Issue.      ****
           D. above is Mary's 'Dear David' of The Letters.
─ ISAAC    = Jane  (         )                          Issue.      **
─ MARY ANN = Thomas ORD                                 Issue.      ***
                    --------------------

                 JANE (WILCOCKSON) = JAMES NICHOL                   **
        |
─ MARY     = Samuel PICKARD                             Issue.      ***
           M. is one of 'The Marys' and married her first cousin Sam.
                    --------------------

             ELIZABETH (WILCOCKSON) = SAMUEL PICKARD                *
        |
─ SAMUEL    = Mary (NICHOL)                             Issue       ***
─ And other Issue.
                    --------------------

    *,**,*** indicate the frequency of mentions in the text.

                                63
```

```
          EDWARD SATTERTHWAITE (1728-1812) = SARAH (PARK)
       E. of Scalegill, Ambleside & Wray, Hawkshead; S. of Skelwith,
                                                              Westmorland.
```

- Michael = Hannah (BALKIN)   M. of 'The Wood' Hawkshead.   Issue.

- EDWARD (8/11/1754) = MARY (PARKINSON) (-1827) Issue see below.
                                    Mary's 2nd spouse = Ralph Alderson of Preston

- William   Of Manchester. Married twice. Issue.

- Mary   = John Rogerson of Preston, Innkeeper.

- ESTHER (SATTERTHWAITE) (1756-6/4/1814) = DAVID WILCOCKSON (1752-   )**
                          David of Wray, nr. Kirkby Lonsdale and Preston.

- John   A seaman. Issue.

- Samuel   Of Manchester. Issue.


```
            EDWARD SATTERTHWAITE = MARY (PARKINSON)
         E. A Clogger and Currier of Preston; M. of Yorkshire.
```

- Edward   =   Hannah Maria (FOWLER).
               E. of Manchester, H. of Tamworth. Issue.

- Michael = i. Hannah (GILPIN) of Stockport. Issue.   **
          = ii. Ellen (WARING)   Issue.

- William =   Jane (CROSSFIELD) Jane of Lancaster. Issue   *

- Samuel =   Mary (CROSSFIELD) Sam. a Currier of Manchester,   *
                                 Mary of Lancaster. Issue.

- Mary   =   Charles HOLMES   Issue.   *
              Charles of Lancaster and Orrel, Wigan.

- SARAH (SATTERTHWAITE)(30/4/1788-   ) = 1817 WILLIAM ORD (-1832) *
                                                William of Darlington.

```
         THOMAS ORD (1822-    ) = MARY ANN (WILCOCKSON)           ***
                                  M. is one of the 'Three Marys'.
```

- Issue = SARAH, MARIA, and ANN ELIZA.   ***

Asterisks (*>**>***) indicates the frequency of mentions in the text.

David Wilcockson, son of James, and his sister Mary (Wilcockson) Harding came from Wray near Hornby. He was a hatter by trade with a small factory at Walton near Preston. At that time a Preston bye-law prevented anyone who was not a freeman from selling goods in the town, except on 'Fair' days. Therefore, on Market days David set up his stall on Walton Brow (a small hill on the edge of Preston) as near to the town as was legally possible. Later when the bye-laws were changed, his shop was in the market place and is now the site of the Harris Library.

Mary (Wilcockson) Harding, David Wilcockson Senior's sister, was a formidable character, usually referred to in Mary's letters as 'Aunt Harding' and 'Aunt Harding and her nonsense'. She, Mary H., with many members of the various clans became customers of Jonathan and in the letters Mary H. has trouble with overshoes.

Isaac Wilcockson senior - Ann Dilworth's elder brother - married Amelia Sennals who was not a Quaker. As a result of thus 'marrying out' of the Society of Friends he was disowned. However, as can be seen from the letters he continued to be accepted by his family as 'a family member in good standing'. This may have had as much to do with his success in life as with the family's tolerance. Isaac born in 1783, was educated at Ackworth, then apprenticed in Preston to Thomas Walker, a printer (at the same time as Edward Baines, subsequently an M.P. and noted local Lancashire historian). After widening his horizons in London Isaac returned to Preston where he became a publisher and owned and ran the 'Preston Review', (later the 'Preston Chronicle'). In the period immediately before the letters Mary's brother, David, had been apprenticed to Isaac who was largely responsible for the latter's acquisition of his own printing and publishing business in Newcastle-under-Lyme. (See Chapter V.) He was a prominent member of the town council and founder of the Preston Gas Company. On at least one occasion Jonathan A. was given a ride home to Preston from Calder Bridge by Isaac and remarked on the latter's kind and charitable, views of Friends.

Esther (Satterthwaite) Wilcockson, wife of David Wilcockson of Wray near Hornby, was the daughter of Edward Satterthwaite (clogger), of Wray near Hawkshead and Colthouse and of Sarah (Park) of Skelwith. The grandson of Edward, one of her (Esther's) elder brothers, was Thomas Ord who married Mary Ann Wilcockson and they and their children, Sarah, Maria and Ann Eliza Ord (see below and tree) figure prominently in our story.

David and Esther (Satterthwaite) had eleven children,

five of whom had issue. The five resulting families of
cousins all appear in the letters; some with their
married surnames. Those cousins are marked * thus below,
and 'The Three Marys' appear frequently.

Sarah* (BROWN)	m. William CAMERON
Eliz.* (BROWN)	m. F. D. NUTTALL
David* WILCOCKSON	m. Ann (SIMPSON)
Isaac* WILCOCKSON	m. Jane (_____)
Mary Ann* (WILCOCKSON)	m. Thomas ORD
Mary* (NICHOL)	m. Samuel* PICKARD
William* DILWORTH	m. Alice (BIBBY)
David* DILWORTH	m. Emma (GOODALL)
Mary* (DILWORTH)	m. Jonathan ABBATT

David Wilcockson was undoubtedly Mary's favourite cousin
and one for whom both she and Jonathan had great respect.
He was a cotton manufacturer by trade, a staunch Friend,
and a member of Preston Council in the eighteen sixties.

Mary's next letter shows how often she saw friends and
relations. In this letter she has visited three homes and
if she saw 'everyone there was to see' - and she notes
none as missing - then she would in this week alone have
seen up to twenty of her cousins in their own homes.

       To: Jonathan Abbatt
              158 Friargate   Preston

Calder Bridge,
27th of 5 Mo 1853 [Friday]

Dear Friend

On 2nd day morning I had the pleasure of receiving
thine, in the first place permit me to tell thee
thou art now beginning to feel more like an 'old
acquaintance' than the 'stranger' thou once did so
that I can now address thee with more freedom.

You had a beautiful day at Fleetwood and I doubt not
a pleasant one.

Last 7th day I was enjoying myself in Wyresdale,
Mary Jackson kindly invited my worthy cousin and I
to join her and Lizzy in a dog cart there. Having
left the conference at J. Kelsalls we set out for a
ramble from which we returned in about five hours,

and partook of tea at our kind friends which was truly refreshing. A little after 7 o'clock we found ourselves communicating to the rest at Vale House the adventures of the delightful day spent.

Ellen could not tell me when I am going to stay there, towards the end of next week I should prefer going; but in a day or two I should hear from her, and then I will let thee know, perhaps I shall hear from thee before that time.

I have been spending a short time at Oaken Clough this week, and often very often was asked how friend Jonathan was and so on. Richard also tells me he met a friend of mine at the station the other evening. I must now draw to a close and remain
Thy sincerely attached Friend
Mary Dilworth

Mary Jackson (who provided the dog cart) daughter of Joseph and Lucy (Holmes) Jackson of Vale House , Calder Vale, later married Harold Adair of Egremont, Cumberland. Mary Dilworth was thus destined to be the sister-in-law of one Mrs. Adair (Jane Abbatt) and the cousin of another - Mary Jackson. There were two children of Mary and William's marriage, Gilbert and Lucy. Lucy subsequently married Ewart Beswick, the son of one of Thomas A.'s best friends, (see later description of Benjamin A.'s funeral). Among other activities the Beswicks bred dachshunds and as a teen age boy the editor was brought up with two successive 'Beswick dachs' which came from 'our cousins'.

Gilbert was a scientist of note, being a Fellow of the Royal Society, Fellow of King's, Director of Physiology Research and of the Low Temperature Laboratory at Cambridge, the first person to grow and describe the haemoglobin molecule. Gilbert was a little eccentric and when at Bootham (Friends school in York) was a somewhat precocious small boy. On one occasion when asked by his cousin, (the author's Father), for help with some Latin prep, replied: "No, it would not be fair to the other boys". One of the author's own vivid memories of Gilbert is of an invitation to lunch in the lab on a beautiful June day in the early nineteen fifties. After a discussion of work, GA's and JDA's,they adjourned for lunch to the cold room (walkin refrigerator) so that they might be uninterupted --- the sherry was served cold. At this time Gilbert, though still eccentric, was charming, humorous, gracious and continued to be kindly helpful.

Jonathan replying to Mary's letter on Monday 30th May, is

obviously pleased with his progress - more like 'an old acquaintance than a stranger - and would like to visit with Mary in Wyresdale in her true childhood surroundings. He is perturbed about the propriety, acceptability and timing of such a visit and asks for guidance, 'I wish to leave the matter with thee as may be most agreeable and shall be pleased to act as thou may suggest.' He goes on to tell of a recent visit to Bolton where he has viewed his brother Thomas' house which is being furnished for his coming marriage to Jane Haworth. Jno. has asked Thomas to 'keep an account of his expenses that I may have guide to serve me, when the time comes.'

Elizabeth Abbatt has just returned from London (where she was having her teeth extracted), 'and am happy (to) say seems so much better, and now that so much of the pain has left her seems much younger and looks less careworn. Sister Jane desires her love to thee --- .'

In reply the practical Mary, gives Jonathan leave to visit and asks: 'How do you propose going to Wyresdale?'

    To: Jonathan Abbatt
           158 Friargate   Preston

    Calder Bridge
    6 mo 1st 1853 [Wednesday]

    Dear Friend

Thanks for thy letter of yesterday. I could not help smiling when I read it and I must tell thee that I thought thou has begun to find out the perplexities of courtship I did not sit down to please thee (forgive what I have already said) No! it is my duty and pleasure to enlighten thee as to my whereabouts. This morning I had a note from Ellen saying she would be glad to see me anytime soon, so I hope if all's well tomorrow morning will find me there and as I am staying over first day there with my _leave_ perhaps thou will be there too, if Joshua should be at liberty and I think it most likely he willbe- you have so long talked of having an out there.

So thy brother is to be married sooner than he expected, will thou have an office at the time?

I was pleased to hear of the welfare of thy Mother must I tell thee I _can_ _almost_ imagine I have seen her, I have heard so much about her from thee.

Wilt thou forgive a short and I fear meandering letter this time from
> thy sincerely attached Friend
> Mary Dilworth

How do you propose going to Wyresdale?

P.S. If anything should occur to prevent your coming on first day or if thou should wish to write to me there, thou must address J. Kelsall, Chapel House, Wyresdale left at Bear and Staff Lancaster they only receive on 7th and 4th days--
> For the present farewell
> M.D.

WYRESDALE

Wyresdale, see map, has changed little in the past century and a half and, the motorway and railway apart, very little since the land enclosure of the 1780s. At the time of Domesday, and before, the land was wild and uncultivated. It was then owned by Roger de Poitou. By the thirteenth century it was described as the 'Vaccary and Forest of Wyresdale'. Vaccary means cow place, dairy house or cow pasture, and in the thirteenth century the whole dale was a single 'vaccary'. Later, probably in the fourteen fifties, it was divided into twelve 'vaccaries' named: Abbeystead*, Marshaw*, Dunkenshaw, Green Bank, Ortner*, Lentworth, Tarnbrook*, Lee, Emmets, Hayshaw, Catshaw. These names still survive today and those marked with asterisks are places with major associations with people and events in this book.

Wyresdale is still rural and the major changes since Jonathan and Mary's time are undoubtedly those associated with the building of the M6 motorway. Dolphinholme, girlhood home of Ann Corless,(Thomas Dilworth's third wife), was once a minor industrial centre with perhaps three thousand people engaged primarily in spinning worsteds. At its peak in about 1800 the Dolphinholme 'worsted works' had the biggest water wheel in England. (Compared with one at Laxey (Isle of Man) it was twice as wide though of smaller diameter!). Dolphinholme's other 'first' in 1801 was in being the first place in 'the kingdom' to be lit by gas. The 'luminant was made at the works and stored in a holder on the east side --- '. As industrialisation proceeded elsewhere the works faded and failed in the middle 1860s. In 1839-40 there was a nasty strike with violence and arson the 'Blacks' who struck and the 'Whites' who did not. Peace came in a field with the ceremonial roasting of a black sheep accompanied by much beer, bread and the playing of bagpipes.

In addition to the mills in Dolphinholme there used to be three Wyresdale country mills engaged in the manufacture of silk, cotton and - important for 'the Families' - felt and hats. By the mid eighteen fifties these mills and most of their workers had also disappeared. Many of the felt makers once lived in the village of Tarnbrook - it is now reduced to two or three small farms; and the hamlet of Haythornthwaite (pronounced '(H)Athernate') has disappeared. At the very least eighty houses disappeared from Wyresdale in the 1800-50 period. This rural population emigration, mirrors the changes which occurred in Lancashire (and the country at large), with the onset and acceleration of the industrial revolution.

Parts of Wyresdale remain good cattle country to this day, though as it is largely Pennine approaches and part of the Trough of Bowland, much of it is open moorland. Many of the houses, farms, cottages and places like Tarnbrook, Newton-in-Bowland and Chipping are virtually unchanged since the days of Thomas, and the times when James and Ann Dilworth left for America with William Penn and when Jennet Cragg made her horseback journey to London and back. The sea and Morecambe Bay are close and can be seen on clear days across the Fylde plain and Cockerham Sands. It is a country of sheep and curlews, of skies and trees, of cattle and streams and still is a place of natural peace.

Many members of the book's families have had a compelling sense of location and have had 'Wyresdale in their bones'. One Oakenclough Jackson (John James 1861-?1935) believed that he knew where home 'was' even on express (non-stop) night trains from London or Glasgow. The truth was, to some, demonstrated by his penchant for pulling the train (emergency) communication cord to achieve non-scheduled stops at Garstang and Catterall Station. (The five pound fines, which increased with each offence, all contributed to father James' permanent displeasure).

From 1800 until about the time the Dilworths departed from the dale there was a Friends School beside the Meeting House in the 'Over' division a mile to the north of the Church (there are two divisions in the dale, Nether and Over Wyresdale). It is said, probably incorrectly, that both Church and Meeting House were largely built with stone plundered from the 12th century Cistercian foundation at Abbeystead. (This foundation was a satellite of Furness Abbey but was abandoned by the monks moved to Wythney Abbey in Ireland in the 13th C.)

Mary's branch of the Dilworths had lived in and stayed close to Wyresdale since 1689 when Thomas 'removed' to

Wyresdale. (See Chapter II.) This closeness to Wyresdale is epitomised by Mary's father and Thomas' great-grandson born in Mary Townson's old house - 'Lower Moor Head in Over Wyresdale' - another Dilworth 'ancestral home'.

JOHN JACKSON and ANN (WILCOCKSON) DILWORTH

John Jackson Dilworth (1786-1870) was born at Lower Moorhead in Wyresdale, the eldest child of William and Mary (Jackson) Dilworth. He was the first of the family to have two given names, for which his mother Mary, daughter of John and Ann (Kelsall) Jackson, was responsible. She had married aged seventeen and was one of the early 'ferocious Jackson women' - domineering, kind, truthful and acutely conscious of family.

John J. D. initially lived, farmed and was involved in felt making at Caton Green. It was through this activity that he and his sister Jane met and married a Wilcockson sister and brother from Preston. (The Wilcockson family seems to have originated from Wray near Caton). John and Ann Wilcockson were married in 1821 in Preston and William, their eldest child, was born at Caton Green. Very soon afterwards the family moved to Ortner in Wyresdale, close to Moorehead, Chapel Cottage and the Meeting House. It was here that they farmed for 27 years before retiring to Calder Bridge, when John J. was sixty-six years of age. It is interesting to note how unchanged and modern were their activities, for example: training for and following vocations, 'starting out', living, loving, educating children and retiring.

Dilworth Abbatt remembered his grandfather, John J. D., as a short man who always wore a black wig, had a fine head and observant deep set eyes. He tended to be of a 'nattery' disposition though he was basically kind hearted and straightforward in his dealings. He spoke in a Lancashire country dialect and called his grandson to him saying : "Hey coom hie tha".

In the Calder Bridge days (and probably before) it was the custom after breakfast for John J. to read a chapter from the Bible followed by a short period of silent devotion. Dil tells of their companion-help, one Margaret Carrick - a plain country body - who, in the middle of silence and on hearing a dog cart outside, rose from her seat near the window looked out and muttered aloud:
 -- "Well I niver, theers that little black devil agean!"

Ann (Wilcockson) Dilworth (1788-1874), the sixth of eleven children, was born at Fishwick, Preston. She was sent to Ackworth in 1798 for three years, after which she was apprenticed to a confectioner in Brighouse for seven years. In her certificate of removal from Brighouse Monthly Meeting in 1811, she was described as being: "of orderly conduct, had no debts and was free from any marriage entanglement'. On her return to Preston aged twenty-three her Father, David 'the hatter', set her up in business 'on her own' as a confectioner in Church St. where she made her own merchandise - it was said to be delicious! Ann's interest in the kitchen continued through her life and in a surviving fragment of her last letter to Mary (written in 1873) she spoke of picking 36 quarts of blackcurrants from Calder House garden.

John Jackson, Ann and his mother Mary (Jackson), are buried beside each other at Calder Bridge Meeting House.

Jonathan visited Mary in Wyresdale on Sunday 5th June, together with his friend, Joshua, and to judge from his letter of 9th June the visit was a great success. In this letter he tells of a Tuesday's 'day trip' to Windermere with 'a party'. They travelled by the early Mail train and reached Windermere by 7 a.m. This must have necessitated an early start from Preston, because the train stopped at Lancaster where they were joined by more Friends including 'four of the Satterthwaites'. During this 'out' and on other occasions he had been teased about his courtship and Robert Benson had asked how 'Friends were in Wyresdale to which I replied very innocently'. He tells Mary that he:

> --- felt at our last meeting a greater freedom and familiarity and fancied that we were more like truly attached lovers than heretofore ---- fancy this feeling is reciprocal and nothing could give me more pleasure than to have an avowal of it from thee ---

The letters were not written for an audience other than the addressees, and were simple, if romantic, vehicles of communication. Despite this, the quality of the English and the richness of vocabulary of both authors is remarkable.

No attempt has been made to paraphrase for clarity and brevity as this is unnecessary and it is indeed simpler and much more satisfactory to 'lift' whole sentences and paragraphs. This permits our authors to 'say it themselves' and they then say and express their meanings <u>much</u> more clearly and succinctly than otherwise would be the case. An early Victorian Ackworth (and Wyresdale sand tray) education was extraordinarily effective.

Mary's letter of reply 13th June gives Jonathan his 'reciprocity' answer and well illustrates the above point of clarity. Sarah Ann Jackson was the first wife of Albert Simpson of Elmhurst, Garstang, later of Burghill Grange, Hereford; after Sarah Ann's death Albert, who was an Anglican and a wealthy cotton manufacturer, married one of Mary's nieces - Lillian Emma Dilworth daughter of David and Emma (Goodall) Dilworth and Mary's niece.

    To: Jonathan Abbatt
           15b Friargate, Preston

13 of 6mo 1853 [Monday]

Dear Friend,

Thanks, for thy kind and welcome letter which found me as thou anticipated at home, having returned the evening before.

I am glad to hear thou has had such a nice out to Windermere, if thou had not been in that part before I am sure thou would like it. You were indeed near being left the other morning, I am glad you were just in time; does thou think Ann Jackson saw thee in the train I understand she was at Preston that day, - as we were going into Meeting yesterday afternoon she whispered in my ear, "I congratulate thee Mary" it is the first time she has ever said anything, but I am far from thinking it will be the last.-

Agreable to thy earnest wish I must now inform thee what my thoughts were at our last pleasant meeting: especially as I have to assure thee of my increasing affection, and feel that ere long I may be unto thee all that the most ardent lover could desire.

Thou has from the first given me every reason to believe that thy love for me was sincere, therefore I do now my dear friend repose my full confidence in thee; and it is my desire to prove myself not unworthy of thine. - Say have I not now humoured thee to thy hearts content? remember it has been my pleasure to do it.

Since my return home we have had some most delightful rain and on looking into the garden, find in large quantities what I should do well to pull up; weed will make its appearance in the garden as well as in the mind. I have planted the <u>white</u> <u>blue</u>

JANE (ABBATT) 1833-1901 and WILLIAM ADAIR 1831-1886
JONATHAN's 'shy sister' aged about 52. Note Henry's double breasted wool coat and the Lakeland sheepskin.

AMELIA (SENNALS) and ISAAC WILCOCKSON Senr.
MARY's uncle Isaac was her brother David's apprentice Master and owner/ publisher of the Preston Chronicle, etc. Note Amelia's moiree silk taffeta gown and decorated buckle. She was not a Quaker.

FRIENDS BURIAL GROUND COLTHOUSE – HAWKSHEAD

Meeting House built 1688 before which time Meeting was held – in the open air – note the original stone seats-flags projecting from the walls. Robert Abbatt the Younger and Agnes Rigge of Swarthmore married here as were Michael and Hannah (Balkin) Satterthwaite and David (The Hatter) and Esther (Satterthwaite) Wilcockson.

JOHN JACKSON and ANN (WILCOCKSON) DILWORTH

MARY's parents, of Wyresdale and Preston, were buried beside each other at Calder Bridge. (J. & J. Holderness, Photographers, 36 Charlotte Street, off St. Austin's Road, Preston.) Note John Jackson's black wig.

bells thou went to such trouble to procure for me, perhaps I should not have said trouble as thou would not I dare say consider it as such; say rather it was a slip of the pen, it ought to have been pains.

I suppose you will have a marriage in Preston tomorrow, my cousin M.N. rather expects to be in town tomorrow so will most likely be at Meeting.

I forgot to ask thee if thou would be at the Q. Meeting at Lancaster this week, I am not thinking of being there. - I will now conclude and remain,

Thine, affectionately
Mary Dilworth.

The M.N. in the penultimate paragraph is Mary Nichol, daughter of James and Jane (Wilcockson) Nichol and later Mrs. Samuel Pickard. After David Wilcockson she was perhaps Mary's most favourite cousin and confidante.

Quaker Family Relations

Quaker relationships are at times extremely complicated and even for Friends themselves are frequently not comprehensible. They were a result of the two factors of individual propinquity in relative isolation and the Society's rule of not 'marrying out'. Until the late eighteen-fifties Friends who married 'out' i.e. who married 'one of the world' were liable to virtually certain disownment by the Society. Many good Friends were lost to the Society during the eighteenth and nineteenth century as a result of enforcement of this rule. In consequence serious young Friends had a limited choice of potential mates and many of those available were distant, or in some cases not so distant relations.

Until the advent of cotton and the industrial revolution the north west of England and the north of Lancashire were always isolated from the rest of the country both in fact and in thought. This isolation was to a large extent responsible for the reception received by George Fox's mission following his 1652 vision, on Pendle Hill - of 'a great people to be gathered'. However, though strong Quaker Meetings existed throughout the area, for the next two hundred and fifty years northern Lancashire remained a static and largely insular collection of communities and people. Intermarriage of families was inevitable. For the Dilworths, the Kelsall's, the Jacksons and others who had all been in Wyresdale for many generations the result was inevitably a series of very complicated relationships!

The following, by no means isolated, examples give an idea of the complexity of relationshsips in Mary's - and all other - generations. All permutations of cousins existed from first cousins/german and **were the norm**.

Mary (Jackson) Dilworth (Mary's grandmother and daughter of Ann Kelsall and John [the Honest Miller] Jackson) married William Dil(l)worth in 1785 and both came from Wyresdale. Mary had three children, of whom John and Jane married sister and brother - Ann and John Wilcockson.

Jonathan Jackson of Spout House, Wyresdale and Calder Vale (see Chapter II - three Jackson brothers and Calder Bridge Meeting House) was father of, among others, Joseph and Elinor who married sister and brother Lucy and Charles Holmes - in 1852 the latter wrote the Jennet Cragg verses in Mary's mss. Journal - again Chapter II.

These interrelationships were the rule and not the exception, and a natural and inevitable corollary was that most Friends were relations and vice versa. In fact, in the still very rural Wyresdale community and society, there was little or no room or time for completely unrelated and unconnected friends. (This was to some extent true even if the friends were Friends!).

A good example of a functioning network concerns the illness of Mary (Jackson) Dilworth in early 1855 at the time of Mary's visit to her brother David in Newcastle-under-Lyme. At this time Jonathan was able, in Preston, to hear regular daily news of his fiancee's Grandmother's progress from three cousins - William Dilworth, Isaac Wilcockson and David Wilcockson. In a similar manner Mary heard of Jonathans's momentous purchase of his own business on the day it occurred, this time from her cousin David Wilcockson. Such net-works operating continuously and reliably lent a dimension of security, cohesiveness, spice and particularity to life, which it is difficult for the late twentieth century nuclear family member to imagine.

Jonathan's reply to Mary's letter above is interesting:

- It illustrates the interlocking information network operated by relations and both male and females:
- It tells us of Mary's forthcoming visits to relations in St. Helens (and elsewhere).
- It tells us of the first formal introduction of the pair - at a tea party given by Mary's cousin, David Wilcockson. (They had previously met at Calder Bridge in Jonathan's apprentice days.)

To: Mary Dilworth
Calder Bridge, Nr. Garstang

Preston
6 mo 16 1853 [Thursday]

My Dear Mary

Thine came to hand on the fourteenth for which I am much obliged and am glad to say that in answer to my pressing request thou has given me entire satisfaction and I greatly prize thy increasing confidence and can assure thee it is mutual.

The wedding as perhaps thou has all particulars ere this passed off very nicely.

After Meeting, Lizzy Jackson came to the shop and from her I got such a rush about visiting Calder Bridge that I have not yet had from anyone, I told her I was fond of an occasional stroll and variety of scenery, but she told me I so often visited one spot she was induced to think me interested in some other object and did I know that I had been seen from almost every corner and she stuck so close I told her I was never ashamed at being engaged in a good cause at which she laughed and commended me.

It was as thou supposed Ann Jackson saw me at the station on our return from Wyresdale and seemed pleased to have caught me. I was pleased to see Mary Nicoll the day she was here and she took the opportunity to tell me slily that friends at Calder were all well, giving me all the time a very significant look.

It will soon be time to go to thy duties at the wedding, and with all thy past and coming experience in these interesting occasions one may presume to think thou has learned pretty well how things are managed and may hope (contrary to the predictions of D. Wilcockson's almanaac which we consulted if thou remembers when I took tea there some time ago in company with R. Veevers) that thou may put thy experience in practice before 1863. I was thankful to him for inviting me to tea that afternoon whilst thou was there. I could scarcely find time to go to the Q. M. but expect to see my Father on his return and perhaps my Mother.

If thou art likely to be at home next first day but

one please let me know that I may come and admire the scenery once more, or shall I have no opportunity before seeing thee at St. Helens, but perhaps thou art scarcely able to let me know yet.

I hope you may have a fine day for the wedding and I doubt not there will be true enjoyment I could not wish a more sequestered spot for such an occasion apart entirely from pomp and vanity.

I was amused with thy description of thy garden and thought the comparison (at least on my part) very good of weeds in the garden, and weeds in the mind, and on viewing my condition find I have a very plentiful crop to pull up and as thou art such a good gardener perhaps I may call upon thee for assistance. I fear if I join thee at St. Helens thou will have something to be ashamed of more than otherwise but I will do my best to bring on thee no discredit.

It is now getting time for me to go to meet my Father, so will now conclude and shall look forward with pleasure whenever thy next of a course of most interesting letters may come, though this is not intended to convey the idea that I wish for one sooner than usual but merely that they are always so acceptable. In the mean time I will subscribe myself as ever
                Thine Affectionately
                    Jon.n Abbatt

Mary's letter of 20th June is noteworthy because it is the first letter in which she addresses him as 'Dear Jonathan', and in it she tells of a forthcoming five day visit to Wyresdale with Mary Nichol. The purpose of the visit was to help with the preparations for the wedding of her cousin Ellen to George Glover. She more or less invites Jonathan to come to Calder Bridge on the following Sunday, as on the next Monday she leaves for Liverpool and her round of visits. After the invitation she goes on to say: 'after an early tea, we may admire the scenery around. My Mother may perhaps be from home at that time, but I dont know that need make any difference.' This letter is but seven brief paragraphs are packed with meaning, feeling and information.

Replying two days later on Friday 24th June, Jonathan says: 'allow me to say that I was very much gratified with the alteration of thy mode of address and led to consider it as a mark of increasing affection --- .' He continues later: ' --- addressed merely as a friend a

something too distant --- I have felt all along something
more than a friend --- .' His other principal piece of
news is of a letter from his brother, Thomas A. asking
him to be groomsman and telling him that sister, Jane A.,
is to be bridesmaid at Thomas' wedding on 21st July.

It is presumed that the planned visit to Calder Bridge
took place, and from the following letters we know that
Mary left to stay in Liverpool with the newly married
Ellen (Kelsall) of Wyresdale, and George Glover. Mary
arrived at the Glovers the day after they had returned
from their holiday (honeymoon) in Scotland.

Jonathan's letter of July 7th speaks of a planned meeting
with Mary in St. Helens (later in her tour), of a letter
from his sister, Jane, but primarily of his and David
Wilcockson's solicitous yet fruitless attempts to see
Mary pass through Preston on her way to Liverpool. 'Thy
cousin David and myself were each twice down at the
railway station last evening to meet you, and as we did
not, concluded you were gone by an earlier train'. David
was correct in that she travelled early the next day.

Mary's next letter tells of her stay at the Glovers:

    To: Jonathan Abbatt
           158 Friargate   Preston

Liverpool
6 of 7 mo 1853 [Wednesday]

Dear Jonathan

On my arrival here on 7 day morning I had the
pleasure of finding a letter from thee, for which
accept my sincere thanks.

I am sorry David and thyself had two needless walks
to the station to meet me, from what thou said on
first day I did not expect that thou would go down,
not that I am displeased with thou going there
contrary to my expectation, no I desire to thank
thee for thy kindness. I came through Preston by the
first train seventh day morning arriving here about
half past ten, George and Ellen met me at the
station, and gave me a hearty welcome. They got home
the night before, having had a delightful vacation
in Scotland. I gave thy message to Ellen, she is
much obliged. The more I see of George Glover the
more I admire him, and think from the little I have
seen, it will be the first wish of each to make the
other happy.

We had a few friends to tea on 2 day evening and W. Wood jnr. came last night and he was <u>wondering</u> when thy brother was to be married of course I did not enlighten him as to the time, indeed I said nothing, when I found that he did not in the least know that I was so much interested in another brother, I quite fancied they would have known about us. I assure thee I get many a good rub from George.

Thou would have a nice day at home on 1st day last.

I am intending leaving here on 6th day and spending a few days with my cousins the Swithenbanks.

It may perhaps be two first days before I am at St. Helens, in my next I shall better able to tell thee. I should like the time thou spends with me there to

be fine it is no nice country I can assure thee, but perhaps the society of each other will make up for that. I have not yet heard from Home but am duly looking for a letter from Mary in the morning, I must not expect that she would spare the time yesterday seeing that her <u>friend</u> would be the there -- Trusting to hear before long of thy welfare I will for the present conclude, and remain
    Thine affectionately
     Mary Dilworth

P.S. My next address will [be] John Swithenbank, Alfred Street, Liverpool.

The 'W. Wood' referred to above reappears later, again in Liverpool, as the jilted lover who confides in Jonathan when his world has been shattered!

In her next letter from Alfred Street, Liverpool, where she is staying with her cousins, the Swithenbanks, Mary tells Jonathan a little more of herself:

--- forgive me when I say that I smiled when I read your remarks on our future home but remember it was a happy smile. I find it a delight to dwell on the future at times and I have no doubt but that the home that thou speaks of with such glee, will be a happy one to both but in looking forward we may not forget that we have a home beyond, another beside our earthly home; do not my dear J. think from the remark I have just made that, I in the least am finding fault with thy style of writing, it is I assure thee such that I admire. I fear sometimes that thou art mistaken in me and I am not that staid

little piece I appear to be, no would that I were
more so perhaps I can talk in a more lively tone - .

Mary tells of a tea party which included her two married
cousins Sarah (Brown) and William Cameron - her next
hosts - who had teased her about leather and cobblers:
'--- there is nothing like leather. I suppose they have
liberty to say anything they like now they are married.
They have had their share and are going to give me mine.'

The second paragraph of Jonathan's reply is one of many
in a similar vein. One may wonder whether the religious
sentiments and feelings of the pair were 'put on' for
themselves and for each other. Judgement from letters of
another time is guesswork and indeed Jonathan is at times
ponderous or pompous (as in this letter where he quotes
as new minted, and for the second time in six months,
the same passage from Chambers Journal). There is no
evidence that either he or Mary were ever dishonest -
pretension in a matter of this kind would have been easy
for the other to detect. They had, moreover, a reputation
with their children of scrupulous honesty, real piety and
both had a strong sense of humour. The editor believes,
that they were completely honest - the reader must judge.

  To: Mary Dilworth/ William Cameron
     Chester Street
     Birkenhead

  Preston
  7 mo 14th 53 [Thursday]

  My Dear Mary

I was very much obliged and agreeably surprised to
have so nice a letter from thee on 3rd day, and am
almost inclined to think thou permits my impatience
to inconvenience thee, but as thou says thou was
alone perhaps it would be an agreeable occupation,
as is always the case with me when I am writing to
thee.

It pleases me too to hear that my remarks on our
future home were appreciated and still more so thy
injunction not to let our anticipated and earthly
home obscure our thoughts of another and more
important one, and yet I do frequently find myself
so thoughtless on this all important subject, that I
have in my sober moments great cause to regret and I
can assure thee my dear Mary I do feel truly
thankful in having met with one in whom, I feel I
shall find a kind guide, and instructor, and though

thou may feel thyself but a weak instrument yet I may most truly say the little remarks (though important ones) thou occasionally makes have great weight with me and in thy last letter most opportune.

As thou thought I was in a frolicksome humour when writing my last and feel that a little indulgence in this way occasionally is decidely profitable. I am of the same opinion as a writer in Chambers Journal who says that
> A little nonsence now and then
> Is relished by the wisest men,

But by this, thou will almost of fancied me preaching a sermon though I assure thee such was not my intention but being led into this train of thought one can hardly stop, and if I carry much longer thou would have a tedious letter to read.

Thou seems to be enjoying thyself well, with thy friends company and sightseeing, when thou mentioned Georges Hall as such a splendid building I was reminded of what old Isaac Wright of Bolton said, that it is only the building that so much resembles Solomons Temple but when I last saw it it was in an unfinished state.

By this time next week I suppose my brother will have got through the all important job and as we shall have four miles to go to get to Meeting I hope we may have it fine.

It seems Thomas Mulliner knows about us and was asking my brother the other day when my turn would be but he simply told him he knew nothing about it. Jos[eph] and Lucy Jackson were at our meeting on first day last when J. spoke to me and Lucy looked as though she would but had no opportunity.

So in thy next I may perhaps be informed when and where I shall meet thee, When I make no doubt we shall both enjoy ourselves and have plenty to say for I feel that if I were with thee more I should hardly be able to stop chattering for a long time but for the present I must conclude and with love I will subscribe myself
    Thine ever affectionate
        Jon.n Abbatt

The content of the letters are a good indication of the mid-Victorian penchant for generalised letter writing, both for information and for entertainment. In the

previous letters over a ten day period there is mention
of six other correspondents (in addition to the writers).
These are: Jane and Thomas Abbatt, Mary Nichol, John
Jackson Dilworth, Sarah Cameron and David Wilcockson.

Mary's next letter from her Cameron cousins' house in
Birkenhead tells of her fondness for Jno. 'how sweet is
that feeling to know that I am beloved by one in whom I
can place my unbounded confidence, may I not be unworthy
of thine --- .' She goes on, having just written to her
cousin Bessie (Mrs. Frank Dixon) at Sutton Nr. Prescott,
to tell her, and now Jno., of the dates of her projected
stay at Sutton; she then asks when she may expect him and
suggests that he might stay overnight on the following
Saturday: 'just do as will suit thee best'. She
concludes by sending good wishes for Thomas Abbatt's
wedding three days later and by half grumbling that she
has not heard from her home for the last four days.

Jonathan replies on the eve of his brother, Thomas'
wedding, on 20th July:

> --- though not quite sure of meeting my brother
> William and his wife'. The main point of his letter
> however is to confirm his visit to Prescott --- not
> being able to liberate myself conveniently on 7th
> day I purpose leaving here on first day morning by
> train at 5 minutes past 8 and expect to reach Sutton
> station in little more than an hour or an hour and a
> half --- would it be agreeable fo thee to meet me,
> dont let this inconvenience thee for I can easily
> find thee out if I be alone.

Mary's next short letter contains both clear and precise
instructions as well as news.

> To: Jonathan Abbatt
>   158 Friargate   Preston
>
>
> Close House
> 22nd of 7 mo 1853 [Friday]
>
> My dear Jonathan
>
> Thine I received yesterday just as I along with
> Frank, Bessie and two of the children were setting
> out for a picnic at Eastham; we met a large family
> at Liverpool all strangers to myself, had the day
> been fine we should have had a pleasant time but the
> rain coming on so soon after we left here put a stop
> in some measure to our pleasure.

Of course I shall expect a long and particular account how yesterday was spent by thee when we have the pleasure of meeting once more.

I omitted mentioning in my last to what station thou must come, and as I know the way to Rainhill and it is also much nearer than Sutton, I think it is far better for thee to come there. I am intending meeting thee (if fine) as I have no wish thou should be <u>lost</u> in a strange land on my account, but if I should chance not to be at the station thou had better ask the man there and he will direct thee to Mr. Dixons where thou wilt find me if I do not meet thee on the road which I hope to do.

Bessie is as usual full of her talk and while I am writing is asking me questions so I will leave thee to fancy what sort of person my worthy cousin is. Hopeing so soon to see thee. I will draw this scribble to a close and remain dear friend thy sincerely affectionate Mary

Dont forget the station Rainhill, I am quite in hopes thou will receive this tomorrow then. Farethee well.

Mary's implicit Victorian faith in the reliability and speed of mail is shown by this letter containing crucial information - if their meeting is to take place at the correct station. It is written on only the day before Jonathan leaves Preston for a new - to him - destination.

Jonathan made his journey to Prescott, because in her next letter (from Calder) Mary mentions having received a letter from Bessie Dixon who sends her 'kind regards to Jonathan'. However, as with their other meetings, we know tantalizingly little of what transpired. Mary was away from home for three weeks during which time she stayed with four families. (Five, if one includes her five day stay with the Kelsalls in Wyresdale). In the thirty month period covered by the letters Mary made three rounds of visits similar to the one just concluded. From the letters too, we know that it was not her first journey of this nature and it is interesting to imagine the society which permitted girls of Mary's age to travel safely, alone, and relatively frequently for appreciable periods 'to visit and see people'. Times have changed.

Jonathan's next letter to Calder Bridge on 1st August, written after Mary's return, is brief and is, in the main, about his increasing fondness for Mary. This takes the form of the lover's question: 'what should I do if thou cast me off ?' He ends with a paragraph which is a presage of change to come because Jonathan and Thomas Mulliner are beginning negotiations which eventually lead to Jonathan's acquisition of the latter's business:

> --- I am very busy this evening preparing a list of my wants for T. Mulliner who I expect to see in the morning and have to square up my accounts etc. with a promise to make amends in my next for this short scribble I will conclude and remain as ever --- .

Mary's response on the 5th of the month is very much shorter than her 'dear friend's':

> --- suppose I give thee the Quaker answer by asking thee the same question. However she goes on to tell him of her affection and then continues: 'S[arah] [Brown] Cameron and her husband [William] is coming tomorrow and Thomas and Mary Ann [Ord] the day after and perhaps William and David [Mary's brothers] so that we shall have quite a company (7) of first cousins. She concludes: --- if thou should chance to see me in Preston next week thou must not be surprised --- if I come I shall have to call on thy shop. <u>Not to see thee mind but to get a pair of boots</u>, if thou has any to fit such a person as myself.
>
> It is our O. Leaf [Olive Leaf = Friend's womens peace] meeting this afternoon, and as I am one of the sisters of peace I must leave my dear friend and attend to other duties --- .

Mary letters are often written on handsomely headed Olive Leaf notepaper and in 1854 we hear more of Elizabeth Abbatt's views of the Preston branch of the movement.

Jonathan's next letter is his most affectionate to date and he looks forward to his next 'out' to Calder -'if fine' on the following Sunday:

> To: Mary Dilworth
> Calder Bridge, Nr. Garstang
>
> Preston
> 8th Mo 10th 1853 [Wednesday]
>
> My Dear Polly,
>
> It was my intention to have written to thee yesterday but thinking likely I would have seen thee

here today, and that thou would hardly receive it before leaving home had I written I deferred, though it seems I was mistaken, however I will now take the opportunity to thank thee for thy last kind and affectionate letter which came promptly to hand.

The weather is now so inviting for an out that if it be fine on first day next I purpose coming to see thee, if convenient, so that there seems a chance of spending at least one fine day with thee once more though it has been so often wet so thou may expect me about the usual time, soon after two.

In replying to my last thou certainly would have answered me as I deserve had thou let me be content with what thou calls thy Quaker answer, but the reassurance of thy never failing affection is certainly delightful to hear and seems as it were to rivet the bonds of love that have bound me to thee, perhaps it was overanxiousness to make sure of thy much prized affection that led me to the supposition I expressed in my last, but since thou has so thoroughly convinced me that I may look for higher and better things from thee, I must ask thy excuse for such a transgression, but thou must remember dear Polly it was <u>only</u> a <u>supposition</u> and not intended to wrong thee at all, no, for it is (and I firmly believe and feel ever will be) my greatest pleasure to please and serve thee.

As to my own constancy thou may rest ever assured and I think thou trusts in me, my prayer is that I may ever be worthy of such a trust and so long as we continue in such fervent truthfulness to each other there will undoubtedly be in store for us a life of happiness and contentment, when the time comes that we will be <u>man</u> and <u>wife</u>!! Perhaps thou thinks me using a strong expression but no more than I feel, for the very prospect of such being the case and at no distant period fills me with Joy unspeakable and to think too of living with one who is in every way congenial to my tastes.

In thinking sometimes of our engagement I am led thoroughly to feel that kind providence has brought us together, and will work for our good, and in return I humbly though too seldom return my thanks and pray for increased strength to serve my God who so bounteously bestows his blessings on those who serve and please him.

My connection with thee I must confess has given

rise to thoughts and feelings before almost dormant, and as I before mentioned in a former letter thy casual injunctions to look above for help and strength to do our Father's will, though perhaps not intended have been taken to heart, I think with benefit.

I have scarcely dared thus to write to thee before, from a feeling of unworthyness and indeed I may almost say it would have been hypocrisy to do so, but for fear thou should think me in too serious a humour this time I will conclude and subscribe myself thine ever to be   Affectionate
                                        Jon.n Abbatt

P.S. If thou art fond of reading and has not read Mrs. Ellis's work entitled Family Secrets or how to make home Happy, and will let me know, I can find thee something interesting , so once again dear Polly
                                        Farewell. JA

The word 'out' for an outing usually of short duration, frequently a day or less, is much used by Jonathan. The expression was still in use in rural Lancashire and the Yorkshire dales in the nineteen thirties and forties.

The planned meeting took place and in the letter following on Thursday 18th he tells of an encounter with Lucy Jackson and this is followed by a long explanation of changes in Sunday train schedules. In future because the mail train will not stop at Garstang on Sunday evenings Jonathan will have to walk home from Calder. ' ---- will make me begin to think of hiring a pony.   ---- I have heard again from home and am sorry to say my Father is no better, it is a lingering complaint but hope to hear of an improvement soon.'

Mary's reply indicates her fondness for Jonathan, she is sure of herself but is not ready for a final commitment:

       To: Jonathan Abbatt
              158 Friargate, Preston

       Calder Bridge
       8mo 24 53 [Wednesday]

       My dear Jonathan,

       Accept my thanks for thy last communication which it is my pleasure to answer, did thou look for my reply yesterday? I feel anxious to hear of thy Father;

how often did I think of thee on first day wondering
how thou might find him. I trust better than thou
expected. I believe it is as thou says a lingering
complaint, therefore there is good ground for hope
that he may recover.

Lucy Jackson has not said a word about thou being
here the other day, and yesterday we had the company
of the Miss Ords to tea, strange to say they never
gave me the least hint, I suppose the news is like
everything else getting out of date with them
however, and quite agreeably so to myself. They had
been saying to Polly that thou was very seldom to be
seen at Meeting or at school, they supposed thou had
to go one first day to Calder Bridge and another to
Bolton; so it appears they look pretty sharp after
thee.

Thou speaks of thy letters as being almost worthless
- perhaps they may be to thyself (like my scribbles
are to me) but by me they are I assure thee much
valued.

Well now for "thy curious but important question"
what will thou say when I do not give thee a decided
"yes" but such dear J must be my answer now, while I
feel that the time may and most assuredly will come
when I can leave the dear home of my parents for a
home and a love untried. Now is not that enough for
thee to know? That I can be the means of completing
thy happiness is sometimes a source of pleasant
thoughts, but may we not look for an altogether
unruffled happiness such is not to be found on
earth; still we may do a good deal towards it .

I must now again say farewell to my dear friend and
remain as ever thy affectionate
$\qquad$ Mary Dilworth

To: Mary Dilworth
      Calder Bridge, Nr. Garstang

Preston
8 mo 25 1853 [Thursday]

My Dear Polly,

I am afraid my reply at this time to thy kind and
affectionate letter, received this morning, will be
of a melancholy character, from being so depressed
with my poor Father's illness which I find is

contrary to what I before stated, being a disease of the heart.

I found him much worse than expectation on first day, being almost unable to speak to me, I watched most part of the night and also all night on 3rd day returning to attend to my business last night, leaving my brothers and sisters who have all been sent for, to attend in my absence, but expect to return again soon.

I am glad to say that my Mother seems more composed than expected and endeavours to feel resigned to what must be, as there is to all appearances not the slightest chance of recovery.

From what I have said my dear Mary thou will be enabled somewhat to judge of my feelings and perhaps will excuse more this time from thy truly affectionate but sorrow stricken
                I may say more than
                        Friend
                              Jon.n Abbatt

To: Jonathan Abbatt
      158 Friargate   Preston

Calder Bridge
8 mo 30 1853

My dear Jonathan

Accept my sincere thanks for thy prompt answer to my last. I felt wishful to hear of thy Father, and am sorry to find from thy letter his illness is of so dangerous a character.

I fancied thee at home again on first day, it will I know cast a damper on thy spirits having so near and I doubt not so dear a relation in so precarious a state. I hope thy Mother still keeps as well as her trying situation will allow.

I had a letter from my friend and cousin E. Drewry the other day wishing Polly N. and myself to spend a short time with them, but we must at present decline her kind invitation. I rather fancy Mother will go this weekend, she has to be in Preston so will (if all's well) go forward. Excuse the shortness of my letter this time and believe me as ever to remain, thine in near affection and sympathy
                        Mary Dilworth

To: Mary Dilworth
    Calder Bridge, Nr. Garstang

Bolton
8 mo 30 1853 [Tuesday]

My Dear Mary.

I have been home all this week helping to nurse my poor Father who I am sorry to say departed this life this morning about half past 11.

I am now so much occupied with arrangements respecting the funeral etc. which owing to Monthly meeting to be held on 6th day is to take place on 5th day.

Perhaps thou will excuse my saying more at this time but as my time to visit thee again is on 1st day next thou will no doubt want to know what I mean to do. I can scarcely say whether I shall come or not but will let thee know again, very likely we shall not leave home again for our respective homes until next week, in the mean time I will subscribe myself
         Thine Most Affectionately
                    Jonathan Abbatt

To: Mary Dilworth
    Calder Bridge, Nr. Garstang

         'Blessedarethe Peacemakers'
              (Headed notepaper)

Bolton
9 mo 2nd 1853 [Friday]

My Dear Polly,

Thine was duly forwarded here for which I am much obliged, and sit down to say that I shall most likely come to see thee next first day next at the usual time if the weather permits, when I am satisfied we shall have a day of enjoyment once more. I have been at home all this week but intend to return this evening or tomorrow morning and shall feel truly glad of the change again when I return once more to my usual routine of duty, for this last week has been a truly sorrowful one to us all, but am glad to say that though my poor dear Mother has had so severe a trial yet considering all things she seems to bear up as well as expectation.

> As I only intend this to inform thee of my coming I shall defer saying more until I see thee and in hopes thou will excuse me saying more at this time I will conclude and remain as ever thine
> truly Affectionate   Jon.n Abbatt

The above series of letters not only tell of the father's death but also of the depth of Jonathan's attachment to Mary. Not only does he write to inform Mary on the day of the death but two days later he has already made plans for a visit to Calder Bridge on 4th September.

Jonathan's relations with his father were never extensive or intimate. At the age of eight he was sent to Ackworth (where there were no holidays) and did not return home again until he was thirteen. After a brief holiday he was then, against his will, apprenticed to his Uncle Fletcher. He again left home to serve his apprenticeship in Leigh, and upon being 'free' immediately went to Preston to work for T. Mulliner as a journeyman.

The fact that father and son did not know each other does not mean that there was antipathy, there was none. Indeed the letters, including those from Benjamin, suggest a real but rather distant and austere, emotional relationship. This consisted of respect and duty from the son and responsibility and duty on the part of the father.

The following notes on Benjamin come from his brother Jame's, his grandson Dilworth, his own letters and Paul Beswick's diary. A clear picture and character emerges.

BENJAMIN ABBATT 1799-1853

Benjamin the third child of Thomas and Alice (Smith) Abbatt, lived all of his life in Bolton. His brother James (1796-1868) said that: "Benjamin had not like some of his brothers an education at Ackworth School, but began work when he was eight years old. In course of time he was apprenticed to Emmanuel Birkett, Basket Maker of Oxford Street, Bolton".

In 1824 Benjamin married Elizabeth daughter of Jonathan and Ann Brown of Standish near Wigan who once lived at the Old Langtree Meeting House. Elizabeth's great grandfather was a convinced Friend who married Elizabeth (Rigby) Brown of a staunch Quaker family from Middleton Hall, Nr. Goosnargh.

In 1823 at the age of twenty-four he began business on his own account in the making of cane 'skips' - the very large baskets that were then much used in the Lancashire cotton mills. As the business grew a number of other cane containing products were added; and by the time the fourth generation were in the firm the weaving of cane seats for railways carriages (cars) was an appreciable part of the business.

Benjamin had felt himself in need of help with his business for some eight to ten years before his death, and this may well have been due to angina because he died after a short illness following a massive cardiac infarction. Originally, Jonathan had been intended for the cane business but this was not to be and after his father's death the eldest son William, who was a master at Sidcot when his father died, succeeded. The business prospered which is not only a tribute to his family successors but even more so to the founder who died young at the age of only 54.

A Friends funeral is well described in diary entries by his friend Paul Beswick of Bolton:

> Monday 29/8/1853. B. Abbatt est presque de mourir on trouve -
> Tuesday 30/8/1853. B. Abbatt died today at 11 1/2 without much struggling he was a true specimen of the British "Quaker" simple and rigid in his habits, with few or no bad habits: kind in his demeanour to all but expecting industry and self denial from all: an early riser, hard worker and temperate in eating and drinking, a good but stern father an excellent advisor but one that allowed few excuses or shortcomings. He had been bedfast for a week. His disease was of the Heart, he will leave his family well provided for, they are all over tw[enty] ---
>
> Wednesday 31/8/1853. Rain v. heavy in night I went to see B. Abbatt today - he had been opened by Drs. Black and Mallett, he is very much altered - bury him tomorrow --
>
> Thursday 1/9/1853 - Rain, I went to B. Abbatt's funeral this morning he was buried in the Quaker manner. The Friends of the deceased are invited to meet at the house the coffin is brou(ght) down placed in a hearse (although it ought by their rules to be carried bare through the streets) and comes to the burial ground, the Friends following after in no particular order, the nearest relations making no difference or outward demeanour (their shops or places of business are not closed) the coffin is received at the Meeting House by no other than the Friends who have walked on a little before, no word

> is spoken - it is deposited in the grave as quickly as possible and all then stand around in thought - nothing is said, the immediate relatives step forward to take a last look at the coffin and retire and all is over, at times however the Spirit they suppose moves someone and he or she will make suitable remarks on the Life and -- to the deceased and follow with a scriptural·discourse. It rained heavily all the time."
>
> ------------------

In the letter written to Mary on 9th September immediately after his Calder visit and one week after the funeral, Jonathan refers to his need to be of service to God and is affected by death bed memories - but he, himself, is very much 'back in life':

> On my return last 2nd day morning, [he had stayed overnight at Calder House], I met both Richard and Jon.n Jackson in their gigs, so thou sees I was caught again, as has been my fortune almost every time I have visited thee, but I always console myself with the reflection that it will be my good fortune to catch something some of these visits ----- though at the same time I feel a pride in being seen with thee and shall feel doubly so (perhaps 12 months from now!!!) when I can truly call thee my wife.
>
> As I have said before I have for sometime had a tendency to more serious thoughts and a life more devoted to the service of my God but after the scenes of my poor Father on his death bed I feel doubly so --- .
>
> I always write as I feel, that thou may judge my character whether it be congenial to thy tastes or not, and shall feel glad if I say anything contrary if thou will name it, we should have a thorough understanding of each other. Having said this much and having some business to attend to this evening I will once more conclude in hopes my seriousness has not been unpleasant and will subscribe myself---

The first and the last paragraphs of spontaneous letters reveal much of the writer's person and immediate 'things on their mind' and this letter tells us a great deal about Jonathan. On the one hand at the beginning we have self consciousness, sensitivity and love for Mary; in the middle we have religious consciousness and a desire to serve, and at the end is honesty, concern for Mary - and 'business' i.e earning a living.

MARY (NICHOL) and
SAMUEL PICKARD
'Mary N.' of the letters – MARY's cousin, friend and confidante, – another of 'the Marys' – who married their cousin, Sam, at Calder Bridge March 1855.

BENJAMIN and ELIZABETH (BROWN) ABBATT of BOLTON
JONATHAN's parents. (Benjamin from a daguerrotype.)

PAUL BESWICK of BOLTON
Boot and shoe maker and 'literary friend' of Benjamin and Thomas A. Was fluent in French, German and Italian, and described Benjamin's funeral and JONATHAN's wedding.

JAMES ABBATT 1796-1868
JONATHAN's uncle – and Benjamin's elder brother – was a tailor in Bolton and Preston. Emigrated 1843 and farmed in Peoria, Illinois, U.S.A.

THE FIRST LOG CABIN in DILWORTHTOWN, PENNSYLVANIA

Built in 1754 by James Dilworth (1720-1769) this log cabin was the first structure in Dilworthtown. The red-brick extension behind is a later 18th-century addition. It is now an excellent Restaurant – Inn-keeper Timothy McCarthy. James D.'s son, Charles, obtained a licence for the tavern in 1770 and in 1820 it became 'The Dilworthtown Inn'. During the British Army occupatin in 1777, after the battle of Brandywine, much damage was done to the Inn by looting and Charles D. made an itemised claim for £820.15.3 which included the 'lost time of a servant lad Patrick Kelley, about 14 years, he went off with the British Army'. See pages 20-22 and 270-72. (This illustration was most kindly provided by Martha Carlsen of Victoria, B.C. Canada.)

Mary replies on 15th September and acknowledges 'thy kind and welcome letter':

> Do not for a moment think that thy seriousness is offensive to mine ear, on the contrary so much more do I admire thy character. Often do I flatter myself with the pleasing thought that he on whom I have bestowed my confidence and affection is found walking (though maybe in a smaller degree) in the footsteps of our blessed Saviour. May thou my dear J. be my teacher in this all important work and may each remind the other that this beautiful world is not our abiding place.
>
> 'Aunt Marys', [Mary (Wilcockson) second wife and now widow of Richard Jackson of Calder House and Bridge M.H.], are expecting a neighbour or two to tea this afternoon and as I am invited to meet them I must of necessity draw my unworthy scribble to a close, for we go to spend the <u>afternoon</u> here and not the <u>evening</u> as you do in town.

Preston at this time (though still quite small) was clearly and definitely 'Town', with town manners and customs, as opposed to 'country' in the Garstang area.

On 22nd September Jonathan writes that his sister Jane:

> - was very poorly but the change seems to have done her good and is now I think quite recovered and since thy Mother has given me an invitation for her to come and see thee I shall be glad to spare her some day next week if thou will say when is convenient --- . --- when I shall be more decided about it, though <u>perhaps</u> thou will say since my visits are so intimately connected with thee that I must ask thy consent before I make my appearance in public, well since I have so far committed myself to the <u>mercies</u> of <u>petticoat government</u> I will <u>humbly</u> ask if it be agreeable to thee, thou must remember they all know and if they do quietly titter at us at first we shall be no worse for it I assume. I dont consider the Railway Company any friends of mine with their [timetable] alterations.

When Mary replies the poor girl is still very self conscious about 'people', despite knowing that 'they all know'. Jonathan had made a brave effort to help her and as a result she says: 'do as thou likes about it --- '. How difficult for Jon.n! It is interesting to compare Mary's lighter touch, when she is gently teazing, with her fiance's cumbersome efforts quoted above.

To: Jonathan Abbatt
      158 Friargate,   Preston

      'Peace Brotherhood Progress'

Calder Bridge
27 of 9mo 53 [Tuesday]

My dear Jonathan,

Again it is my pleasure to acknowledge thine of 22nd for which accept my thanks.
In the first place thou must give my love to your sister, and tell her that we will be most happy to see her at our house (if convenient) tomorrow. I think there is a train about one o'clock, I shall (if alls well) be at the station to meet her, she must not fix a time to return, so thou will not need to look out for her reappearance in Preston for a few days at least; I quite hope the change will benefit her.

Cousin David was over here on first day what a day to be sure we had for wind and rain; thou would be glad I dare say to stay quietly at home.

Now about thee coming on first day morning; I dont quite like the idea of it: will it not be well if the idea is worse than the reality, perhaps it may be so, therefore I will say do as thou likes about it, now thou will have to call me generous I am sure.

Polly N. and self talk something about going to Fleetwood next week but it is quite uncertain if we get off. Aunt Jane being from home Mary cannot leave until her return, she is at cousin Bessies. Hoping to be favoured with <u>one</u> or <u>two</u> of thy well filled sheets before long in return for this <u>most interesting</u> and lengthy one, I will say farewell and remain - Thine affectionately
                                    Mary Dilworth

P.S. Mind and dont forget what I have told thee to tell thy shy sister.-
                           M.D.

Aunt Jane (Wilcockson) Nichol, is mother of Mary N. and Cousin Bessie is Bessie (Pickard) Dixon of Prescott. Jane Abbatt stayed for four days at Calder Bridge and the visit must have been a success as she stayed longer than originally planned and it was repeated later. Jane's stay with Jonathan was probably to provide her with a 'change' after her Father's death and to enable her to meet her future sister-in-law. Jane's visit changes the now established routine leading Jonathan to enquire on 30th:

--- perhaps I will trip over on third or fourth day afternoon next week and come by the same train as my sister did, and then for 1 month or more we may save ourselves from being gazed at by the worthy friends in your quarter, perhaps thou will favour me with thy opinion about it.

Mary's reply is, as usual, more than clear:

To: Jonathan Abbatt
    158 Friargate   Preston

Calder Bridge
3rd 10mo /53 [Monday]

My dear Jonathan

In thy letter recd. on the 7th day thou wished to know if it would suit me to have thy company on third or fourth day, such would have given me pleasure had I not been expecting to be in Preston so soon, and as thou may very likely see me there I think there is no need for thee to come here.

I hope to leave here by the first train on fourth day morning accompanied by M.N. we go to Fleetwood the day after.

I was glad thy sister appeared to enjoy herself with us, I hope she got safe to Preston on 7th day night we left her very shabbily at the station, but we were afraid it would rain before we got home, else we should have stayed to see her off. I almost think it would have been impossible for us to have prevailed upon her to stay longer, she said many times on 7th day 'I shall see my mother tomorrow' well dear lass I do not wonder at her. We often talked about thee she likes to speak a good word for her brother Jonathan, all which I was well enough pleased to give ear to thou may rest assured --
Perhaps <u>sometime</u> I may know thee as well as thy sister appears to, but really now thou must not tease so, to know when that <u>sometime</u> must be; time and patience will work wonders and will I have no doubt if we are spared for each other see the

pleasing picture thou has often drawn realised. Now do not be saying dear friend that I am writing to thee in a cool and calculating way no it is the language ofa heart affectionately sinceretoward thee.

I must now for the present conclude and remain dear Jonathan thine Truly
      Mary Dilworth

To: Mary Dilworth
   Thomas Drury
   Dock Street Fleetwood

Preston
10 mo 6th 53 [Monday]

My dearest Polly

I have been thinking since last I saw thee that I shall hardly come to Fleetwood on first day, for it is now so long since I saw thee to be in thy company long at once, that I shall prefer seeing thee at home, where we can enjoy each others company more privately, for when with strangers we can scarcely do so.

Perhaps thou will let me know when thou will be at *home and if thou would prefer my company on the first day or some week day afternoon.

So thou was not at the Book meeting, well now if I had known I should like to have spent the evening with thee, but more of this when I see thee.

It is is now so near posting time that I must conclude to be in time so will once more say farewell and remain my dearest Polly
    Thine
      Affectionately Jon.n Abbatt

It seems, from Jonathan's letter to Fleetwood, that it had been suggested by the 'two Marys' when they were in Preston, that he should have one of his 'outs' to see them there. His unusually short letter tells us that he he did not like the idea of a second threesome so soon! In addition he had 'business' on his mind as he was becoming impatient for the changes in his work which would provide a basis for marriage.. He wished to talk all this over with Mary and did so at their next Calder meeting the following Sunday.

Following this Calder talk with Mary he wrote on the 18th telling of his frustration and impatience:

> I have had T. Mulliner here today but he seems not to think of any change as he did not even hint to the expiration of my term but as there (are) rather more than five months yet he may think it too soon, though let first month [January] get here and I can read him the <u>riot</u> <u>act</u> but thou will again be saying patience, patience, though in my opinion there is nothing like going ahead and my motto is onward and onward I must go. ---- so I must desist, and as Wm. Jackson [one of Jonathan's personal Oakenclough friends who later, and after a severe illness, married Jane Gardner] has just come in and it is past shutting up time, and my sheet is nearly full, I must conclude though I can fancy thou saying what excuses for a finish as though I could not turn W. out, shut up shop and write after, and if the sheet be full get a fresh one but really my dear Polly thou must excuse me so with unfailing love I remain sincerely and affectionately
>
> Jon.n Abbatt

Jonathan's reference to reading the 'riot act' and Mary's probable response of 'patience, patience' was a sign of things to come as Mary was placid, dryly humorous and temperate in her counsel. Jonathan, while easy going and superficially placid, was not always so. Many Abbatts have been hasty tempered and quick to anger, and according to his eldest son, Dilworth, Jonathan was no exception. Another side of his, and the Abbatt family's character, again according to his son, was his speech. Both Jno.n, his brothers and sisters as well as Elizabeth and Benjamin spoke what, in another age, would have been called 'Oxford' or 'standard' English. This is odd, and the reasons are quite unknown, they certainly did not include pretension and if desired Jonathan could be an excellent mimic of accents in (mostly humorous) stories in a wide variety of dialects. Why should a Lancashire cane manufacturer and his family of no particular rank or pretensions speak relatively unaccented English? (John Jackson Dilworth, who was no less and perhaps more literate, spoke with a broad country Lancashire dialect) The most obvious and perhaps a major contributory reason is that the language of the home is a potent influence but beyond this and a (most unlikely) genetic influence, it remains a minor and inconsequential mystery. The 'phenomenon' was carried to three succeeding generations!

The next planned visit is delayed by early rain, and writing on Sunday 23rd October Jno.n begins:

> It was so wet and unfit for walk this morning that I at once concluded to defer my visit until 3rd day afternoon, and shall leave here about one o'clock, when if it be fine and agreeable to thee it would please me if thou would meet me. [at the Railway Station]

Garstang and Catterall railway station (now closed) is a little over three quarters of a mile from Calder Bridge and provided a pleasant walk 'home'. J. and M. could either go direct or even better for lovers and only a little further, by the banks of the River Calder much of it tree lined, with wild daffodils (Lent Lilies) in spring, sparkling water, stones and pools, trout, wagtails and sand martins. The love letter continues:

> I have thought lately we have scarcely seen each other sufficiently, to promote that loving interest for each other that is desirable, not that I have experienced any decrease in thy much prized love and esteem ---- but we have been so long separate, with one short exception, that I have almost said --- . Perhaps thou thinks as is said in that piece of poetry we were used to repeat at Ackworth entitled 'Isle of Beauty' that: "Absence makes the Heart Grow Fonder". I can scarcely sanction that as truth exactly though it certainly produces in me a greater longing for thy company ---- .
>
> Well now Polly as I hope to see thee on 3rd day [Tuesday] perhaps I may venture to conclude without too many excuses, [it is already quite a long letter] and as I suspect you have the company of D.W. [her cousin David Wilcockson from Preston] perhaps I am as well here today, so wishing thee but a short farewell this time before I see thee --- .

The next letter tells of William and Thomas 'getting established' and of Jonathan's desire to follow suit:

> To: Mary Dilworth
>   Calder Bridge Nr. Garstang
>
>
> Preston
> 11 mo. 2nd 1853 [Wednesday]
>
> My Dear Mary,
>
> After a full weeks silence I think it time I should again address thee for if I defer longer it will seem so long before I hear from thee.

I have this morning received a letter from my dear Mother telling me of the changes that have taken place since I was there, brother Thomas has dissolved partnership and as thou will see by the enclosed card has opened a shop himself, brother Wm. too is what I believe permanently settled in my poor Father's old established business, and now comes <u>my</u> turn next and then ----- dear me what does thou mean by leaving such a blank? Cant't thou guess, I think thou can, but still I can almost fancy thee saying have patience and dont run away from Preston by any means, but I am afraid if there be no chance here soon my impatience will drive me elsewhere, however time will settle the matter.

In my Mother's note too she tells me of their <u>glorious</u> success in behalf of the Anti-slavery Bazaar having obtained some most excellent contributions, my Aunt and cousins at Leigh have forwarded a box containing nine or ten pounds worth of articles and altogether they seem in excellent spirits about it, I expect to be over in Bolton before long to see them as I wish to obtain the best advice I can in my arrangements with T. Mulliner.

I mean to make out a list of what I shall require to commence business and shall have a good guide in doing so with the present stock as regards prices etc. which will help me well in making my purchases if it so happens that I do commence instead of partnership, but I must not bore thee with business matters which are at the best of times shockingly dull subjects.

I begin to feel I must make some more excuses for writing a long letter and will perhaps make amends in my next visit to thee which is now about three weeks too, for I prefer chatting personally to scrawling over so much paper, especially when I derive so much pleasure as on my last visit, though perhaps thou sets me down as a young man with too much nonsense about him, but thou must not forget as thou has seen me and knows me otherwise.

Well now I think I must once more take leave of my dear Polly for the present so will conclude remaining as ever
                Thine affectionately
                Jon.n Abbatt

His thoughts of leaving Preston for Bolton evoke an immediate response from Mary because this would have taken him, and therefore her, appreciably further from her familiar surroundings, home, and relations. Her reply and counsel on 10th November is very clear:

> Now dont thou begin to frighten me by saying thy inexperience will drive thee away from Preston. No thou must on no account leave, though I quite fancy the good folks at Bolton will do their best to get thee near them and I do not wonder at them, but thou must have a little more patience again say I. ---- only I must remind thee not to be in too great a hurry: but for fear thou should think and feel that I sat down to preach a sermon on paper, I wish thy agreeable permission to drop the subject --- . ---- love to Jane please ---- it is indeed [the Anti-Slavery Bazaar] a most praiseworthy object on which to bestow ones labour, though we in this quarter do not work for it, still I trust we are friends and warm ones too if the poor share.
>
> On 3rd day [Tuesday] Cousin Mary Ord [from Preston] came on a visit to this quarter, she Mary N.[ichol] and worthy self were at Lancaster yesterday it being our M. Meeting there and a very fine day we had, we had to leave as early as 7 o'clock in the morning and did not get home again until 6 at night so find lots of time for gossip, as I suppose thou will think that almost indispensible but thou will be saying 'now Polly dont make be out so bad'. My aunt E. Wilcockson came yesterday on a short visit to Aunt's [Mary (Wilcockson) Jackson] she has not been well of late'.

Jonathan's next letter is long and affectionate:

> To: Mary Dilworth
>   Calder Bridge   Nr. Garstang
>
>
> Preston
> 11 mo. 16 /53 [Wednesday]
>
> My Dear Polly
>
> I almost fear thou will think I have been transgressing in not writing to thee before this but when I explain personally what I have been doing in the meantime, thou will I think excuse me.
>
> Thine came to hand last sixth day, but thou must not call me *too* impatient when I tell thee I had looked for the postman pretty eagerly on 4th and 5th days

so thou may be sure its contents were devoured with avidity.

I am expecting to be in Bolton next first day when I will faithfully deliver thy message. I shall have some matters of importance to talk over and will let thee know the result when I see thee on third day, but first of all allow me to ask will third day be convenient.

Now I have thee fast Polly thou <u>must</u> write to let me know if it will suit thee otherwise <u>perhaps</u> I may not come, so thou sees I consider thee bound to let me have another letter ere I see thee; it will be a good idea to <u>invent</u> something if possible of this sort to get early replies but when the time comes that I shall have thee here and shall have only to trot upstairs to enjoy thy company at any time, then shall I consider myself a happy man and shall try all I can to make thee a happy little <u>wife</u>.

I can almost hear thee saying did anyone ever hear such stuff, and thou may say too I am ever fiddling on one string, then I must tell thee tis the one with the sweetest music in it, and since it affords me so much pleasure may I not indulge it, and <u>do</u> I not indulge it to our mutual satisfaction.

Perhaps thou will remember during my last visit whilst appealing to thee <u>most</u> <u>pathetically</u> (telling me O dear thou art laying it on) meaning I suppose a bit of flattery, now my dear Polly under these circumstances what am I to do, if I be a long time in replying to thy letters thou must not be surprised, since thou has placed me in such a difficult position, for if I give utterance as the <u>spirit</u> <u>moves</u> me (as we friends say) thou makes light of me and laughs, <u>even</u> when reading this, however this may be, I must try and convince thee I am in earnest when next I see thee that is if thou won't laugh at me.

I almost begin to think a partnership with T.M. would do well for me notwithstanding the bad times in Preston we are doing several pounds better weekly than last year, which I consider a good sign our business is nicely increasing.

Thou should have seen me in Sam Jespers parlour last evening, we were transacting some first day school business and about 10 0'clock when we finished for the night Sam and I played several tunes he on the

flute and me on the flutina while Sam's sister
accompanied us with her voice so that we had quite a
concert, to be resumed again tomorrow night. Should
we not look sheepish if Jos. Jesper were to come in
in the midst of it.

Well now I must make more excuses for a finish, in
the first place it is almost shutting up time for we
now close at 7 o'clock then again our shop is so
cold that I am cold too and further if I continue
writing much longer my dear Polly will find it
tiresome to read so much of what is truly <u>laid on</u>
(that is the ink on the paper) so rather than
fatigue thee with too much of my scrawl I will
conclude and remain as ever truly loveing
                Thine   Affectionately
                              Jon.n Abbatt

    P.S. I have no time to look it over so thou must
    excuse blunders.

Jonathan was musical and not only played the flutina -
presumably a 'mini' flute - but much enjoyed his own
performances. In this taste he was a very 'advanced'
Friend as music was only just beginning to be introduced
into some liberal minded Friends' homes in the sixties
though the practice was far from general. Through-out
the nineteenth century the Preston Meeting (and no doubt
many others) used a dinner bell rather than an instrument
for the game of musical chairs at childrens parties.

Mary's reply is short 'light and loving', and tells much
of herself and her activities:

    To: Jonathan Abbatt
           158 Friargate   Preston

Calder Bridge
21st 11mo 1853 [Monday]

My dear Jonathan,

Once more I take my pen for the purposes of
addressing a few lines to thee; in the first place I
must ask thee if thou could come on 4th day or any
other day of that week, as I have an engagement
tomorrow afternoon, I hope it will make no
difference to thee.

What this important engagement is I will tell thee
when I see thee, I dare not put it on paper for fear

thou should laugh. I assure thee I am not alone in laughing; does thou never laugh at me? Well well, better do that at times than be sad.

Nice young man you are indeed, to think of your having private concerts, I wonder if you will ever have them public, I will promise to come once when you have. Thou will get a first rate hand.

Thou would love a nice day at Bolton yesterday I trust thou found all well.

I have to go to Garstang this afternoon so thou must excuse this shabby note as it is quite time I started, to be home before daylight has gone.

Allow me to remain as ever thine in dear affection

                          Mary Dilworth

It is sad that we shall never know what was the nature of Mary's appointment on Tuesday afternoon 22nd November but we do know that Jonathan paid another of his Calder Bridge visits on Wednesday the twenty third and events moved rapidly in his affairs. On this fourth day (Wednesday) he took a letter just received from Thomas Mulliner offering to sell him the Preston business. One can imagine that the serious Jonathan and his girl had a major talk on 'matters of importance'. We know too from the next letter that he told Mary of a precise date when he hoped that they might be married.

    To: Mary Dilworth
           Calder Bridge   Garstang

Preston
11 mo 26th 1853 [Saturday]

My dear Mary

I have pleasure in sitting down to address thee this time though I have seen thee so very recently yet in this short time business of importance has been transacted.

I found on getting to Preston the night I last saw thee that the last train was so late that I should have found my folks in bed if I had gone, so that I went by the first train in the morning, after showing my brothers and my Uncle the letter I had received from T.M. and [after] considering the different features of the affair, they concluded I could do no better than accept his terms though of course I made every effort to get the business <u>under</u> his terms but of no avail, for on the first onset he told me point blank it was his determination not to swerve a <u>fraction</u> from what he had offered, and also told me he rued having made the offer and insists on having cash down; on mentioning this to my Uncle he said immediately "Oh I'll be bound with thee two hundred pounds" and throughout the matter he has been excedingly kind to me.

He at first thought that one hundred pounds [was] a large sum to pay but upon considering the trouble anxiety and expense of beginning a new business in the face of so much opposition as I should have to contend with he thought it better to pay the 100 and have an established business at once that now brings in 200 clear so thou sees I can pay the 100 the first year comfortably.

T. Mulliner is to come next 3rd day to take stock, when I enter on the business at once, but business matters are a dry subject to thee I don't doubt so will teaze thee no more at present with it.

Well now thou must remember what I told thee to expect and hold thyself prepared to say <u>yes</u>, though if I <u>should</u> be <u>four</u> months longer than I gave thee to expect I should want thee to say this <u>leetle</u> word thou must, my dear Polly <u>sympathise</u> with me in my <u>distress</u> in not being able to press it.

I've been told already, does thou know that we are going to be married next summer. I told them I was rather surprised as I had heard nothing of it, but be this as it may I must get my affairs a little straight first before the happy day comes.

It now begins to look as if I was going to settle in Preston instead of running off to Bolton, which thou seemed so afraid of, and I must confess tis a comfort to me to stay here I like the town so well.

I just mentioned to my Mother about Richard Jackson's house being to let when she seemed to jump at the idea of living there almost, and requested me to ask the rent, she has quite a fancy for living in a country place among friends. Yet I fancy she would find it a hard matter to leave Bolton and it is so uncertain that I would wish it not to be <u>mentioned</u> at <u>all</u> nevertheless thou can let me know the rent, though if you think of going there I am sure she would not prevent you.

Having written so much thou must excuse more at this time and shall be glad to hear from thee again at any time.

So now my dear Polly I will again say farewell and remain
                 Thine Affectionately
                         Jon.n Abbatt

The above letter and Mary's reply on 2nd December are models of what such letters should be, informative, clear, honest and 'sharing'. Jonathan's conceals nothing, thinks of others than himself - even at this time - and is affectionate. Mary listens, counsels, understands and acts - in that her Father has been sent to talk with Richard Jackson about housing. (This would be no hardship since John J. D. lived beside the Meeting House and they were kinsmen and near neighbours.)

Jonathan's purchase of his business was to put it mildly, 'facilitated' - and was made possible - by his Uncle and old Master John Fletcher of Leigh. In addition to advice and encouragement, John F. spontaneously offered to lend - "Oh I'll be bound with thee two hundred pounds" - at the crucial time of T. Mulliner's offer to sell.

John Fletcher and his wife Mary both had the reputation of being autocratic, old fashioned, strict, stern, 'stand no nonsense' Quakers. However, Jonathan specifically mentions his Uncle's kindly help, so that old John was not without the milk of human kindness. We may presume too that Jon.n had been a 'good' apprentice. Old John, who was to die at the end of 1854, was a Clogger and Leather Cutter in Leigh (8 miles SW of Bolton). He was much valued in Leigh and as his funeral passed though the town all shops closed and blinds were drawn. As we will hear later Jonathan was somewhat involved with his affairs before and after his death.

We do not know the details of T. Mulliner's offer to Jonathan beyond the fact that the latter had to borrow so that he could pay cash down. Since the premises were rented/leased, almost certainly the offer was for the sale of business goodwill, with stock to be bought at valuation - as agreed by T.M. and J.A. John Fletcher's loan was for two hundred pounds at five per cent/year with an additional 100 pounds to be immediately available on the same terms, should it be needed. Jonathan's estimate of the business ' --- that now brings in 200 pounds clear --- ' proved to be an underestimate and in his first year he took 250 pounds.

The editor has not solved the problem of relative values of money and goods for 'then and now' - housing costs compared with food costs were low.

Interest rates at 5% (which would not be the top rate) are comparable (sometimes) with today.

Rental of Calder House 1853/4 = ten pounds per year. (Mary's letter of 2nd December)

Emma Goodall, who married David Dilworth in April 1855, see Chapter VI, kept a diary and the Newcastle-under-Lyme December 1855 entries include the following:

- pound of bacon   = 10 pence
- pound of butter = 16 pence
- pound of beef   = 30 pence
- dozen eggs   = 10 pence

One pound sterling until c.1969 = 240 pence.

At this time Jonathan's capital was limited to the hundred pounds he had received on his Father's death. (In his will Benjamin left "each of my children, namely William, Thomas, Jonathan, James, Jane, Alice Ann and Elizabeth the sum of one hundred Pounds to be paid to the youngest on their severally attaining the age of twenty one years --- ." The residue was left in trust with the income for his widow Elizabeth.) As a result the material basis for 'setting out on his own' was probably sound, though there was little margin for disaster. Although there was no 'safety net' or social support system, none was expected and Jonathan had confidence in his world. He believed that things were getting better and better for ever and ever! This provides confidence.

It is not known what, if any, unseen influences operated to allow Jonathan to 'set up on his own'. Thomas Mulliner was a Bolton relative, as well as Jno.n's employer, at the time of the sale, his wife, too, was a friend of Elizabeth Abbatt. John Fletcher, was both the apprentice's old Master of seven years, and the husband of Mary Brown of Standish - Elizabeth A.'s sister. They would know both the facts and the need, and would, too, be very conscious of Benjamin's recent death and Elizabeth's bereavement. Knowing all this, it is probable that they were predisposed to help, particularly since they thought well of Jno.n. However, they were unlikely to be unduly influenced, because, though a staunch Quaker, Uncle John was at the same time a sound and careful Lancashire business man.

After his purchase, Mary tells Jonathan - 'thee should not be too anxious' - a very 'Mary' piece of advice!:

    To: Jonathan Abbatt
           Friargate   Preston

Calder Bridge
12 mo. 2 /53 [Friday]

My dear Jonathan

Thou will doubtless have looked for a letter from me before this makes its appearance but thou must not think I forget thee.

Thine was received on first day morning just as I was starting to meeting thou may rest assured it was quite welcome. My cousin David (who came the evening before with Mother) told me thou had taken T. Mulliner's business so thou sees my mind was soon at rest; well I am very glad thou has done so; and thou must now allow me to beg of thee not to be too anxious.

Thou says I am to remember what thou told me, well, I do remember, and then again thou wants my sympathy, in what way am I to sympathise with thee? I do not see thou has need to disturb thyself; never fear but we shall be married time enough, although as thy friend has told thee, it may not take place next summer.

How strange people should get such ideas, why Lucy Jackson (the other day) said to Mother as bold as possible "When is Mary going to be married I hear he has gone into business" we shall both be able to stand these remarks shall we not?

My cousin Bessie Dixon will now be in Preston perhaps she may have called upon thee, we are expecting her in this neighbourhood on 7th or first day, we shall not be lost for want of conversation I guess.

Thou would be quite busy on 3 day I hope you came to an agreeable arrangement.

My Father has spoken to Richard Jackson about us

going to their house, but it will be some time
before it is at liberty, and it is quite uncertain
our getting there: so that if we should not we shall
be very glad to have thy Mother and sisters for
neighbours.

Should we go our house will be at liberty and I have
no doubt J. Jackson would put it in nice order, the
rents are 10 pounds a year I believe. I think with
thee that thy Mother will not like to leave Bolton
after residing there so long.

It is post time so thou my dear Jonathan must excuse
more from thy truly attached
                                                    Mary

P.S. I shall be on the look out for a letter
towards the end of next week.   Fare Thee Well

The speed of word of mouth information flow from Preston
to Garstang is an excellent example of the efficiency of
'the network'. Faster than the daily Post!

The scheme for Elizabeth Abbatt to move to the Calder
Bridge/Barnacre area came to nothing, and the Dilworths
did not move from Calder House into Richard Jackson's old
house. Calder House is a good sized house with an
excellent large garden, it is well situated and as we see
from the letters, easy of access from north, south, east
and west. Rental of ten pounds a year in 1853 from J.
Jackson would be an economic, though not an exorbitant
amount. Rents, like life styles, have changed.

There are only two more letters for 1853, Jonathan's on
9th December tells of separate visits he has received
from Mary's cousins, Bessie Dixon and Elizabeth Drury,
both of whom are newly married. Both had, no doubt, been
to see the new 'young man' soon to be their cousin. He
makes a 'date' for his next visit the following Tuesday
when he hopes for: ' --- a fine frosty day so that we
could have a nice ramble --- .' Such winter days which
can be crisp, clear and whitely sparkling are in the
editor's opinion the best of all Garstang days, even
better than the spring or summer. Jno.n adds a P.S.,
having seen Ann Dilworth (before post time) and hearing
that Mary has a cold, he commiserates and also tells her
that another cousin, Margaret Swindlehurst, has: ' ---
lost her little one after something like two months
illness.'

Mary replies on the 19th December and is expecting
Jonathan: ' --- tomorrow [Tuesday] when I suppose I am to

look for thee at the old time.' (The previously planned visit had been postponed because of M.'s cold). She tells of hearing from her cousins Elizabeth Drury above, and Ellen (Kelsall) Glover. The two Mary's (Dilworth and Nichol) have been to stay with Ann Wilcock and were visited by: ' --- William Jackson came in on 7th day evening [and] the young ladies from the Vale [Calder Vale, built by Jno. Jackson] were at tea on that day.'

The Wilcocks appear quite frequently later. Margaret (Wilcock) Jackson (1800-1843) had been wife of John Jackson (1789-1845) of Spout House, Wyresdale and later of Oakenclough.

The year 1853 ends, in the letters, with a presumed meeting at Calder on Tuesday 20th December and no mention of either Christmas or the coming New Year.

Neither Jonathan nor Mary, mention or reflect in writing on the passing of the year; this is in contrast with 1854 so it is not Quakerly reserve. Friends were acutely conscious of the significance of Christmas, but every day is holy and no one day more than another. They were, moreover, wary, and as Jonathan remarks in 1854, well aware of the growing commercialisation of Christmas.

Whether they reflected on 1853 or not, it had determined the course of their lives. In this year Jonathan made his first formal approach to Mary and her parents in January/February. He was accepted by the Dilworths with little delay. His stern father, Benjamin, also gave his blessing and approval, but after appropriate enquiries.

Benjamin probably never met John Jackson and Ann Dilworth or for that matter, Mary. Elizabeth, however, must have completely approved of the arrangement since within a month or two of her bereavement she was considering going to live in a Jackson house as a very close neighbour of the Dilworths. Indeed Elizabeth, who knew of Mary before Benjamin, no doubt helped to sway her irascible husband when Jonathan ask their blessing of the proposed union.

Five months after the engagement, on 31st August, Benjamin was dead and by early December Jonathan had 'started out on his own' in Thomas Mulliner's Preston business that he had been managing since his apprenticeship ended in 1850.

The enduring enterprises, of the engagement and the business, were to be with Jonathan and Mary for the rest of their lives.

V GETTING to KNOW YOU - 1854

Practical Joke Problem - Increasing Affection and Letters Cross - More Jacksons - Marriage deferred - Wax flowers - David Dilworth - Mary D. & Mary N. to Newcastle - Sarah Ord - James & Eliz. Labrey/Jackson - Jno. to Calder and Woodlands - Increase in Jno.'s business - Teetotalism - Jno. meets David D. - Eliz. A. & daughters to Preston - William Abbatt - Elizabeth & Alice Ann Abbatt - Thomas Abbatt - An 'Out' to Windermere - Speed of Mail - Mary Ann Ord - Business competition - A Valuable Collection of Manuscripts - Sarah Ord's Concern - Railway Excursions - New York Tribune - Jane to Fleetwood and the Town - An Escaped Slave - James Abbatt - Hereditary Rat Poisoning - Dr. Annie Jackson - Education of Abbatts - Sleep in Meeting - Jno. to Liverpool - More and More Wyresdale Relations - Visit by Jno. and James - Illness and death of John Fletcher - Anti-Slavery Bazaar - William Jackson and TB - Jno.'s Landlord Problems - Jno.n's Furnishing begins - Aunt Mary Harding's Overshoes - A Working Cobbler - Eliz. A's Earnestness - The Olive Leaf Movement - Book Meetings - John Bright - Jonathan stocktakes at Christmas and Mary goes to Jackson Parties.

For Jonathan and Mary eighteen fifty four is a year of calm during which 'nothing very much happens', when compared with the year before and the year after. It is full of everyday interest; whereas '53 was full of major change and 'formal happenings' (deaths, engagements, business purchases) and '55 will have house acquisition and preparation, wedding notices and finally the wedding.

While Jonathan is consolidating his business position, resettling his Mother and sisters in Preston from Bolton; Mary is, less obviously, mentally expanding, while preparing herself for the change from country to town and for her change in status to a married woman. It is interesting to see how a relatively slow engagement process has, by June 1855, ripened into an inevitable marriage. During the process we learn something, because she shares them, of Mary's doubts and uncertainties.

After a meeting at Calder Bridge immediately before Christmas Mary pays a visit to Preston where the couple met at Thomas Ord's. They also played some kind of practical joke on Jno.n's friend, Harrison, which misfired and on 9th January 1854 he tells M.:

>   I may just inform thee that our joke on Harrison

worked wonderfully, but his brother Richard who was shown the letter and gave Harrison such sage advice believing the silly letter to be genuine,is sadly vexed and talks of making an apology (which if we refuse) (which we do) of taking it to the overseers, so thou sees it assumes a rather serious character but I can inform thee more ere long, for the present we wish nothing said of the matter. --- Wm. Jackson and S. Jesper are waiting for me so perhaps thou will excuse my hasty conclusion and believe me to --

Friends 'Elders' were spiritual overseers of the Meeting, and because there were no ministers they were never (or should never) be 'nominal people'.

There is now a gap before Jonathan's next letter on 13th February 1854 due to Mary Nichol's illness and a meeting in Preston where Mary had stayed with her cousin. The casual mention, which is not repeated, of smallpox sixty years after the 'discovery' of vaccination by Edward Jenner is a good example of the slow spread of invaluable preventive measures. It is also a Victorian view of one of the world's deadlier diseases.

    To: Mary Dilworth
           Calder Bridge   Nr. Garstang

Preston
13 of 2nd mo. 1854 [Monday]

My dear Mary,

I have no doubt thou has thought me somewhat negligent since last I saw thee, but thou must not say forgetfull! for thou art the subject of my thoughts many times daily. On 7th day I was too much occupied with business to write and yesterday I was in Bolton where all were glad to hear of thy recovery and send their love to thee.

I can scarcely describe to thee how delighted I feel in thus resuming our interrupted correspondence, for though thou has has been here so long and I have seen thee occasionally, yet it has been with a feeling of restriction that I have gone into a strange house, and not to compare with the true and pure feelings we can express _even_ in writing "what then when I see thee at home"!! but I must not lay too much stress on the pleasures of thy now happy home, or perhaps thou will be adhering to it so fondly (when <u>the time comes</u>) that I shall find difficulty in persuading thee to come and make me a sharer of the joys I so long to taste, whilst at the same time, instead of diminishing, it is my fervent wish, and <u>shall</u> be my greatest desire to <u>increase</u> if possible what thou now enjoys.

I look forward to my next visit with great pleasure and now my imagination is dazzled with the prospect before me, replete with enjoyment, gloomy winter is taking leave of us, the days are nicely brightening, spring is coming with its delightful accompaniments, we shall once more enjoy our outdoor rambles mid sunshine and green fields with birds carroling forth their sweet song of freedom, when I contemplate these things provided for our enjoyment by an all wise creator, and picture to myself the loveliest of women by my side who can appreciate these bounties. I am drawn insensibly to feel deeply thankful and can feebly, praise God from whom all blessings flow.

Thou will be thinking me somewhat sentimental but somehow I seem led from one thought to another so unpremeditated.

I have not yet enquired thy health and how thou got home etc. but hope thou will give me all particulars, I was not aware till near week end that thou was gone from home for I was down at the Station on 3rd day at 1 o'clock yet I did not see thee. I shall be very glad to hear from thee sometime this week, it will be quite a novelty to have one from thee again.

How does Mary Nicholl with the small pox I hope she is well again and shall be glad to hear of thy Father being well again.

Being now almost closing time and having to write to my brother James I will for the present conclude and remain as ever
    Thine
     Sincerely Attached
      Jon.n Abbatt

Mary's failure to even mention smallpox, in the 'sickness report' of her 13th February, letter serves to emphasise the non-remarkable nature of the disease. These two letters crossed in the post and in his next skittish and affectionate letter of 19th February Jonathan says:

How singular (may I say) truly sympathetic we seem to have been writing perhaps at the same time, and

both entertaining fresh bright views of gladsome
spring with its sunshine and flowers, and where are
they now! gloomy winter once more --- .

In her reply of 23rd Mary tells of:

R. Jacksons have got into their new house, Mary
[Nichol] and I went to get tea with them on first
day last, it is indeed a grand spot. I wish they may
have their health to enjoy it. I suppose James
Jackson [of Oakenclough] is to be married [to
Elizabeth Labrey] the last week in next month.

I am expecting thy worthy cousin [H. Fletcher]
coming to go with me to our friend Thomas Marsdens
this afternoon so thou must excuse my writing more,
and another reason I have, namely my Father and the
above guest are so busy talking (and have been)
about their cows and so on that I might put
something down that would not be of much interest to
thee --- .

James and Elizabeth (Labrey) Jackson of Oakenclough lived
at Oakenclough until their respective deaths. James was
only 13 when his father, John, died in 1845 leaving a
somewhat complicated trust to be administered by his
brother Jonathan (of Vale House and later Brooklands) and
nephew Richard J. (the latter married James' sister
Elizabeth - his own first cousin). James ultimately
succeeded to the Oakenclough paper Mill and farms,
failing his elder brother Richard (celibate and lived at
Woodlands). Elizabeth died in 1875 aged forty one and
James after problems with his eldest son - John James -
left an even more complicated trust arrangement than his
father and was eventually succeeded at the Mill by his
third son Harold.

One of James and Elizabeth's grandaughters, - Millicent,
the editor's Mother and daughter of Frederic and
Florence (Dilworth) J. of Woodlands (see map), married
her (Dilworth) second cousin Geoffrey, son of Frank and
Sarah Maria (Peile) A. of Bruna Croft, Calder Bridge (son
of Jonathan and Mary A. If it is remembered too, that
John Jackson Dilworth's mother was Mary Jackson (still at
Calder Bridge at the time of the letters) it gives some
idea of who is, was, and became what and who! The above
complexities are by no means unusual (though first cousin
marriages are not common) in many Quaker families.

In his next letter Jno.n tells Mary:

Since friend Harrison has concluded to associate no

more with young Quakers I think I can hardly spend
my first day [Sunday] evenings more pleasantly than
in addressing myself to thee, for being in the
weekdays in the company of Sam Jesper, Wm. Jackson
etc. I find it quite an agreeable change, though
this evening I ought to go to a teachers meeting but
choose to write to thee first. --- I have some
little matters to communicate when next we meet,
interesting to us both --- what if I tell thee I am
thinking of deferring our marriage a little longer
perhaps instead of 10th month [October] the 5th or
6th month of 1855 though all this will cause me a
severe trial --- .

To this Mary responds on Thursday 2nd March:

Well now about this important deferring of our
marriage. Thou thinks I may find thee somewhat
changeable, must I tell thee I have never thought we
could or should be married in the 10th month
therefore the change is quite agreeable to me and
did not come in the least unexpected.

I only hope that if we are ever permitted to bring
this courtship to so important and I may add happy
(as I hope it may be for both of us) conclusion, we
may not do so until the right time; if we have that
affection for each other we ought to have, can we
not manage to wait.

Mary and Mary Nichol are very soon leaving to stay with
Mary's brother David D. at Newcastle-under-Lyme, but
before this there was another of Jonathan's visits to
Calder on Tuesday 7th March when he was again observed by
Joseph Jackson. He writes on the eve of her departure:

    To: Mary Dilworth
          Calder Bridge   Nr. Garstang

Preston
3mo. 12th 1854 [Sunday]

My dear Polly,

I once more sit down to my first evenings task,
hoping thou will excuse if this be rather shorter
than sometimes for I am not in my best humour for
writing.

Thy wee' little note came to hand just in time to
prevent my having a further journey but thou may

expect me at the Station on 4th day morning, all well.

I am expecting to be in Bolton tomorrow evening having so[me] business there as well as Manchester, but shall be back I hope on 3rd day.

I suppose thy cousin David will be with you today what a pity! for we have had a long supplication from S.O. [Sarah Ord] today as usual at 12 o'clock pleading for the overtime and masters dispute, also the disturbance with Russia etc., but perhaps thou will be calling me to order if I go on thus, but some parts seem so much cooked beforehand that I am a little tempted to roll it over again, though I must confess that time spent in looking to my own failings would perhaps be more profitable for at times feel how utterly neglectful I am on this all important point, resolves for future amendments are easily made, but had I only a register of these resolves made in my serious reflecting moments, here to look at, I verily believe I should have great cause to be ashamed; temptations are so many and I do'nt sufficiently look for help from the right source on these grounds as I make my way.

Thou must excuse these effusions of sentiment and feeling from me, for it seems somewhat a relief in giving expression to them especially when I know tis to one in whom I can confide.

I dont know that I have anything fresh to convey of interest and having filled my sheet will conclude and remain   Thine Affectionately
         Jon.n Abbatt

P.S. I omitted to say I was just nicely in time for the train the other night, I passed Joseph Jackson and another young man on the way but they had to run a little to get in time. Joseph opened the carriage for his friend where I was sitting but dont know whether he observed me or not.

Sarah Ord (a Wilcockson/Satterthwaite relation), of whom we shall hear more later, was a weighty Friend and a frequent speaker in Meeting. Jno.n clearly felt that her offering was not as 'the Spirit moved her', but, 'in parts much cooked over'! He may have been influenced by Sarah's timing - at twelve o'clock i.e. the end of Meeting; but her concern about: ' --- disturbance with Russia etc.' was the weighty matter of The Crimean War.

Mary's reply from her brother's home in Newcastle tells of making wax flowers for indoor decoration. (This was a popular Victorian activity and the editor has a wax bust of a 'Quaker Lady' made by Mary's daughter Caroline.) In his next letter on 19th March Jonathan asks for: ' --- a nice bouquet to adorn my own mantle --- .' He also includes greetings to the 'two Marys' from his mother Elizabeth and speaks of her staying with him 'until 5th day when she purposes returning --- (but) having a pressing invitation from the Ords will --- etc.'

DAVID DILWORTH 1824-1902

David was the second son of John Jackson and Ann Dilworth and like his sister, Mary, had been born at Ortner in Wyresdale. He went to Ackworth at the age of 13 with Thomas and Abraham Kelsall. The latter, a brother of Mary's friend Ellen, came from the old time Dilworth home - Chapel House, Wyresdale. In addition to Abbatts his Ackworth contemporaries included Mary Nichol (later Pickard), Esther Pickard (later Shaw), Ann Eliza and Mary Ann Ord. Jonathan did not clearly remember David from school - though they later became lifelong friends. In his will, signed at Hillside 150 yards from Calder Bridge and dated 2nd January 1901, the executors were: my friend Jonathan Abbatt of Fulwood in the said county Gentleman', and his son and son-in-law - John Jackson Dilworth, Surveyor and Frederic Jackson, Tea Merchant.

When David left school he was apprenticed for seven years to his Uncle Isaac Wilcockson. Isaac, printer, publisher and owner of the Preston Chronicle, was largely instrumental in helping David to acquire his own business in Newcastle-under-Lyme, Staffordshire.

David's business, bought in 1848, was an old establised printing and publishing firm previously owned by D. Mort. Like his Uncle, he also published a newspaper - the 'Staffordshire Advertiser' - until shortly before handing the business over to his son Frederic in 1884. (One of the great sorrows of his life was the sudden death of that son in 1889.) The initial site of David's business - Number 44 High Street, Newcastle - was used by one Peter Gillworth who was printing books and publishing broadsheets there as early as 1670. (The direct business of printing and publishing on the site was very briefly interrupted in 1712.) The business prospered in David's time and the high quality of his books and their leather binding was noteworthy. A collection of 'great grandfather' David's books, now in the editors's care are of very high quality and are a joy to behold.

David, like Mary, was small of stature, and described, by Jonathan among others, as a 'merry little fellow'. He was apparently virtually always cheerful but was basically of serious intent. He had an ingenious, inventive mind and some of his money came from inventions which made a profit. One such idea which yielded no profit (due to patent fraud) was the invention of triangular blotter pad corners - to hold blotting paper flat and uncreased. David accepted this particular setback with equanimity and merely told Jno.n, apparently with a smile, that he would otherwise have retired twenty years earlier!

Like his elder brother William, David 'married out' of the Society of Friends, and his bride, Emma Goodall, of Staffordshire was a member of the Church of England. On their marriage in April 1855 her diary entry reads: "Our Wedding day May God's Blessings rest on us". David assumed at this time and acted on the assumption, that he would be automatically disowned by Friends. A little later we hear of Mary's first meeting with Emma, and there was immediate approval and liking, this ripened to affection and was reflected in the fondness of the two resulting sets of cousins. One example of this continuing affection was that one of the main reasons for Frank Abbatt's (Jno.n's second son) retirement to Bruna Croft (two hundred yards from Calder Bridge) was to be close to his cousins Frederic and Florence (Dilworth) Jackson at Woodlands. Because Bruna Croft and Woodlands are one third of a mile apart this further cemented the ties; it was probably the reason for their children's marriage (Fred J's rolltop desk is now being used by the editor.)

David and Emma's seven children were all brought up in their Mothers' faith (most of them were both christened and baptised on separate occasions - ? to make certain). Two of these children, Lillian Emma and Florence married actors in our story: Albert Simpson the widowed husband of Sarah Ann Jackson (and her brother James' trustee) and Frederic Jackson, James's son.

David and Emma had a comfortable life in Staffordshire with a town house in Newcastle and a country one at Whitmore near Emma's old home. In 1884, when David retired in favour of his son, he and his family went to live at Low Abbey, Ellel in Wyresdale. William (D.'s elder brother) retired at about the same time to John Jackson's old home at Ortner and the two couples spent some happy years in close touch with one another. There could have been no clearer way for William and for David to have shown love for country and origins than by this return to Wyresdale. Widowed in 1894, David went to 'Hillside', Bowgrave, on the 'doorstep' of Calder Bridge.

The next two letters tell us of Jonathan's increased attractiveness to Mary when she is from home, and of her brother's more 'relaxed' less Quakerly household:

> To: Jonathan Abbatt
> Friargate
> Preston   Lancashire

Newcastle
3 mo 23/1854 [Thursday]

My dear Jonathan

I was pleased to hear again from thee perhaps thy letters are more acceptable from home than at home, at any time however it is pleasant to be again and again assured of thy sincere affection.

Since I last wrote we have been out several times in a friendly way to tea and suppers. We do not I am sorry to say keep such good hours as the friends, I am now talking of and would think proper for young ladies such as me; but we do as the saying is "When you are at Rome do as the Romans".

Mary and I were at Stoke Meeting on first day afternoon - the morning was so very wet so we staid in the house, there were but few friends there. We have some thoughts of going this morning. The weather could not be more favourable for our visits, every day we have had a walk somewhere. When next we meet it will afford me pleasure I am sure to tell thee of our goings on but do not flatter thyself with the thoughts of seeing any of my productions in the waxflowers line. No what I make here are for my brother. Well done thee nothing like asking for a thing before you need it, however I think I may venture thee a promise that if I live to share thy fireside with thee as thou so often talks about, and if I do not forget how to make them thou shall have some waxflowers to adorn thy mantlepiece, now then is that a nice promise?

Thy Mother will be leaving thee today I suppose, if still with [thee] send her my kind love.

In return for <u>all</u> <u>this</u> I shall look for a long letter [in return.] I have made a mistake so I think it time to conclude remaining as ever thine
affectionately
Mary Dilworth

To: Mary Dilworth
        David Dilworth
        Newcastle   Staffordshire

Preston
3 mo. 26th 1854 [Sunday]

My dear Polly

Thy very acceptable and interesting letter came to hand on 6th day, and was glad to hear you are having so nice a time for your visit, the weather has certainly been most delightful and with your frequent walks and out door exercise I hope to see thee next time with a little more colour, for thou may remember I told thee thou was looking rather paler than usual, and now you have got more than one week over I may hope to see thee again ere long.

Well Polly after all, thou art a queer lady, for in answer to my begging for wax flowers for our own mantle piece I thought it rather characteristic when thou exclaims 'well done thou art asking in time' just as though thou delighted to teaze me a bit by letting me know how long I have to wait, at the same time thou must accept my thanks for thy kind promise but remember that in 15 months from now I quite expect thy name will undergo a change when I call thee my dear little wife.

I have just had an offer from Sarah Ord of a bed, bedsteads and bed hangings etc. that belonged to Cousin Sarah for 9 pounds but on looking at the bedsteads I felt almost inclined to think myself insulted that they should offer one such an old fashioned lot and purporting to be a bargain too, however I declined them, and hope when I do furnish to get something more suitable to the taste of us both. Thou may be thinking me in a hurry to be looking after furniture now, but the Ords wanted the goods out of the way and I thought if it was a bargain I might get them to my lodgings and keep them until the long looked for day arrives when we twain shall be one, I am very and frequently asked how soon I am going to furnish and a many such questions.

Having a little spare time this evening I have just been looking over a number of thy letters and am most certainly pleased to have such an interesting correspondence, on a second perusal they recall so many pleasant incidents that I find it quite a treat to turn them over again and am sometimes led to think when there is one so congenial to my mind "why wait so long" but I must subdue all such expressions or thou will think dear me what an impatient fellow, if I find him so when I am <u>Mrs. Abbatt</u> I shall have a weary time, but I'll give him a lesson or two to teach him different, is it not so?

Well now having said thus much I will once more say Farewell and remain as ever
                              Thine Affectionately
                                  Jon.n Abbatt

Sarah Ords's offer of bed and bedding makes good reading, evincing the following comment from Mary on 30th March:

So thou would have nothing to do with S. Ord's <u>bargain</u> well I must tell thee we [M., David D. and Mary Nichol] had a good laugh for I suppose she has long wanted to speak to thee on the subject, I hope her mind is now at rest.

James Jackson will I suppose be married [to Elizabeth Labrey] today, if a wet morning has anything to do with future happiness of such, there is but a poor look out for them, we will hope that theirs is a love no rain can damp. --- (James was <u>not</u> Mary's favourite Jackson). --- So thou thinks it almost time we said something about turning our steps home, but as all is going on so well at home and we are not tired of being here we have leave granted to stay another week, I hope to have my brother's company back, so that thou will have a chance of seeing this strange relation of mine.

Jonathan now writes on a Sunday and Mary on a Thursday:

    To: Mary Dilworth
           David Dilworth
           Newcastle   Staffordshire

Preston
4 Mo. 3rd 1854 [Monday]

My Dear Polly

I can fancy thee wondering what is the matter (since I received thy letter in good time) that I did not write yesterday but when I inform thee I think thou will not withhold thy excuses.

Well then the day was so very fine and I had such a pressing invitation to accompany S. Jesper and T. Lester in a ramble that I consented and at about 10 minutes after 10 after an exceedingly pleasant walk we found ourselves seated at Calder Bridge Meeting after which we were so separated that we lost T. Lester who rode with the Jacksons to Calder Bank [Oakenclough] expecting we were going to follow in which they were mistaken. So after vainly looking for us he concluded to stay the night.

I took dinner at thy home and found all, I fancy I may say almost well, I was pleased to see thy Father looking so much better, in the afternoon we took tea with R. Jackson at the new house which is a beautiful place, and at about 7 o'clock returned home on foot arriving there too late to answer thy interesting letter though my thoughts were often with thee.

The Jacksons are quite alive to the brides visiting this next week which I suppose you will be back in time to attend, it will be quite an era in Calder Bridge History. I am glad to hear thy brother purposes returning with thee I have almost a fancy I remember him for we were schoolfellows at Ackworth but am not quite sure.

Well now having written such a lengthy letter as this in business time I think I must beg to be excused more at present and perhaps at our next meeting I may talk the more to make amends. Still I dont wish by any means thou should follow this example but let me have a good long letter in reply, it is so pleasant to stroll in thought on thy interesting chat and whilst I have it on paper I can, and do, look and read again and again with satisfaction and am only afraid my scribble is only a fair return for thine so acceptable, nevertheless thou must make all due allowance and admit I do make an attempt.

I feel very grateful for thy cousins kind notice and desire my kind regards to her, I thought Calder looked rather lost without you.

Hoping this may be accepted as pretty as if thou had received it this morning I will once more My dear Polly say Farewell and remain as ever

      Thine Affectionately
       Jon.n Abbatt

Mary's last letter from Newcastle is dated 8th April:

> So thou was at C.B. on first day [Sunday], it appears that thou can come when a certain person is not there, you had a fine day. We, that is David [Dilworth] Mary [Nichol] and two of our friends had a long and delightful ride round by Trentham that afternoon --- --- we hope to arrive in Preston at 20 min after 3 the second day [Monday] --- am I to expect to see thee at the Station? ---- I am sorry to say that my brother cannot return with us, he would like to be in Preston when Isaac [Wilcockson] is home so must leave him to come after.'

On Good Friday 14th April Jonathan writes:

> I am now labouring under a disappointment (by the trains travelling today as on first day) in not being able to visit thee and enjoy thy company --- but I purpose --- . I am this afternoon engaged to go to Longridge with T. Salthouse and Sam Jesper etc. and am expecting a fine airing on the fells.

Visits such as the one just mentioned have connotations of returning to origins, and Jonathan's great grandmother was a 'Longridge girl'. Jno.n and his friends are, to some extent at least, Victorian 'fresh air fiends'. His next letter follows a Calder meeting:

> To: Mary Dilworth
> Calder Bridge Nr. Garstang

Preston
4 mo. 23rd 1854 [Sunday]

My dear Polly

Having as usual some spare time this evening it affords me much pleasure to address thee especially as it secures me some much prized and interesting message in return.

I went to Blackburn as I gave thee to expect to hear the American Total abstinence Advocate J. B. Gough and was really well rewarded for the journey.

For the first third of his address I was disappointed and thought him rather common place, but as he warmed in the subject he made ample recompense and thrilled me with feelings indescribable, his comparisons and anecdotes were calculated to send his hearers home with love for the man and an inclination to be stronger teetotalers than ever.

I was favoured yesterday with J. Jacksons new wife becoming a customer of mine acccompanied with her sister etc. Mary Jackson, she was looking very bright and happy as I expect most newly made wifes do (and perhaps thou may say husbands too) well I admit they either do or <u>should</u> do for I already feel such will be my experience <u>ere</u> <u>long</u> but I can fancy thee saying really what a queer fellow thou art, thou lets no opportunity to pass when thou can refer to this <u>momentous</u> <u>crisis</u>, I do wish thou wouldst not pester me so, but thou must really bear with me a little longer, for so long as thou art so far from me, I firmly believe I shall continue <u>perhaps</u> what thou calls a pest though I must use all the patience I can.

I was much pleased with thee when we were sitting in our <u>mountain</u> <u>retreat</u> when I told the the remark that some make about courtship being the happiest time of life when thou replied "it was a pity if it were so", yet to me such is the case <u>so</u> <u>far</u>, what wonder then when the foretaste is so sweet that I should be so impatient for our union, well <u>now</u> will thou call me a queer fellow, and can thou excuse my impatience, when I say I can fully coincide with thee in believing the foregoing remark to be erroneous where true love exists.

After my visits to thee I often interest myself with musing on our conversation during our delightful rambles and am invariably led to long for the time when we can not only have them more frequently but enjoy each others society more constantly.

This week I am expecting to be very busy preparing for my Mother and next week hope to see them something near settled.

I think I must now bring my scribble to a close and whilst waiting for thine in return I will remain
                Thine Evermore
                    Affectionate   Jon.n Abbatt

Jonathan's interest in teetotalism was real and though he never drank spirits he was never rabid. He drank beer for breakfast as a schoolboy at Ackworth, and later supplied lunchtime beer to at least one of his grandchildren - Philip Dilworth A. - with the saying: 'A little beer to

make him feel queer'. However he never drank spirits.
Mary clearly says she is not a teetotaler though it is
not certain that she ever drank even a glass of wine.

>   To: Jonathan Abbatt
>   Friargate   Preston
>
> Calder Bridge
> 4 mo. 27/54 [Thursday]

My dear Jonathan

Accept my warmest thanks for thy kind and welcome
letter.

I have been to the train to see my brother off, he
has as usual had but a short stay with us, short but
I may from my heart say how truly sweet has his
visit been to me. He said he should call upon thee:
I often wish he was nearer his family and friends,
but we cannot have everything we would like can we:
and indeed it would not be well for us: for what
unreasonable wishes we should sometimes have, and
were they to be granted perhaps we might forget to
prize the numerous blessings it is ours to enjoy.
But thou will be saying I am growing quite a
sentimental young lady, that and 'queer lady' will
not sound very well together so I will drop the
first; and if thou will still persist in calling me
a 'queer lady' well I cannot help it I suppose thou
must have thy way in that as in every other thing.

I am glad thou was so much pleased with J.B. Gough
the other day evening - tho' not a pledged
teetotaler myself I like thee all the better for
being one.

So thou thought J. Jackson's bride looked bright and
happy the day she was in thy shop. I have no doubt
she is what she appears to be and her husband too.
Yes and all husbands ought to be, I am quite sure on
that head, or why do you trouble yourselves about us
I wonder? - are we not made to make you happy? I
believe thee to be a woman's friend or perhaps I
might not think so well of thee as I do, am I right
on that score? The last time thou was here thou
asked me what I thought of myself: and having
confided so much matter into thy keeping thou may
well ask that question after receiving such a letter
as this I think. But may I not ask in return has
thou not confided as much and perhaps more into my
particular charge?

OAKENCLOUGH (CALDER BANK)
Built by John Jackson (1789-1845) of Spout House, Wyresdale and in MARY's day the home of James and Elizabeth Jackson.

JAMES JACKSON
1832-1890 of OAKENCLOUGH
(CALDER BANK)
Son of John of Spout House, younger brother of Sarah Ann and not MARY's favourite relation.

DAVID 1824–1902 and EMMA (GOODALL) 1830–1894 DILWORTH
Likenesses taken about the time of their wedding in 1855.

QUAKER DRESS
A Collage Picture probably made by Caroline Abbatt.

The little rain we had this morning has made quite a delightful change in the appearance of everything around. Well but I must conclude or perhaps thou will get tired of reading my scribble, and then what shall I say, so hoping to hear from thee some time before long.
      I will remain Thine Affectionately
              Mary Dilworth

The Mary Jackson who accompanied the newly married Elizabeth (Labrey) Jackson of Oakenclough to buy shoes from Jno.n on Saturday 22nd April 1854 was James J.'s eldest sister who, in 1857, married Joseph Harlock.

Jonathan's last and next letters clearly shows his happiness as do those from Mary:

To: Mary Dilworth
   Calder Bridge Nr. Garstang

Preston
4 mo. 29th 1854 [Sunday]

My dear Polly

Thy truly endearing missive came to hand yesterday, which allow me to say, seems to be a breath of such pure love that thou has not hitherto so ardently expressed to me, yet my dear Polly thou art not by any means to run away with the idea that I mean to insinuate thou has been too apathetic no, for I have every cause to think differently, thou has most certainly not been too forward in entrusting thy love and feelings towards me, to any charge, yet at the same time had I not been able to read thee aright, I might have fancied thee rather too backward, but I know thou does not give expression to thy feelings till truly satisfied of them, and such being the case I tender thee my sincere thanks for the little effusion of what I am convinced is true love which is dear to me and must tell thee I have greatly admired thy prudence and caution in entrusting to me thy womans love and confidence, whilst encouraging my address, and am rejoiced to know and feel that thou unbosoms thy sentiments to me with less reserve and sincerely hope to prove to thee that I am a womans friend in reality.

I was much pleased for the visit that thy brother paid me though was out first time he called, I dont wonder at thy being so fond of him for certainly he looks an affectionate merry little fellow though not exactly what I fancied him to be. I expected him somewhat taller and more slim altogether, I see considerable resemblance in some respects to William.

On 4th day Sam Jesper, Wm. Jackson and myself had a most delightful ramble together as far as Red Scar about four miles out of town, I got permission from Squire Cross who is resident there to ramble through his grounds, where we collected some specimens of ferns etc. for glass shades as I am about to get myself, and got a good tea after some difficulty at a nicely clean farm house and after much enjoyment got home about 8 o'clock ready for bed.

Thou has no doubt before thou has read to this, wondered what could induce me to send thee this parcel today, but tomorrow is no day for carrying parcels, and being wishful thou should have some tangible token of my sincere wishes for thee to enjoy a many happy returns of the anniversary of thy birthday, I hope thou will do me the favour to accept it, not that I wish to secure thy love (which I believe I already have) by presents, as I would despise the woman who would look to barter love for trifles, for in my opinion where such is expected but little love exists, yet even in a family of brothers and sisters I often think it a trait of good feeling to see trifling presents bandied from one to another and even on the occasion of a present from a Mother, of whose love we are sure, it is on the occasion of a birth day a really nice memento to look at in after years, and believe thou will look at it in this light.

The house I have taken for my Mother I am glad to say is now almost ready and famously have I been complimented on my choice of papers etc. which I hope thou will have the chance of seeing ere long if, yes thou does well to say if I can fancy thee saying, well now really I dont see any need for ifs and buts, so when thou comes to Preston again to say a bit thou may at least peep in on the sly if thou objects to being seen.

This being Market Day I must cut my letter short with a hope again to resume it before long in personal conversation and in the meantime will remain
    Thine Sincerely Affectionate
      Jon.n Abbatt

The Brother referred to in paragraph two above is David Dilworth and the resemblance noted is to M. and D.'s elder brother, William. By 6th May Jonathan writes:

> I once more address thee, and from <u>home</u> too, Mother and sisters having arrived here on 5th day morning and with hard working have managed to get things almost straight.
>
> I hear from thy brother Wm. that he is about furnishing house now thy cousin is giving up housekeeping, and I also heard from Mrs. Sandlehurst who professes ---- that she heard on good authority that Miss Dilworth was coming to be her brothers housekeeper. I fancy Thos Ord is again either unsteady or from home for he was not at meeting today. (Note: Concern about Thomas Ord's health recurs - he was fond of drink, how much is unknown.)

On 8th May Mary replies:

> To say that I am obliged for thy beautiful remembrance seems small and commonplace; but I must beg of thee to accept my warm and heartfelt thanks for (as I believe them to be) thy kind and sincere wishes, and also for thy (as thou may may rest assure it will be well prized) present: which it is my pleasure to do thee the favour to accept.
>
> I was at Oaken Clough [Calder Bank] the day before yesterday to meet the bride and bridegroom again [James and Elizabeth J.]; the evening was spent in an agreeable manner, I got home soon after 10 --- .
>
> So thou thinks we might as well put away all <u>ifs</u> and <u>buts</u> now, not yet, dear J. we must wait a short time longer -- perhaps a long time ---- .

By this time the reader may have become used to Quaker phrases and language, - "Thee", "Thou", first day etc. The reasons for this usage stem from the early days of Quakerism when Friends were, in a way, challenging the world and its ways. By dressing in a simple and unostentatious manner with no frills or luxuries (this later became almost a uniform) and by using direct speech 'thee and thou' etc. they were attempting to remind the 'world' and the worldly that they (the world) were forsaking the reality of the Saviour. This has been well described as a form of spiritual truculence and in truth it was just that. The names for days of the week and the month were seen as, pagan words and usage - which they are - and the early Friends did not compromise.

With time the continued usage became anachronistic, and lost much of its 'point'. Despite this the habit died hard and many Friends continued to use the 'old' Quaker terminology and practice long after the point had been lost. The author's grandparents spoke in this manner until their deaths in the mid-twentieth century.

In 'routine' letter Mary writes on Thursday May 11th:

> We had a large meeting yesterday for our M.M. I just saw Sam Jesper [Jno.n's friend and hardly a stranger] ---- he was about the only stranger we had I think. My Mother went to Preston this morning to see about "William beginning housekeeping", and I can inform thee on the best authority that Miss Dilworth is not thinking of being his housekeeper: so Mrs. S. has got hold of the wrong story --- . ---- My Father has come in for his tea so to attend to his needs I must leave thee and remain as ever thine in true affection
>
> Mary Dilworth

The last paragraph of this letter implying that Mary is going to get John J. Dilworth's tea is one of the very few occasions when there is any indication of Mary doing any 'domestic tasks'. At this time her Mother, Ann, was 67 years of age - she was 33 when she married - and as we know she was still energetic. She was a notable cook and housekeeper, and judging from her fairly frequent absènces from home there must have had appreciable other domestic help in addition to Margaret Carrick. Until her marriage, Mary's domestic role was that of 'decorative daughter in training'; with 'stand in' duties only.

A Calder meeting took place and Jonathan wrote on 25th:

> We had thy Aunt Jane to tea this afternoon along with Alice Salthouse, was glad to hear little Johnny was improving.
>
> I found on getting home on first day my Mother considerably improved [she had had a cold] and is now enjoying her usual health, my brother Wm. too was over and had been disappointed at my being from home, --- however he did not return till morning so we had some time together.

Mary's Aunt Jane (Wilcockson) Nichol was her mother's sister and Mary N.'s mother; on 30th May Mary writes:

> William Jackson will feel rather discouraged, as the doctor has said he must not go to Preston again for

several months, I hope --- . [William J., one of Jno.n's original Preston friends had tuberculosis.] ---- My Cousin Bessie wrote to me last week, she desired me to give her kind regards to Jonathan, she and Frank [Dixon, B.'s husband] are going to London sometime next month she wants me to join them: but I find her cousin M.D. must stay at home. I suppose the book meeting will be at O Clough next week, will thou be there? Well now I must again bid thee --- .

We now have the next of many business progress reports:

    To: Mary Dilworth
           Calder Bridge   Nr. Garstang

Preston
6 mo. 4th 1854 [Sunday]

My dear Polly

Thou must not at this time expect a very long letter from me as my brother Wm. and sister Maria and child are here today, but thinking thou would be disappointed should I omit writing I thought it better to write even though but briefly, so thou must excuse and accept the will for the deed and a promise to make amends sometime else.

I am glad to say my business is increasing so nicely notwithstanding we have had so much depression here, I have done 50 pounds worth or more this past week and though I took 46 pounds corresponding week last year I consider this small increase good, considering circumstances, but perhaps as business matters may be a bore to thee I will desist.

I think it rather improbable my being at the book meeting on 4th day though Mary Jackson gave me a kind invitation for sister and myself but think my business will require me here.

Although I think I shall not be at Oakenclough I fancy there is more pleasure awaiting me the week following on 4th day perhaps, as I suppose your O Leaf meeting will be held on 3rd day perhaps thou will say when thou writes.

Hoping thou will make all due allowance for this shabby scrawl I will once more conclude and with dear love remain as ever -- Thy Affectionate
                                  Jon.n Abbatt

WILLIAM ABBATT 1825-1901

William was the eldest child of Benjamin and Elizabeth A. and went to Ackworth at the age of nine, remaining there for four years. He then had a spell at home working for his father in the cane factory. However he was, and remained, keenly interested in education and after teaching for a time he went to Flounders Institute which was opened in 1848. At this time Flounders was situated close to Ackworth and initially was a training college for male teachers, (it was later moved to Leeds). William then taught at Ackworth, Bootham, Rawdon (as Superintendant), and Sidcot. On the death of his father in 1854 he forsook teaching, returned to Bolton and took over the family cane business.

William married Maria Lucas (1827-1856), in 1853 while he was at Sidcot. After Maria's death, he married Ann Mulliner (1824-97) of Bolton. (Ann's father, Jonathan M. was a brother of Thomas for whom Jno. worked as a journeyman and from whom he bought the Preston business). By his first wife, Maria, William had two children one dying in infancy and four children by Ann.

Education and the Society of Friends were the real concerns - perhaps passions - of William's life. His educational interests were manifest early in life - as a teacher and after 1854, by his dedicated public service in the cause of public education. When the national Education Act of 1870 was passed William became one of the first members of the Bolton Education Board and on his retirement twenty years later was presented with an illuminated address and a purse of 100 guineas. In this work William was a genuine social pioneer. It is often forgotten that prior to the 1870 Act, even elementary education was not available to any except the somewhat privileged members of English society.

In the early seventies he also served with some prominence 'in the Liberal interest' on the Bolton Town Council. At this time he publicly condemned the magistrates when there was rioting and police violence at the time of the Dilke riots. In his interest and concern for public work, William was unlike virtually all Abbatts of his own and other generations. (This does not mean that they did not serve, but almost never in a public manner. One recent senior member of the family remarked 'doing it in public is not in my line'!) William was equally active in his own Meeting of the Society of Friends, and indeed Jonathan comments on one of his letters: 'that he is getting to be quite important --- '.

Dilworth Abbatt, William's nephew, remembered him as sincere, almost earnest, with a tender streak of great kindness. He was robust and breezy in manner, but unlike Jonathan, his anger could be hasty, explosive and public. He apparently enjoyed confrontation in his public work, particularly when he gained his point, -- he was described as a 'bonnie fechter'.

Dil told a delightful story of how, shortly after leaving Ackworth, William was sent to deliver a note some distance from Bolton. In sight of the house, he asked a man whom he thought was the potential recipient: "Please art thou John Smith?" to which the reply was: "Who taught thee to thou me , thou young dog?".

In a brief letter on 6th June, Mary makes the country person's comment on all "townees".

> --- short as it was, I dare say thou will be on the lookout for an answer --- I was at the Book meeting yesterday [at Oakenclough and Jno.n had decided not to go], I enjoyed the afternoon very much and we had a long ramble after tea - some of the Preston ladies will be feeling the effects of it today I fancy.
> ------.
> P.S. I forgot to ask thee, to bring me (that is if thou has no objections) a pair of summer boots, perhaps thou can manage to guess my fit -
> --- Faretheewell

On 18th June Jonathan reports:

> --- I have again had a good week, an increase of 7 pounds over the corresponding week last year, --- [but] --- this is a love letter yet when our interests and prospects are so intimately connected --- I think such information may not be displeasing.
>
> I was well pleased with my out to Lancaster [he had been to Monthly Meeting] --- the Pickards were quite disposed to joke some about thee at times, especially Sam who amused me with the interest he showed in looking for your return from T. Hadwin's Senr. that he might get a peep at Mary I suppose.

The Pickards were a large and complicated family whose Lancaster branch intermarried with the Satterthwaites, Walkers, Wilcocksons, Peiles, Dilworths and Jacksons. As a result Mary had a multitude of Pickard relations.

Jane Abbatt and her cousin Ann Fletcher from Leigh visited Calder, and in her next letter of 23rd Mary says:

I trust Jane and thy cousin got home safe and feel no worse for their country outing. It was an agreeable surprise to see thy Mother here the other day, though we had very little of her company.

We are expecting Mary J[ackson] of Oakenclough and M.N. [Mary Nichol] to tea this afternoon and yesterday I was at J. Marsdens so what with one thing and another think myself quite throng ---- [and later] ---- Mary J. tells me that she has rather better accounts of her brother [William with TB] since first day, the first few days he was at Lytham he was worse I believe. ['throng' in this sense means busy with people]

In Mary's next she acknowledges a letter now lost:

--- thou does not need to fear putting me out of temper with talking of business, no I think it kind and considerate of thee to tell me how thou art getting on; I believe we are neither of us so romantic as to think we can do without it even when the <u>time</u> <u>comes</u> thou <u>sometimes</u> talks about and I hope thou will ever find in me a true and sympathising friend. Our O.L[eaf] meeting will not interfere with thy next visit as ---. --- My cousin Mary Ann Ord is staying at Aunts [R. Jackson's widow] and they have sent for me to help them quilt, so thou sees what a useful lady I am. But I fancy thou wilt be saying "self praise is no recommendation" --- .

I am much obliged for thy kind offer to lend me "Fern Leaves from Fanny's Portfolio", I have not read all the pieces in it, so if thou can without inconveniencebring it with thee sometime I will - .

Jonathans reply written is amusing and full of news:

  To: Mary Dilworth
     Calder Bridge Nr. Garstang

Preston
7 mo 2nd 1854 [Sunday]

My dear Polly

It is again my pleasure to write once more in reply to thine which I received on sixth day, and though it is evident my thoughtlessness has caused my dear Polly some pain, I am glad to find my apology was so timely, and should any doubt of my trust in thee remain I shall only be too glad to kiss it away when next we meet, for had I only thought then as I have done since I should not have made the slip, I am so fully convinced of what I said in my last.

My Mother and sisters took tea with Isaac and Ann Fearon the other day when Ann Fearon mentioned thee as a <u>nice</u> young woman and thought Jonathan had made a good choice, so thou sees if thou does not use self recommendation as thou talks about, others will do it for thee much to my satisfaction and if thou will say I'm flattering thee I'll say not without occasion.

I was quite ashamed of myself the other day for I met with thy cousin M. A. Ord in the street and some way or other I felt quite bashful, a thing so unusual when I see or speak to her, for I fancy all along her disposition is so much like thine, and I dont often feel so shy with folks like you, perhaps it was with seeing her so unexpectedly, for I could scarcely find anything to say, though she will perhaps excuse me, for I fancy perhaps I might have felt rather shy at seeing thee at one time though I think that is over with me now.

Well now after all this delicate confession does thou really laugh at me or <u>pity</u> me, a "<u>poor bashful thing</u>" did thou think. I was so easily outfaced on thinking about it after perhaps it might be what Sarah Ord said that made me feel so unusual.

I saw neither M.A. or Thomas Ord at meeting today perhaps they are both with you.

My Mother has gone to Bolton to meet my little sister coming from Ackworth and is stopping with my brothers for about a week, it seems quite lonely without her and if she stays till next first day I think of going to bring them back.

I thought I was going to have a miserable quiet business week for up to 5th day night I did not take 3 pounds ten but on 6th and 7th day it brightened up and I took more than 20 pounds, I was not alone for trade throughout the town was very dull.

I have to write something like 3 other letters this afternoon so thou must excuse more at the present time.
        Thine truly Affectionate
                      Jon.n Abbatt

- Isaac and Ann Fearon, worthy Friends from Cumberland, built and rented Woodlands to the Jacksons. (Their daughter Deborah and Allan Peile of High Pow Cumberland were the editor's Peile g.g.grandparents).
- Mary Ann (Wilcockson) Ord - one of the 'Three Marys' - was Mary's 'first cousin german', being the daughter of John and Jane (Dilworth) Wilcockson the brother and sister of John Jackson and Ann D.
- The 'little sister' coming from Ackworth' is Elizabeth who became: one of "the two little aunts".

ELIZABETH ABBATT 1840-1886

Elizabeth was the youngest child of Benjamin and Elizabeth A. and like her sister was at Ackworth for only three years, all the older members of the family had four year spells. After leaving school she spent her time looking after her Mother, other household duties, initially in Preston at No 3 Bank Place and 35 Fishergate Hill. Later, and after Elizabeth Senior's death, she lived with Alice Ann at Mere Street in Bolton. She was interested in childrens' relief and Sunday School work. Elizabeth died of pneumonia aged 45 years; and was remembered as having a sense of humour, and leading a simple, quiet and useful life. Elizabeth's 1851 Ackworth sampler is beneath Mary's in the editor's sitting room.

ALICE ANN ABBATT (1838-1914)

Alice Ann was the elder of the "two little sisters" who were both below average height. Alice Ann's three years at Ackworth from 1849-1852 left her with a very warm place in her heart for the school and for many years she was years a well known figure at Easter Gatherings.

In partnership with Eleanor Jesper (later Fisher) Alice Ann took over her elder sister, Jane (Abbatt) Adair's baby linen business in 1859 and traded for many years at 109 Fishergate as "Abbatt and Jesper". (Eleanor Jesper was the sister, of Jonathan's friend, Sam Jesper - both mentioned frequently in the letters). After returning to Bolton with her sister, Elizabeth, in about 1871 she continued to run the business in Preston but became more and more concerned with her sister in social work. Her own special concern was for crippled children. After their Mother's death in 1873 the two sisters' 'holidays' became visits to friends and relations in Preston and to the Adairs at Maryport, Cumberland. At the very end of her life Alice Ann's mind failed and she died at the Retreat in York aged 76 years.

On 6th July Mary comments on the Mary Ann Ord encounter:

> Well I did get <u>quite</u> a laugh when I read thy last about seeing my cousin M. A. Ord she would not notice anything peculiar in thy manner I dare say though thou might fancy she did, she would have told me if she had. -----. ---- Thomas Ord should come for Mary Ann today, but perhaps the wet weather may stop him, we had him, Isaac [Wilcockson] and my brother [William D.] over on first day afternoon.

Jonathan replies on the ninth:

> I am much pleased and delighted with the prospect of once more enjoying thy company on 3rd day [Tuesday] and shall make it a good excuse for writing a short --- . My Mother returned on 6th day [Friday] bringing my little sister [Elizabeth] with her from Ackworth - famously delighted with her Preston home.

Jno. replies after visits to Calder and Bolton:

> To: Mary Dilworth
>   Calder Bridge, Nr. Garstang

Preston
7 mo. 17th 1854 [Monday]

My dear Polly,

I dare say thou would feel a little disappointment at not hearing from me this morning, and though desirous of doing so myself I was prevented by a journey to Bolton which I enjoyed very much in company with my brother Thomas, the day was delightfully fine until 9 o'clock in the evening.

My brother Thomas's wife talks of coming to spend some time with us next and most likely if fine and agreeable to thee I may trip over some afternoon with her, she is a little agreeable body and should like you introduced to each other, perhaps when thou writes thou will say if I may bring her.

I have thought since seeing thee, that I shall not fix any regular and stated time for coming but 'as I am sometimes caught out with a wet day' come when the day is fine, and as opportunity offers, it is so delightful to have such pleasant strolls together of which we are debarred when wet, and perhaps too may come a little oftener, I think it will be well to see more of each other and for my part will enjoy it much. I expect you would be quite throng yesterday, it was pleasant too for you to be so fine. Although my Mother was so little acquainted with thy Aunt she was full of sorrow to hear of her decease.

Thou will no doubt have been too much occupied to read much but shall be glad to hear how thou likes and if I can find out thy taste for reading perhaps I may supply thee occasionally with something pleasing. I have just been getting bound a whole series of Chambers Journal which are a really interesting collection to grace our bookcase with which with some other select additions will not be despised.

I have had another good week and am altogether looking forward to the future with something like a feeling of confidence though I dont by any means wish to get too sanguine about it.
Hoping thou will excuse my unintentional neglect I will once more subscribe myself
                    Thine truly attached
                            Jon.n Abbatt

Mary's Aunt Mary (Wilcockson) Jackson 1779-1854 was the second wife of Richard Jackson whose first wife had been Elizabeth Labrey 1788-1818. See Chapter III and Jackson Tree 'The Builders of Calder Bridge Meeting House'.

Mary replies on Tuesday 18th July happily agreeing to the proposed visit of Jane Thomas A. and mentioning the funeral of Mary (Wilcockson) Jackson attended by many.

Thomas Abbatt was the brother to whom Jonathan was most attached and the latter's son, Frank, (though he did not have asthma) was strikingly similar to Thomas both in looks and temperament.

THOMAS ABBATT 1827-97

Thomas and Jonathan were fast friends and remained so throughout their lives. As were his brothers and sisters, Thomas was born in Bolton and went to Ackworth at the age of 9 where he remained for four years. On leaving school he was apprenticed to Mr. Bradbury, a Bolton printer, and later as a journeyman he worked in Manchester for some time with 'Bradshaw and Blacklock' of railway guide fame. In 1851 he returned to Bolton in partnership with R. Kenyon as a Printer and Stationer and two years later set out on his own in Market Street, Bolton. By the eighteen seventies he had three shops and a printing works in Corporation Street which he ran until the business passed to his eldest son Benjamin.

In 1854 Thomas married Jane Haworth (1823-1910) of Liverpool. Jane was not initially a Friend, but became one by convincement, and was accepted into the Society in 1853. There was some initial confusion in the family with two Jane Abbatts (one of whom later became Jane Adair), this was resolved by Jane (Haworth) becoming Jane Thomas. (Her signature became Jane T. A.)

Because of their friendship Thomas and Jonathan visited each other frequently, to do this they often walked one way to or from Bolton, (or Preston). These jaunts were described by Jon.n as: "he would run over to Bolton to see Thomas", and by the latter who would: "pop over to have a chat and cigar with Jonathan." It is nineteen miles from Preston to Bolton.

Thomas was a moderately severe asthmatic; he was short, slight and always neat and dapper in appearance and dress. In manner he was quiet with a keen dry sense of humour. He was keenly interested in Friends' affairs, and an Elder of his own Meeting. Thomas was, like Jonathan, catholic in his interests being widely read and largely self educated. His friends included Paul Beswick, whose diary entries described his father Benjamins's funeral.

The next three letters, two on one day, tell of an invitation and arrangements for a day trip to Windermere:

    To: Mary Dilworth
           Calder Bridge   Nr. Garstang

Preston
7 mo 20/54 [Thursday]

My dear Polly

Does thou not feel surprised to hear from me so soon again and wonder what it can be for, and as I have been a long time detained with a traveller I shall explain myself briefly.

Sam Jesper his sister and cousin are intending to take the advantage of a trip to Windermere on 3rd day next, there and back for 3/- leaving here at 6 o'clock in the morning, they want my company, and as the weather promises a fine out I thought perhaps my dear Polly and her cousin M. N. could like to join us, which I can assure thee will be truly agreeable to all, and would constitute a strong party, if you should conclude to go and can find anyone wishing to join us we shall be glad of their company, and as the train I believe does not stop at Garstang you would have to come to Preston the 2nd day night previously.

If <u>others</u> decline I hope <u>thou</u> will come I should enjoy myself so much and have no intention of going without thee though I hope thy cousin will come too.

We had a few young friends to tea here on 3rd day when I played them a few turns and Emily Jesper was so pleased she wants me to take my music to the Lakes which I have no doubt will sound nicely on the water.
I have but little time till post time so will conclude and hope to hear from thee soon if you conclude to go, and if convenient I trust to having your company, in the meantime I remain as ever
      Thine affectionate
       Jon.n Abbatt

'Out of town' mail delivery on the day of mailing makes it possible for Mary to reply on the same day <u>after</u> she was able to find and invite Mary Nichol, make complex arrangements for her part of the trip and then reply to Jonathan. All of this was done without the aid of phones or any other devices and depended solely on walking and word of mouth. The arrangements included train times and dates (? a visit to the railway station) gig transportation to and a bed in Lancaster.

 To: Jonathan Abbatt
    Friargate Preston

 Calder Bridge
 7 mo. 20 1854 [Thursday]

 My dear Jonathan

I am much obliged for thy note received yesterday and shall be glad to avail myself of thy kind invitation, tho' I fancy I shall have to go alone from this part as I have not been able to prevail on Mary N. to accompany me. I do not quite like the idea of being the only one, but Mary did not seem willing to go therefore I did not press her much. I am quite in hopes of enjoying myself however, and as thou art one of the party perhaps I shall not feel so very lonely.

It is my cousin D.W.'s north journey on second day so I think I cannot do better than ride with him to Lancaster in the afternoon and as I had a kind invitation in a note from Sarah Pickard this morning saying if I had any thoughts of going to Windermere she would be glad for me to lodge there: so that I hope to be ready to reach you at the train on third day morning. I rather fancy the Pickards have some thoughts of going, I wonder if my cousin M. A. Ord would like to go if thou has no objections would thou ask her please.

Thou has said nothing about provisions etc. but I suppose we shall have a pic-nic dinner, but perhaps I shall hear from thee tomorrow. In hopes this may find thee well and after again thanking thee for thy thoughtful kindness I am thine as ever
                                    Mary Dilworth

Mary's use of the word pic-nic with a hyphen is interesting, and clearly Jonathan intends to pay for the food - though it is not clear whether they each pay their own fares or not. In this connection there is no clue in the letters as to how Mary's spending money was provided, though clearly she did have such discretionary money.

    To: Mary Dilworth,
        Calder Bridge   Nr. Garstang

Preston
7 23 /54 [Sunday]

My dear Polly

I was pleased to hear from thee this morning and am delighted thou has concluded to go. I gave thy message to thy cousin M. A. Ord who thou will be pleased to hear intends to accompany us.

I also saw thy cousin David and told him he might expect a freight with him to Lancaster tomorrow though I did not say how <u>precious</u> or to be carried <u>with</u> <u>care</u> but trust he will know sufficiently the value of his cargo to need no caution.

Not knowing exactly who may join us at Lancaster Sam

> Jesper will provide picnic dinner for his company only, and not being skilled in these matters myself, may I engage thee to make the needful provision for taking a picnic lunch on one of the islands as is intended or would thou prefer dining at an hotel, I dont mind much which, but I think the former much more pleasant in which case thou must charge all expenses to my a/c.
>
> Hoping the pleasure of being in thy company and spending a most delightful out together I will for the present conclude and remain as ever
> Thine Affectionate
> J. Abbatt

We do not know how well the expedition fared though it may not have been without problems - there are clues in Jonathan's 30th July letter.

> I was glad to get home on third day as indeed we all were. Thy cousin Mary Ann [Ord] was quite knocked up for want of tea - I felt quite sorry we managed so badly, I have not seen her since though she called in the shop one day I was out to tea.
>
> It was quite an adventure to return home in thy brothers rough coat for the servant came to let me in chattering as usual but stopped short at seeing me with my coat, and my stick over my shoulder and my carpet bag at the end of it - wondering what stranger it was in the dark, it was 10 o'clock when we got home and I think the coat prevented me getting a cold. Hoping thou art none the worse for thy out which I think was enjoyed by all.

From this we not only know that the party was late but that, in addition to Mary Ann, Jonathan himself liked his tea and left his shop to take tea! Throughout the letters there are frequent references to tea and tea drinking both at Calder Bridge and in Preston. We also learn that Elizabeth Abbatt and her daughters and son had at least one servant at their new home at No 3 Bank Place, Preston. Jno.n at times carried a carpet bag!

On Sunday 6th August Jonathan, tells Mary:

> I have again had a most excellent week in business and feel greatly encouraged in my prospects although I have increased opposition to contend with in the form of <u>another</u> shop almost opposite to me, but I feel it will act only as a spur to increased exertion and will most likely do me good.

--- an earnest talk with my landlord about altering the premises so as to make us a convenient house and have drawn him a plan of my notion of things which seems to please, but I can say more of this when I see thee when I hope we may have it fair, so as once more to enjoy a quietly happy stroll which I always do most thoroughly enjoy especially when rambling about thy own home where most things seem familiar and leaves us less excited than when in a strange place, and more inclined to dwell on each others love which is far more preferable to any scenery.

How he proposed to increases his exertions is not clear, but the opposition itself failed about six years later. The next letter tells us of a freed black slave and family who stayed with the Abbatts while speaking in non-conformist abolition meetings in Preston and other Northwest towns. The identity of this family is not known to the editor, but we do know that the anti-slavery movement was very dear to Elizabeth A., and Jonathan too seems to have been more than sympathetic.

    To: Mary Dilworth
        Calder Bridge   Nr. Garstang

Preston
8 mo 13 1854 [Sunday]

My dear Polly

I once more sit down to make a further contribution to thy valuable collection of manuscripts which when complete would contain matter of interest for a large circle if permitted to view it!!!

I hope in thy next to hear of thy foot being better, being a little anxious about it.

Since I saw thee I have frequently thought of thy poor old Grandmother and am sorry she has felt my apparent neglect of her, though I have frequently thought of seeing her when taking leave, and have only been restrained from a doubt of its being agreeable, however now I know and shall always remember her.

I suppose thou wil have heard what a scare there was at our Monthly Meeting on Sarah Ord making known her concern to visit friends in Scotland etc., how backward friends were in expressing their unity with her etc. but I can tell thee when we next meet again, poor woman, I was almost sorry for her.

The fugitive now with us is about giving some lectures this week the Mayor to be chairman on 4th day night, I am glad to say Michael Satterthwaite is going to be there too, I like much to see friends attend these abolition meetings, though when he was here before no one would look favourably on him, but he is now likely to have a many friends amongst the Methodists (of whom he is one) and a many others.

My sisters are returning or rather going to Bolton tonight for a short time and having to go with them to the railway I shall cut my letter short and make it an excuse for so doing though I fear I should not prolong it much if it was otherwise.

I feel in good spirits about business having had another <u>extra</u> good week <u>if</u> it would only continue as the last 3 months I should be doing really excellent I should make at least 250 pounds after paying expenses but I can scarcely expect that yet awhile so shall make myself content with something less.

Mary Ann Holmes I see is in town today, at meeting too, I thought her looking well.

How's Mary and Sam getting on yet, has he been again today. I find myself quite interested in them and often wonder what will be the denouement as Margery would term it in Weary-foot Comn.

I have just risen from tea and if thou had been there thou would have been famously amused with the tricks of this little coloured child staying with us, it is about 3 1/2 years old and I dont know a more intelligent little thing anywhere and even now whilst writing it is trying to know who to.

I find myself writing on at a good rate but as my sisters are getting ready I must bid thee Farewell and with love remain as ever
     Thine Affectionate
      Jonathan Abbatt

Sarah Ord was a worthy, though at times, to Jonathan, Mary and others, a somewhat trying Friend. Nevertheless she later did go on her mission to the North. In the twentieth century Sarah had at least two interesting descendants; one being the late Brigadier Rudolf Ord an enthusiastic soldier, and his brother the late Boris Ord,

Fellow and Director of Music at Kings College, Cambridge, a notable mediaeval and choral musician.

In her letter of 17th August Mary comments on Sarah and on Mary Nichol's affair with Sam Pickard - which made rapid progress and they married at Calder Bridge in 1855.

> I had not heard about Sarah Ord until thou named it in thy letter --- I hope her visit may be of service to friends in Scotland and also to herself, if she is going in the right spirit I have no doubt it will, not else, but I have room to question that, my own sinful heart tells me, no !!!
>
> Thou asks how Sam and Mary are getting on, I cannot tell thee what the denouement may be, but, I should fancy much the same as Robert's [Esther Pickard is now engaged to Robert Shaw] proved to be; if anyone should ask thee anything about it please do not tell them anything I have told thee --- .
>
> Joseph Jackson, Lucy and M.A. [Ord] were here today and yesterday they are gone to the Lakes today for about a fortnight. I suppose there will be another trip there on third day [Tuesday] I want Father and Mother to go; I think if the morning is fine and all goes well they may go.

Railway excursions began to be introduced as the railways were completed and by the eighteen sixties they had become extraordinarily popular in a whole variety of forms. To a major extent the growth, and popularity of excursions was a direct sequel to the Great Exhibition of 1851. The railway companies at this time had vied with each other to provide excursions and 'specials' to London from all over the country. Some, such as the football excursion, were attended by drunkenness, hooliganism and other manifestations similar to those of the present day. However, others such as day trips to Windermere and similar resorts presaged the beginnings of Victorian holidays. Holidays in the sense of absence from home for any period over a day, only began in the early middle century and then only for the more affluent, they were not known until about 1840-50. Later in the century holidays became a fashion to be copied by all except the very poor.

The Lakes were very popular with 'the families' but on 20th August Jonathan tells of the virtues of Fleetwood:

> My sisters [Jane and Elizabeth] returned from Bolton on 5th day night much pleased with their out but

quite ready for home again although away for so short a time and Jane has since not been very well, ---- I have been thinking of getting her lodgings for a week or two at Saml. Hopes at Fleetwood [Sam's wife, Margaret (Mason/Kelsall), Samuel Hope was yet another member of Mary's Wyresdale 'families'.] thinking the change and sea air may do her good, they went to Leigh to my Uncle John [Fletcher] and Cousin Ann [who visited Calder Bridge with Jane A. forwarded me the enclosed piece of poetry which is an answer to my asking what she thought of thee.

The poem entitled "Farmers Girls" is from a "New York Tribune" of 1854 and was enclosed with his letter above.

FARMERS GIRLS

Up in the early morning,
Just at the peep of day,
Straining the milk in the dairy,
Turning the cows away,
Sweeping the floor in the kitchen,
Making the beds upstairs,
Washing the breakfast dishes,
Dusting the parlour chairs,
Brushing the crumbs from the pantry,
Hunting for eggs at the barn,
Cleaning the turnips for dinner,
Spinning the stocking yarn,
Spreading the whitened linen,
Down on the bushes below,
Ransacking every meadow,
Where the field strawberries grow,
Starching the 'fixens' for Sunday,
Churning the snowy cream,
Rinsing the pails and strainer,
Down in the running stream,
Feeding the geese and the turkeys,
Making the pumpkin pies,
Jogging the little ones cradle,
Driving away the flies,
Grace in every motion,
Music in every bone,
Beauty of form and feature,
Thousands might covet to own,
Cheeks that rival spring roses,
Teeth the whitest of pearls,
One of these country maids,
Is worth a score of your city girls.

Jonathan ends with a typical postscript: 'Hurrah for another good week though a wet Market Day.

On 24th August Mary says:

> I am sorry to hear so poor an account of thy sister Jane and hope a change to Fleetwood will do her good --- I dont think she could have more suitable lodgings than with S. Hope they are both very kind people.
>
> Yesterday Sam Pickard drove Robert Shaw over here (he that my cousin Esther Shaw is about to bestow her hand upon), ----- ; Robert tells me they are to be married this week (if alls well). He is very much disappointed that so few of Esthers relations are to be there, I think it looks rather hard myself that we cannot go.
>
> --- I suppose I must submit and receive thee "with a welcome as ever", but it must not be on 3rd day [Tuesday] as my Father has invited some friends to spend the day with us. I must again trouble thee to bring me another pair of boots, this time they must be for winter, I think thou knows the size, I fancy I take them somewhat larger in winter; so if thou will be so kind I will be obliged.
>
> What a grand piece of poetry thy cousin has sent thee --- I thank thee for it.

The reason for the non attendance of the Dilworths and other relations at Esther's wedding was that she was 'marrying out' of the Society - in a church. By the eighteen fifties Friends had realised, that they were only one denomination among many, and hence, not the only true believers, which they had believed to be the case in the early days of the Society. This made it much harder to defend exclusiveness. However, the Society had also realised at this time that declining numbers were in part due to 'old fashions' - such as disownment for 'marrying out' - and the marriage regulations were changed in 1859 so that Friends could and did 'marry out' and thus brought in fresh blood and conserved good stock.

For old fashioned and conscientious Friends, perhaps a little before our period, the difficulties of mixed marriage were very great. A staunch Friend believed it to be wrong, for example, to be married by a paid priest, to attend communion, to use any luxuries, to address individual people as 'you' rather than thou. It could thus be difficult or impossible to find middle ground in a marriage without the conscience of one or both being compromised.

Fleetwood at the mouth of the River Wyre was the site of one of Jonathan's 'outs', (letter of 21st May), and later on 20th August as a 'spa' for his sister Jane 'to build her up and restore her to health'.

Fleetwood was a Victorian 'new town' in the sense that the first house was erected in 1836 on the site of a desolate rabbit warren. The town owed its origins to transportation and in 1840 the Preston and Wyre railway was opened for traffic with branch lines in 1846 to Blackpool and Lytham. By 1851 the population was 3,121 though growth slowed somewhat in the next twenty years. Tourism and trade were the twin attractions of Fleetwood and initially, as a watering place, it attracted more visitors than its slightly older rivals of Blackpool and Lytham. The town became temporarily fashionable when, as part of the Queen's first visit to the Royal Duchy of Lancaster, Queen Victoria and Prince Albert arrived in the town in the "Victoria and Albert" and left by train for Preston. In the town's early days shipping was very important but was not without its disasters, as when the barque "Hope", carrying a cargo of American lumber, foundered in a storm in the harbour.

On 27th August Jonathan writes to confirm that: 'quite delighted to hear from thee, but shall be more pleased to see thee though I have to wait till 4th day. -- will to think on about thy boots and think I know the size now.'

In this letter he mentions, among others, his sister Jane, now in better health, and Mary's brother, William, who does not approve of the 'Mary and Sam' courtship' as 'he thinks Mary too good for him'. William later married Alice Bibby of Condor Green who was not a Friend. After the visit arranged above he is full of chat:

>   To: Mary Dilworth
>   Calder Bridge   Nr. Garstang
>
>
>   Preston
>   9 mo 3 /54 [Sunday]
>
>   My dear Polly

I am glad once more to have what thou was pleased to call this troublesome job to get through again and can assure thee I feel great pleasure in it.

It seems S. Ord and Maria were going to attend Wm. Satterthwaites wedding when I saw them on 4th day and not as I thought on her ministerial mission.

Neither thy cousins David, Mary Ann nor T. Ord were at meeting today I hope Thomas is not drinking again, Mary Ann I suppose is still at thy cousin Bessy's.

The weather continues so nice and warm I hope thou has got nicely better of thy cold again. I have often thought of thee since I returned and should be glad if I could pass this pleasant evening with thee, perhaps thou feels rather lonely now that Sam gets so much of thy cousin Mary's company on first day nights but thou can console thyself with the prospect of a <u>coming change</u> by which I hope to be a gainer too. I am just about writing to my brother James this afternoon I think it likely he may take a situation with Wilson and Jespers before long who have discharged their foreman Thos. Mackbeth and will consequently be wanting another assistant soon, we are quite pleased at the prospect of having him so near us again and shall be enabled to have more family meetings.

Yesterday a woman obtained two pairs of boots from me under false pretences which I soon found out and have to attend the town hall tomorrow to give evidence against her - quite a drunken body. I was very busy and had hardly time to question her; quite a good week again, twice as much as same week last year, it is really quite encouraging.

We are expecting our coloured friends to leave us on third day and are quite glad at the prospect of again enjoying in usual course our own comfortable home without interruption, we have been so much upset with such a large addition to our small family. Has thou read the narrative and how does thou find it?

Though I am afraid my dear little Polly will find this a rather uninteresting letter yet I must bring it to a close and in the meantime whilst waiting for thy much prized return I will subscribe myself with true love   - Thine sincerely affectionately
                                Jon.n Abbatt

The narrative mentioned above was a description (now lost) of the vicissitudes of the escaped American slave who had been for the previous three and a half weeks at the Abbatts in Preston. Jonathan was liberal, open-minded and referred to the visitors as 'coloured', and it is interesting to notice how the 'respectable' way to describe other races has changed with time and place.

JAMES ABBATT 1831-1898

James was the fourth son in his family and Jonathan's youngest brother, he was not a healthy child, and as a baby his life 'was despaired of' when he had 'water on the brain'.

The following has been culled from James' short biography where he describes the next threat to his life: "One of the first incidents I can recall to memory, was going into the Willow Warehouse [Benjamin's cane factory] where my father was sorting 'rods' for his workmen. Seeing there some five or six piles of oatmeal of a conical shape I sat down contentedly close by one of them, polished it off till none was left and then went to tell my father. Without a moments delay he picked me up, tucked me under his arm, and ran with me to Dr. Shorrock's, a little shop in Hotel Street, half doctor, half chemist. He must have given me an emetic, and then I was taken home and presently sat at the tea table. All in the house, especially dear Mother, had anxious looks on their countenances whilst I swallowed a basinful of bread and milk, so far as I can recall, with considerable relish. Some while afterwards I was told that the oatmeal I had partaken of contained arsenic and had been placed there to destroy the rats."

Some things may well be hereditary as the editor had a similar small boy experience nearly a hundred years later. On this occasion, also after eating rat poison at Woodlands, and a hurried car journey to Oakenclough he was treated in the kitchen by Dr. Annie Jackson, daughter of James and Elizabeth (Labrey) J. On this occasion the treatment was with mustard emetic and followed by a 'meal' of uncooked flour and water dough. That meal was not appreciated. (Dr. Annie Jackson was a general practitioner and Honorary Anaesthetist to the Derby Royal Infirmary until her death in 1933. She had kept house for her brother Harold until his marriage in 1896, when at the age of 34 she decided to study medicine. This necessitated 'matriculation' in Latin, which she had never studied. After matriculation she went to Edinburgh to obtain her medical qualification. As remembered, by the editor, she was a gentle but extremely formidable little woman, with a strong and very dry sense of humour. There are many stories of Annie in 'practice' in Derby and her medical 'American Watch' is still working and on the author's desk. She did not seem - even at the time of the emetic - to be old!

James attended a number of 'dame' schools before going to Ackworth in July 1840 at the age of nine - he remained there for four years. On leaving school he spent a year helping his father and was then apprenticed to a Stockport tailor - John Philip Milner. His apprentice indentures include the following: 'The said James Abbatt shall and will at all times during his apprenticeship appear and act in dress and other respects as a consistent member of the Society of Friends'.

After Stockport, a year in Colchester, a spell in Preston (with 'Wilson and Jespers') and an illness, he worked in the cane factory with his brother, William. In 1858 he opened a tailoring business on his own account in Leigh, only to move to Preston in 1866. This move to Preston was not new in the family sense as his uncle James (Benjamin's brother), who also went to Ackworth, had a tailoring business in Preston before emigrating to the U.S.A. In 1874 James moved yet again to one of the shops built by Jonathan at 154 and 154a Friargate.

In 1860 James married Hannah Mary Lamb, a governess,of Penketh, Warrington (a Quaker school founded 1834). For thirty years they were an exceptionally happy couple.

Like his brother William, James was much more interested in teaching and religious matters than in anything to do with money. In 1880 he accepted a position in charge of 'The Pales School and Mission', near Pen-y-Bont in Radnorshire, 'within the compass of Hereford and Radnor Monthly Meeting'. Here he and Hannah spent the next five years in the heart of Radnor living in a thatched cottage beside the Meeting House. The meeting and Mission prospered and James describes this period as being a particularly 'joyous one'. In 1884 he was recorded as a Minister in the Society; this was an 'ancient' position, (it was not that of a priest), which was abolished by London Yearly Meeting in the nineteen twenties.

In 1888, he and Hannah Mary were transferred from St. Ives, by the Friends Home Mission Committee, to the Isle of Wight where Hannah Mary died of a stroke - James was desolated. By this time James' health was poor and he was bereft and worn out, until he met and married, Anna Mary Enock. They lived in her Sibford home until James' death in 1898. Anna Mary survived him for twenty-three years until 1918.

James' life was happy only in 'parts', until, after a peripatetic and unsatisfactory early life, he found what was to be his true niche with the move to Radnor in 1880. This was followed by eight particularly good years. He had no children by either of his marriages.

THOMAS and JANE (HAWORTH) ABBATT and FAMILY
Front: Beatrice and Gilbert.
Middle: Jane, Thomas and Eliza (Vickers) Abbatt.
Rear: Frederic, Washington and Benjamin.
(Thomas 1827-1897 was JONATHAN's favourite brother.)

ANNIE JACKSON M.D.
1836-1933
An early Edinburgh woman Doctor of Medicine. Of Oakenclough and Derby.

MARY (WILCOCKSON)
HARDING 1771-1859
MARY's 'Great Aunt Harding and her nonsense'.

DIMPLES
Home of James and Martha (Labrey) Jackson, ¼ mile from Calder Bridge – once a Roman Catholic priest's refuge.

Mary then writes on 7th September:

> So thou art likely to have thy brother James in Preston, perhaps I shall sometime have a chance to see him, it will be nice for you all to be so near together. I often wish that my brother D[avid] was not at the distance he is. It seems that my cousin David [Wilcockson] was in Yorkshire on last first day so that will account for him not being at meeting. Thomas Ord went to see M[argaret] L[abrey] at Bessies [Dixon]. My cold thank thee has taken its departure, I hope Jane [Abbatt] keeps nicely. ---- I saw W. Jackson at meeting yesterday but did not speak to him, his sister tells me he does not appear to be any better for his break.

On 10th September Jonathan asks:

> Does thou think of going to Quarterly Meeting next week or not to see thy Liverpool friends etc. It is so long since I was there and in fact never since coming to live in Preston; that I think I shall accompany my Mother there and see some of my old schoolmates, W. Wood etc. I think I must tell him I heard he was going to be married soon, and ask him when.
>
> Sarah Ord is away from home but if I understand Sam Jesper aright she was not intending to proceed on her religious visit.
>
> We had a very nice but short address from J[oseph] Jesper [Sam's father] today and what was singular he took the text I had been thinking to speak from. I saw even J. Jesper himself almost overcome with sleep and though not myself asleep my thoughts were not as they should have been, when from what I saw and from my own state too, the words of Christ to his disciples in the Garden of Gethsemane. (What! canst thou not watch with me for one hour) seemed to strike me with some force and I was pleased to hear J. J. speak from the same, but I seem as if I cannot settle my mind as I ought.
>
> I cannot give expression on paper as I should of my thoughts and feelings on these subjects, neither do I feel inclined to speak to others about it, yet I fancy if I had thee there as my dear wife I could enjoy especially on a first day [Sunday] afternoon, Yes, I may say a little holy communion with thee, for if there are times ----- .

It is believed that Jonathan did not speak in Meeting until he was in his sixties, but here he had obviously intended to speak if he had not been pre-empted!

The problem of somnolence and sleep in Meeting was a real Friends' concern and was the subject of formal 'Queries'. In particular a fine warm day, in a peaceful meeting with no address, or even worse a long winded and pompous one, can be a most potent soporific. An effective stimulant can be a short relevant address - as from J. Jesper! (At the very least it wakes the sleeper).

In her reply Mary has news of W. Wood and of Sarah Ord:

    To: Jonathan Abbatt
           Friargate   Preston

Calder Bridge
9 mo 14 1854 [Thursday]

My dear Jonathan

I very much enjoyed reading thy nice letter received on second day morning.

I am glad to hear thou art intending to go to Liverpool, I do not expect to be there as my Mother is going, thou will I fancy see William Wood - so thou art for asking him when he is to be married, thou will get but a sorrowful look I fear, must I tell thee I have been told (quite in confidence tho.) that he has met with a sad disappointment his lady has turned him off - what he has done amiss I do not know. I had intended to tell thee when thou was last here but I forgot.

I was at Lancaster yesterday at the M. Meeting, thou will be pleased to hear that Joshua Kelsall has got nicely better again, I knew his father.

My Father and Mother have gone to Thomas Marsdens to tea so am left alone. Thou will be rather surprised when I tell thee that E. Burns was united to her dear W. on third day last, she told me a week since today when it was to take place, rather sooner than I had expected; they are now in the Lake District - How soon some people are ready are they not? Well, well, I suppose the <u>right</u> <u>time</u> <u>will</u> <u>come</u> either soon or late; if people are only happy that is the main thing.

I am glad to hear of thy business still doing
nicely, truly we each have much to be thankful for;
thou does I have no doubt often like myself feel
very unworthy, need I tell thee how sweet they
confidence is to me; and if we are spared to be
united in a still nearer bond than now, my prayer is
each may assist the other in temporal as well as
spiritual concerns for without a Heavenly hand to
guide and bless how can we expect or look for new
happiness; and I do think I have met with one on
earth who will indeed be my friend and tho. he finds
in her he loves many things he would rather had been
otherwise, yet may there be that left that will
brighten with the keeping.

I heard yesterday that Sarah Ord had gone on her
visit to Scotland, and E. Fellows of Lancaster is
with her.

Two of the Satterthwaites of Lancaster are at J.
Jacksons, I am to meet them at Richards on 7th day
afternoon, I will not say that we shall be a very
quiet party, for I think I never heard such talkers,
they were at O. Leaf Meeting on 3rd day last. Well
now Jonathan I must say farewell and remain in my
affection thine sincerely attached

             Mary Dilworth

- Joshua Kelsall (1781-1854) whose father - Joseph K. -
was known to Mary (para three above) was one of 17
Kelsall grandchildren of Jennet (Townson) Cragg.
- The E. Fellows of Lancaster who accompanied Sarah Ord
was one of the editor's Pickard/Walker great aunts.

In Jonathan's letter of 17th September he tells Mary:

Though I am expecting to see thee as usual on third
day ---- thine was awaiting me on sixth day [Friday]
morning after my return from a journey to the south
as far as Stafford and Stone in company with Thomas
Mulliner [his old employer], where we have been to
see the shoe manufacturers and to make some cheap
bargains which we have managed so as to pay our
expenses etc.

On 5th day [Thursday] morning we went to see
Stafford Castle and found it a beautiful walk from
the town and were much pleased to be shown over the
premises, and see so many old fashioned things of
which I can say more when I see thee.

I was much pleased with reading thy nice letter and

surprised to hear of E. Burns wedding, really Polly we are a long way behind some folks and shall be thought by some to be very cool in our courtship, never mind --- and later ---- I hope to bring thy Mother's shoes on third day though I have not got them yet. I had Mary and Elizbth. Jackson from the Vale [Vale House, Calder Vale] as customers yesterday and although so very wet I had a pretty good draw.

The number of boots and shoes known to be 'consumed' by Mary and her family, not to mention other 'friends and relations', is an indication that the boot and shoe trade was at least demanded and profitable, because it dealt in a Victorian necessity. Despite trains and horses, Victorians walked a great deal in their every-day lives and therefore wore out a great deal of leather footwear.

Following a meeting at Calder on 19th September, Jonathan writes on the 24th to report on his trip to Liverpool. In one brief overnight visit we see the extent of contact with others (he mentions David Wilcockson later). The nature of Mary Jackson's misdeamenour is not known.

> I spent a very pleasant time at the Q. meeting and enjoyed the out very much, took dinner with W. Wood who was very pressing for me to do so, poor fellow, I feel sorry for him, he was wonderfully confident with me and told me all his troubles, it seems it has been through some misunderstanding in reading Wm.'s letter and he has since been to her beyond London to explain himself all to no purpose, he thinks there is someone there who has done the mischief.
>
> I saw Jane and Sarah Pickard there [at] Q. meeting looking very bright and lively, I just spoke to them, there seemed hardly any Jacksons there except Jon.n and his daughter Mary, what a pity there should still be an objection to the query on her account it does not tend to produce any very favourable impression of her.
>
> I have just bethought me to enquire if thou art going this week to Wyresdale for should it prove anything like fine on first day [Sunday] I intend to be there if thou does go. I had no opportunity of speaking with Margt. Glover [M.'s cousin] though saw George [G] and got a very pressing invitation to dine with them but was previously engaged. Perhaps thy Mother would call on them I was glad to see her at Wm. Wood's.

To: Jonathan Abbatt
      Friargate   Preston

Calder Bridge
9 mo 28th 1854 [Thursday]

My dear Jonathan

So thou would have thought well of a letter last 6th day, well I think thou ought to think better than common of this, more particular when I tell thee I take a delight in writing it and thats more than she could have said at one time, thou will say I fancy.

I can assure thee I was well pleased to see my Mother home again last evening she seems to have spent a pleasant time with her friends at Liverpool.

Thou too appears to have had a nice day; W. Wood I dare say would be glad of thy company, poor man he will want someone to tell his troubles to, I feel sorry for him, but still he may think well he has missed her, if she can so soon give up for another.

Father had a note from J. Kelsall on 4th day giving the mournful intelligence of his Father's death, which took place on 2nd day about two o'clock in the afternoon. We were very much shocked to hear of his sudden departure as we had not heard of him being any worse, E. Drury mentioned in a letter I had from her on first day that he had taken cold but was somewhat better the day she wrote. Truly we know not who must go first yet sudden as the call has come to our good old friend he would have no doubt been found waiting, he will be much missed in the neighbourhood. My Father and Mother have gone to the interment today. I had fixed to go to Wyresdale this morning, this however will put a stop to my journey there.

I have had a walk to Garstang today and found it exceeding pleasant, the weather is quite tempting for one to be out and enjoying the sunshine while we can, for we cannot expect to have it fine for very long, now that winter is so near; my cousin D.W. will have been agreeably disappointed this time. I suppose (if alls well) we shall see him on 7th day on his return from the North. I must now once more say farewell trusting thou will believe me to remain thine as ever

                              Mary Dilworth

There are a tangle of Wyresdale relations in the above:

- 'J. Kelsall' (John Jackson D.'s second cousin) is Joseph son of Joshua and Mary (Swindlehurst) Kelsall.
- Joshua was first cousin to Mary (Jackson) Dilworth and died at the age of seventy three.
- 'E. Drewry' is Elizabeth (Kelsall) Drewry - wife of Thomas of Fleetwood. Elizabeth's sister and brother-in-law were Ellen (Kelsall) and George Glover a Clogger of Liverpool who appear frequently in the letters and were sometime Liverpool hosts to Mary.
- The 'agreeable disappointment' for David Wilcockson was that he had had good weather for a Yorkshire journey when he had expected storms.
- Chapel House (the old Dilworth home) was now the Kelsall's Wyresdale home.

To: Jonathan Abbatt

Calder Bridge
9 mo 29th 1854 [Friday]

My dear Jonathan

I just write a hasty note to tell thee I have changed my mind about going to Wyresdale, they seem wishful for me to go, indeed they quite expected me there yesterday (so all being well) tomorrow I intend starting.

Father and Mother had a nice day yesterday and got well home in the evening. They had a large funeral.

It has come to something when I write every day to thee but I thought thou would like to know my whereabouts and if thou should feel inclined to come, thou cannot tell me thou did not know I was there.

I suppose if thou does come thou will find thy way to the meeting house or Chapel House sometime in the morning.

I should not mind if the weather would keep as it is now for the next week.

Hoping this scribble may find thee well I will remain affectionately
        Thine
           Mary Dilworth

After visiting Wyresdale with James on Sunday 30th:

    To: Mary Dilworth
            Calder Bridge, Nr. Garstang

Preston
10 mo 9th 1854 [Monday]

My dear Polly

Thou would no doubt feel some little disappointment at not hearing from me this morning but circumstances prevented my doing so though I made a commencement but my time was so short I gave up the attempt in preference to writing now.

We received word from my Uncle Fletchers at Leigh that since the Q. Meeting my uncle has been unwell and gradually getting worse, he went last week to Manchester to consult a doctor who says it is a disease of the heart and will require him to exercise with great care, I went over yesterday to see him and left him very nicely they were very glad to see me and quite expecting I should come.

So thou sees I have not willingly neglected thee.

We have also heard from my brother James who is engaged to come to Wilson and Jespers on or about the 6th of next month we are glad of the prospect of being all together once more.

I suppose thou knows that James and Martha Jackson have been on a visit here, last 5th day we had quite an enjoyable party to meet them and after tea enjoyed ourselves with a course of games, quite a second edition of thy cousin David's party at the Q. meeting, Isaac was there too and treated us to a song or two.

James and I got nicely home in good time on our return from Wyresdale I don't think I got cold but with rising so early and extra exertion together with some of James's biscuits which I did not think very wholesome I was quite knocked up and tired.

Well I suppose tomorrow is your O. L. meeting which thou will be able to attend this time, for does thou know Jane Crossland who corresponds with my sister Jane mentioned in her last that as she heard Mary Dilworth missed attending their meetings occasionally she fancied perhaps my Mother and sisters were busy getting some sewing done for me as she judged there was something going to take place soon. What really sharp ears some folks have and how soon they jump to conclusions. I wonder if anyone has told her or whether it was her own invention, for I believe her cunning enough to invent this herself she is so full of frolic now and then.

Poor James Little I suppose Mary ran off directly after Meeting and he had no chance to meet at all for Joshua informed me they are keeping company; she is a really queer body I dont fancy I should like to be served in the same way - it is a sort of courtship beyond my comprehension. I fancy I should feel ridiculous if I came purposely to see thee and thou did the same, however I think it most likely if nothing prevents that I shall come on 3rd day as usual when I hope to be more fortunate, but as I hope to receive thy always welcome reply previously, thou will of course say if inconvenient. In the meantime I will subscribe myself ever affectionately
Thine
Jonathan Abbatt

- The identity of 'Mary' who seems to have jilted James Little is unknown - as is the rest of the story.
- James Jackson, son of Jonathan and Elizabeth (Robinson) J., lived at Dimples 1/4 mile from Calder Bridge. James had seven children by Martha Labrey, only two of whom - Herbert and Leonard - had Jackson issue.
- The 'tea, games and music' party for James and Martha J. was held at Michael Satterthwaite's and as we see Mary's cousin, Isaac W., like Jno., played and sang.

On 12th October Mary sends an <u>appreciable</u> contribution of ten shillings to Elizabeth A.'s Anti-Slavery bazaar and comments on James Little and 'Mary':

--- thou thinks it rather strange kind of courting does thou when the young lady will not stay and speak to the young man of her choice, "well young ladies are queer sort of folk and no mistake" thou will say I fancy: we are not <u>all</u> queer are we? Poor James I wish him better fortune next time, perhaps he may not like her any worse for getting out of his sight, for I have an idea (tho. perhaps I sometimes get a wrong idea) that men are rather strange at times, some men at least.

Thou will have received a small parcel I expect from Hugh Lamb, if he has not sent it down to thy shop will thou be so kind as to send for it. I am almost ashamed to send such a trifle, but we in our neighbourhood seem less inclined to work for the bazaar; but I must not forget to tell thee I have received ten shillings so if thou will send the things before I see thee will you give that sum to your Mother and I will repay thee when thou art here next week.

In a short letter Jonathan includes every topic except politics. The reference to the necessity for William (Dilworth) to solicit his cousin David Wilcockson for business is a pointer to the way in which business was done by Victorian Friends (and others).

    To: Mary Dilworth
            Calder Bridge   Nr. Garstang

Preston
10 mo 15th 1854 [Sunday]

My dear Polly

Thine I gladly received on sixth day as usual and though I now sit down to answer thee thou must not expect anything lengthy from me as I hope to enjoy thy company on 3rd day. It is so thoroughly wet today I hope it will get all done by 3rd day that we may have a pleasant walk again.

I see Mary Jackson is in town today I spoke to her about William she thinks him better but says he is scarcely likely to come to Preston again I feel rather sorry for it, we passed many a pleasant time together.

I received thy very acceptable present for the Bazaar from John Lamb and being an article not frequently seen will be well appreciated. My Mother is at present in Bolton working for the Bazaar and is intending to return on 5th day with the articles collected there and to exhibit them along with the Preston collection in the ante rooms of the Meetinghouse for which friends give their consent and I fancy will manage to make a tolerable respectable display, notice of which will be given in the newspaper. I must thank thee on Mother's behalf for the donation thou has in hand for the above object and can assure thee she will be famously pleased, she is so very warm in the cause and most wonderfully persevering.

Trade here generally is rather quieter though I am
still doing more than last year so have no cause to
complain. Thy brother William too I fancy is
pushing his business I frequently see him going out
amongst his friends and acquaintances etc. and have
no doubt it will pay him well to do so, he was going
the other day to solicit thy cousin David's
patronage who he says has scarcely anything from him
since he got in business. I should think it will do
well to rub him up now and then about it.

It is now getting on towards meeting time so I will
excuse myself saying more at present and in true
affection will once more describe myself as ever
        Thine Jon.n Abbatt

After another meeting at Calder on Tuesday 17th Jonathan
writes again on Sunday 22nd. In this he follows a now
established pattern; after each meeting he writes first,
on the following Sunday, - as he says in a much earlier
letter - 'to establish thee in my debt'. The pattern is
not immutable and they also write as the need arises.

At my Mothers request I enclose thee an invitation
circular to the Anti-Slavery Bazaar collection and
if thou does come to Preston this week I hope thou
will get in time to see the things contributed, I
seem to feel unusually interested with being so much
among the stir for our folks are as full of it and
as busy as possible. Jane is dressing a doll as a
Friend and has also made a couple of Sweeps which
really do look odd figures, but will no doubt ---.
Sarah Ord Senr. has contributed five shillings
without being solicited or even expected. ---- hope
to see thee again soon and as I see M[ary] N[ichol]
is not here today I thought it likely you might be
intending to come together ----
      Thine dearly Jonathan Abbatt

It is interesting to see in the last para that Jon.n
'knew' who had, and who had not been to town. times have
changed.

In Mary's brief note of 26th she manages to cram in a
deal of news. She and Jonathan both use the word 'stir'
in the sense of a busy gathering, - if one had several
bazaars, a book meeting and a wedding in one week our
pair would have been 'throng with all these stirs'!

Aunt Mary (Wilcockson) Harding, daughter of Isaac and
Mary (Gilpin) Wilcockson, was Mary's maternal great Aunt
and at this time was a somewhat forbidding old Quaker

lady. A pastel from the editor's dining room, see page 151, gives an idea of this most formidable old Friend.

Jonathan writes on 29th October to 'My dearest Mary', before Mary's Preston 'Book Meeting' visit, this address is a far cry from 'Esteemed Friend' of the earliest letters. It is probable that when William Jackson is described as being in 'better spirits than ever I saw him' he was probably displaying the euphoria of tuberculosis. William recovered after a prolonged period of ill health. (Advanced pulmonary tuberculosis, now relatively uncommon in England, may produce in the patient, a false sense of euphoria or well-being.)

To: Mary Dilworth
    Calder Bridge   Nr. Garstang

Preston
10 29 /54 [Sunday]

My dearest Mary

I was glad to receive thine on 6th day morning though must I tell thee I [was] almost too much engaged to read even one from thee.

Although thou art coming tomorrow I felt quite a pleasure at the thought of writing to thee though this may be very brief yet important [letter] when I give thee an account of the transactions of the week which has been one of unusual anxiety to me!! (dear me whatever is coming) well dont be in too great a hurry and thou shall know soon, only aint it delightful to be kept in suspense well, this is a comical letter, really how soon does thou mean to tell me; well now be all attention then thou shall know all.

The landlord has been talking about dividing the premises over my shop and shaped for making so shabby a place and really not fit to live in, (unless I would make all the alterations myself which would have been very expensive) that I told him that I could not take it upon such terms and have to pay another rent elsewhere, he then made one other proposition which I can explain some other time but will let it suffice for the present to say he agrees to let me have the shop and fitting room as it now stands and at same rent, for which I gladly accept for a term of 7 years so shall have to look out for a house elsewhere which I think will

suit us both a great deal better in nearly all
respects so now thou sees I am at liberty to
commence housekeeping as soon as I will without
being tied to wait for the premises being altered
and consequently, (now this is of the most
importance) shall want thy consent to become my
housekeeper not later than 5th month, perhaps thou
may say - oh plenty of time to talk about that, yet
thou canst allow me to give thee plenty of notice
that thou may feel prepared for this greatest
engagement of life.

I hope to have some opportunity whilst thou art in
town of spending some time in thy company when we
can talk these matters over so will not trouble thee
with further details now. I quite intend to be down
at the Railway tomorrow evening and my lad with me
to carry any luggage thou has with thee.

I had a call from Wm. Jackson yesterday and thought
him looking very well, better than ever I saw him
and he seems to be in very good spirits.

Sam Jesper is gone to fetch his sister back again
after a stay of about 8 weeks, poor fellow he has
been quite the bachelor, thou would have been amused
to see him last first day evening making tea and
afterwards down on his knees sweeping up the hearth
what a pity no one was sympathetic with his
loneliness; but I must be making a finish or get
some more paper and for fear I could not fill it
with sufficiently interesting matter I will conclude
and remain as ever
      Thine Dearly attached
        Jonathan Abbatt

Jonathan's reference to meeting Mary at the railway
station 'and my lad --- to carry any luggage --- '; is
interesting and shows that he is, thus early, an employer
of labour both at home and in his shop.

After the 'Book Meeting', Jno. writes on 7th November to
explain his failure to 'see Mary off' at the Station:

I had the company of my two elder brothers [William
and Thomas] on first day [Sunday] they stayed all
night, and this morning my brother James arrived
from Colchester and will I suppose go to Jespers
[Jesper and Wilson's the tailors] sometime this week
[to start work].

How did thou get home on 7th day [Saturday] perhaps

Mary [Nichol] would think me rather inattentive to
thee in comparison to Sam [Pickard], for not seeing
thee off, but 7th day is a busy day for tradesmen in
my position so thou must excuse me yet with all my
attention I have I believe had two pairs of boots
stolen from my shop this afternoon, but sometimes I
am busy in the back room and they must have been
taken then, I am glad to say my business still keeps
up in the face of all the complaints I hear, yet I
ought to have some return for I have expended 25
pounds in advertising and distributing bills the
result of which is I have taken now as much as all
last year and have 2 months yet to improve on. I
was glad to see thy Father this morning and was
looking for him as I passed through the fair ---- .

Mary's short letter is full of news of people:

- David and William in para one are her cousin and
  brother, David Wilcockson and William Dilworth.
- Father John Jackson D.
- Mary's 'Uncle and Aunt Wilcockson' were John and Jane
  (Dilworth) Wilcockson, parents of David above. John
  and Jane were brother and sister to Mary's parents
  Ann (Wilcockson) and John Jackson Dilworth (i.e.
  brother and sister married sister and brother). John
  Wilcockson was a Hatter of Preston.
- The Wyresdale 'young person' was a servant girl.

    To: Jonathan Abbatt
           Friargate   Preston

Calder Bridge
10 of 11 /54 [Friday]

My dear Jonathan

It was an agreeable surprise to me to receive thy
letter the other morning, I scarcely thought thou
would write before first day, but it appears thou
art more attentive than some perhaps might give thee
credit for. I did not expect to have thy company to
the train the other night so thou need ask no
excuse, David and William were there to see us off
and we got nicely home just before dark.

Since my return I have had a visit from one of my
old fashioned head colds yesterday I felt so much
out of sorts that I did not feel inclined to write
even to thee, today I am thankful to say I am partly
all right again.

My Father told me he had seen thy brother, he will be nice company for thee.

My Uncle and Aunt Wilcockson were here on second day last, Aunt was saying she had seen thee pass their house that morning just before they started, it is the first time she has seen thee.

I was well pleased with the evening spent at thy Mothers, though I must tell thee now it was somewhat of a trial to me to go; my being rather quieter than usual, thou will, I doubt not, be able to account for. ---

My Father was in Wyresdale yesterday and brought a young person to stay a night or two with us.

I will try to give thee a longer letter next time, news in this quarter seems rather scarce just at this time, so I must now take an affectionate leave and remain as before
Thine
Mary Dilworth

Mary's feelings about her visit to Elizabeth Abbatt are quite clear. 3 Bank Place was Elizabeth's new and first Preston home, it is easy to imagine the ordeal for a prospective daughter-in-law making <u>her</u> first call.

Mary <u>does</u> have an inordinate number of colds (and some other illnesses) in the letters, and one is reminded of the Wordsworth's perpetual colds - though not of William's toothache. Oddly enough, there is no mention of anything resembling asthma in the correspondence and this is odd, as in married life Mary suffered severely from asthma. The condition was so disabling that Dilworth A., as an old man, told the editor that he had frequently expected his Mother to die during an attack.

Sunday 12th and Jonathan is now 'engaged with the all engrossing thought of furnishing --- ', but first:

> We heard from my brother Thomas yesterday who says that Jane has presented him with a little boy this last week and that both are doing so nicely. Thomas will begin quite to feel himself a responsible being, with all the joys it may bring it involves a great deal of care.
>
> I have chosen a piece of print to hang my second best bed with this last week and expect to have my Mother and sisters [Jane and Elizabeth] at work for

me so thou sees I am still engaged with the all
engrossing thought of furnishing and housekeeping.

To think there is only seven more weeks in this year
and then for 1855 and its important events, really
how times does pass, it will be time to remember thy
half made promise about making some [wax] flowers
soon and other exquisites that only you ladies are
so clever at, but I must refrain from praising you
so much or perhaps thou will be having too great an
opinion of your ability.

The letter from Calder House is expressive and amusing:

    To: Jonathan Abbatt
           Friargate   Preston

Calder Bridge
11 mo 16th 1854 [Thursday]

My dear Jonathan

Thy welcome letter came duly to hand and for the
same accept my thanks. How soon the weeks seem to
pass, really this year will (truly too soon perhaps)
be at its close, it appears to have been a very
short one tho' I suppose it will have had the usual
number of days in it.

We have had quite winter weather since my return
from Preston, what with that and my cold I have not
been out much. I was at Garstang tho' on third day
at M. Kelsalls to tea and a right pleasant evening
we spent. Thou will judge that my cold has vanished
now that I have got to visiting once more.

My Aunt Mary Harding is at Lancaster she went to M.
Meeting last week and has not since returned. I
believe whenever shoes do not fit, she believes she
will have to visit Jonathan herself, and as for
sending [them] with me again, that she will not do,
for she is sure that if thee and I are together we
shall not talk much about her shoes - poor old lady
she is quite full of her nonsense.

So thou art going to have thy Mother and sisters at
work for thee, and cannot be content but thou must
find something for me to do too, really Jonathan I
dont know whatever you would do without us; though
you do try to set us down a peg sometimes, yet for
all these things we seem to get along ever so well

together; truly man was made to command a woman to a --- no I wont say that little word now then.

Perhaps thou will think me short of a subject and made me write all the above, it may be so but I will drop it.

Thomas Swithenbank was interred last third day, he has I believe been a great sufferer at times, his sister will miss him very much. I feel very sorry for her she has a large amount of trouble of one kind and another. Father was invited to the funeral but did not attend.

I am glad to hear that thy brother Thomas is the happy Father of a hopeful son, I trust that both are still nicely.

I am reading a slave tale entitled Ida May a nice thing very, though perhaps my time might be better employed, but we mortals like something amusing do we not?

It is nearly dark so I must say Farewell and once more remain as ever affectionately
                                        Mary Dilworth

Jonathan writes of Bolton visit and of picking his brothers' brains and house furnishing costs:

   To: Mary Dilworth
          Calder Bridge Nr. Garstang

Preston
11 mo. 20th 1854 [Monday]

My dear Mary

Thou would no doubt fancy me from home when thou missed hearing from me this morning, I had intended writing to thee on 7th day but could not get an opportunity I was so busy and yesterday I spent very agreeably with my brothers in Bolton and found Jane and her little one doing very nicely.

This last week has been a very busy one with me and having been so closely engaged I felt it quite a relief to get out on first day, after soleing with gutta percha something like 8 or 9 pairs of shoes a day with my own hands, does it not sound like being industrious.

I got a famous lesson from my brothers on purchasing furniture and find my brother William has an inventory of all his goods with their prices which will be a good guide to me as I am still adding to my stock and shall find it serviceable as it gives me an idea of the value of things a many of which I am entirely ignorant of. What an amount of preparation we men have to make before you consent to say "I will".

I was quite amused at thy last and in talking of 1855 being soon here thou would almost make me believe thou was getting timid at its near approach and important results and <u>perhaps</u> induce me to think thou art afraid of trusting thyself to me, but I think this is not thy feeling now or I have made poorly out with my 2 years courting is this was so, perhaps I shall have to come a little more frequently to make thy trust in me last from one visit to another, I must try to inspire thee afresh when I see thee next on 3rd day as usual, but for fear thou should think me too much in earnest I will stop saying more at present.

I am sorry thy Aunt's overshoes dont fit she will have lost the use of them this last wet weather, but I must endeavour to bring a pair that will fit when I come.

I was glad to hear of thy cold being better and that thou has been enabled to enjoy thyself so nicely at Garstang.

I have been so frequently interrupted whilst writing this thou must excuse blunders and being just about shutting up time I will once more conclude and remain as ever Thine truly
Jonathan Abbatt

In the above letter Jonathan is still very much a working shoemaker soling his own shoes with gutta percha (OED = rubber like flexible substance obtained from juice of some Malayan trees). He is also clearly concerned that Mary Harding's overshoes/galoshes did not fit and that she has 'lost the use of them this last wet weather'! Quite soon he became one of Mary H.'s favourites as she thought him 'a very kind and gentle young man'.

Mary's reply is short and mentions: 'My cousin Esther' who was Esther (Pickard) Shaw who 'married out' and lived in Leeds - of whom more later, and the other two of 'The Three Marys'. These were the cousins Mary Nichol soon to

be Pickard, Mary Ann (Wilcockson) Ord and 'our Mary'.
They remained, close friends throughout their lives.

To: Jonathan Abbatt
    Friargate,   Preston

Calder Bridge
11/23/54 [Thursday]

My dear Jonathan

It scarcely seemed like second day [Monday] morning when no letter arrived from thee. I had not long to wait however for the next post brought the expected epistle. How soon we get accustomed to anything, I could not have thought once on a time, that I should have looked with such keen interest for one of thy letters, yet so it is and I have no reason to wish it otherwise at the same time, (now do not blame me) I do wish 1855 at a greater distance than it is, bright as the picture is at present, it has its clouds, so thou need not wonder if I am sometimes a little timid at its near approach, but perhaps I have said enough on that subject at this time.

I suppose my cousin Mary Ann Ord and her little ones are still down at Lytham. I had the pleasure of receiving a long letter from my cousin Esther, the first she has favoured me with since she was married; she tells me that her brother Daniel is to fetch his Lucy to Leeds in the second month; and that there is a report out that Sam and Mary N. are to be married in the same month, I dont know if the last is true or not.

So thou art coming on third day [Tuesday] next, somehow it seems a long time since we met, I dont know how it is, but I do not think of thee as much at Preston as I do when I see thee here, I suppose I dont feel quite in my right place.

I have nothing worth while getting another sheet for, so I will conclude and remain
                    Thine sincerely   Mary Dilworth

Mary's timidity and apprehensions about marriage appear again in this letter and the reason(s) is/are not known. It may have been merely that she was the only daughter and a country girl very deeply attached to her home and family; and that the there was a great influence of her 'Dear Octopus' relations. Undoubtedly the eighteen fifties web of 'the families' and their innumerable Garstang relations was formidable and all encompassing. Even in the editor's youth, in the nineteen twenties and thirties - when the families were much attenuated - their influence was still pervasive and powerful. Jonathan, at the time of the letters, though an entirely acceptable young Friend from Bolton/Preston, was still a relative stranger to Mary and not yet one of their 'own'.

The 'families' relied on one another in most things, a good example being in their choice of executors. Those chosen were occasionally friends, but this was not common and relations were the rule - but with absolutely no distinction between a blood and a non blood relationship. (There may even have been some preference for 'in-laws').

Jonathan writes after a 28th November meeting at Calder:

    To: Mary Dilworth
           Calder Bridge Nr. Garstang

Preston
12 mo 3rd 1854 [Sunday]

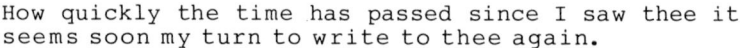

My dear Polly

How quickly the time has passed since I saw thee it seems soon my turn to write to thee again.

I found my walk to the station a real splashy wet one but I got home in good time, thy brother William called soon after I returned to learn the result of his letter to thee, and seemed a little disappointed that thou has not concluded to come, and says he does not want to keep thee any longer than is agreeable, he would have written again but was expecting to see his father yesterday, but as I did not see him I concluded he had not come, so thou will perhaps be hearing from him soon. Thou should come in time to be at the next book meeting which I understand is expected to be an interesting one there being either three or four essays to read.

My Mother and sisters attended on 5th day the O. Leaf meeting here and were quite in disappointment at their way of doing business here, and think them sadly too timid on the subject, there had been a proposition to supply them with a number copies of John Brights letter on the war (which is a capital production) to distribute in Preston as it is just the time for peace folks to make a stir, but they were afraid to distribute them for fear of being mobbed, and at the same time other circles are distributing them and I should think it will do good.

I am almost afraid in my Mothers earnestness in the cause they will begin to think her a busybody, she is desirous to have the meeting held somewhere else than a friends house when most likely a many wishing to join the society will feel less objection and less of a feeling of intrusion - when they all meet in one common place, the plan has answered well in Bolton and Mother has made the motion here which to some is more agreeable but of this I will tell thee more next time we meet.

Since my last visit I have thought I may occasionally vary my letter (as thou art so fond of poetry) by occasionally copying any choice piece I may meet with, the idea was prompted too by reading one evening in Chambers Journal (a back number) a little piece that somewhat took my fancy and will enclose it along with this as my first sample, and if approved will contribute more.

Thou may perhaps think my letter this time rather irrelevant to courtship, and maybe not without cause, I have not much mentioned ourselves to be sure, yet I have hitherto so unfolded myself to thee that there seems nothing else to disclose, especially as I believe thee to be quite ready to become mine with the exception of this leaving home feeling which sometimes intrudes.

I presume thou has written thy Cousin Esther an answer, and will thou consider me inquisitive if I ask what month did thou say we were to be married in, was it 4, 5, or 6? Perhaps thou will treat me in this particular in this as thou did when reading Esthers to me, jump over it, but what if I tell thee I am a party concerned and ought to know - will it induce thee to tell me. Thou must try to get over thy prejudice to 5th month and let me know next time I come; but I must stay my pen for I have almost filled my sheet and think I have done cleverly to write so much, and hoping to have a good one in return I will this time conclude and remain as ever
                Thine affectionately
                   Jonathan Abbatt

We have again heard from my Uncle John Fletcher who has been considerably worse again but is now somewhat better, he has been pressing the doctor to

say what his complaint is, but he calls it the
rheumatic gout in the liver and says the best thing
that could happen to him would be a good fit of gout
in his toes, but with care I think he will be better
again.   J.A.

John Bright the Lancashire Liberal and Quaker politician,
was for the Abbatts and many other North Western Friends,
one who could do no wrong. In addition to his national
views on war, poverty and corn laws, he had in 1850 been
one of seven members appointed by The Lancashire
Quarterly meeting to attend a special London "Meeting for
Sufferings" considering property seizure from Friends for
non-payment of church tithes. (Other members we have
'met' included Michael Satterthwaite and William Jackson
Senr.). These local and national activites almost
guaranteed him their support. But, in addition, John
Bright had been to the Friends school at Newton-in-
Bowland (as well as Penketh, Bootham and Ackworth). Of
Newton (where he carved his name on a desk - still
visible in the nineteen thirties) he later said that he
learnt: "to fish, to take wasps nests and to eat
oatcake". He was one of their very own and Thomas
Abbatt (with another) was, later, to write the address
after Bright's death.

The Little Teacher

With dark foreboding thought opprest,
  I wandered forth one summer day,
  Hoping abroad to ease my breast,
                And grief allay.
Methought with sympathetic smile,
  It seemed to pity and reprove,
  And thus my bitter care beguile
                With words of love.
'Sad mortal, cease these anxious sighs,
  Why sit you thus in sorrow here?
Does not each leaf that meets thine eyes
                Reprove thy fears?
Although a mean unheeded flower,
  My daily wants are all supplied,
  And he who brought me to this hour
                Will still provide.
The light and dew, the sun and rain,
  Are hourly sent to foster me,
  And fearest thou God will not deign
                To think on thee?
Ashamed I rose, rebuked my care,
  And blessed the teacher of the sod,
  Resolved to chase away despair,
                And trust in God.

To: Jonathan Abbatt
        Friargate   Preston

Calder Bridge
12 mo 9th 1854 [Saturday]

My dear Jonathan

I received thy long letter as usual on second day, for which thou wants a good one in return, now what am I to understand by a good one - a long one I suppose thou would like, but I very much fear thou will not receive that this time, as I feel in no very first rate mood for writing. My friends the Jensons are here today and I am to return with them tonight for a day or two.

I hope thy Mother will be able to stir the ladies of Preston up in the cause of peace, we could do with such an one in our circle, I think we are quite as backward as any, I am sorry to acknowledge.

I think it very likely I shall have to be in Preston next week we have engaged a young woman to be with my brother a short time but he will have me to go too, so I suppose I must go on second day evening.
I hope thou took no harm with thy walk to the station the other night. I thought after thou had gone it was a shame to turn thee out on such a night.

I have not yet written to Esther, (Oh! for the shame) and if I had I should not have told her what month we are to be married in, because I am not aware that any month has been fixed upon, however not with my consent. So thou thinks me quite ready to become thine; the pretensions of some folks!! - I wonder what thou will have to say to me next.

Forgive my nonsense and allow me to say that if I were not well assured that my friend would be the same he has until now been to me, I could not even yet leave my happy home to become his. Sometimes I almost think I shall never be able to fulfill the duties of a wife, and then again the thought will come, if Mary has a kind husband she can perhaps do wonders for him at least. But I must say, indeed I have now said more than I thought I should.

Thank thee for thy poetry I think the idea a good one, I am very fond of poetry and shall read with pleasure any thou may find to send.

I hope thou now feels satisfied with what I have written, so that I may venture to conclude remaining as ever thine very faithfully
Mary Dilworth

'Book meetings' were very popular with young Friends at this time, though they were not confined to the younger generation. Though some of the books discussed were intentionally 'improving' and religious works, they also included travel, poetry and fiction. From time to time, as at Preston, which was more serious than Calder Bridge/Wyresdale, essays were written for, and read at, book meetings. A major feature of any regular 'get together' of this nature was of course the forum it provided for the exchange of news and of the gossip arising therefrom.

By his comments Jonathan gives a good idea of his mother, Elizabeth's, 'earnestness' which anyone except a Quaker son might have called ferocity. She was apparently, in pursuit of her 'causes', indomitable and forthright. Mary once told her son Dil that his grandmother, when campaigning, was a frightening old woman. Mary herself was much concerned about peace and the work of the Olive Leaf League (more than anti slavery) and her desire that Elizabeth should 'stir the ladies of Preston' was real.

Mary's fondness for poetry was genuine and though 'Chambers', as we know from the letters, was an early source, she later became very fond of the Lakes poets.

On Christmas Eve 1854 and 28th December there is an exchange of letters, and these give some idea of their writers' respective Christmases. Jonathan's is much the more sombre - even with the prospect of: 'to be quite frank a Christmas party', (which ultimately he did not attend). Mary's due to the lighter touch of the Jacksons was, both in prospect and in reality, much more festive.

In the seventeenth and eighteenth centuries Friends were apprehensive about worldly display, feasting and partying. At the beginning Quakerism was very much a return, to what were believed to be, simple origins shorn of pomp and hypocrisy. Their feelings about the rest of society were well expressed in their talk of "People of the World", and those who adopted "the ways of the world'. By the mid-nineteenth century much change had taken place in the Society and among individuals marked by an increased acceptance of worldly ways. However, changes of this nature are slow and Jonathan and his family were at one end of the Quaker spectrum of 'worldliness' which then proceeded through the Dilworths and Jacksons to the other end occupied perhaps by David Dilworth, as he was leaving the Society through marriage. Another facet of this 'private Quaker conservatism' is represented by the continued use of 'thees and thous'; these fashions were abandoned first 'in the world', or in public, and only much later in the home and with family. Many Friends are still, in this sense, bilingual!

To: Mary Dilworth
    Calder Bridge

Preston
12 mo 24 /54 [Monday]

My dear Mary

Thou must excuse me saying very much this evening for my Mother, sisters, and brother have just returned from Bolton but as I should have less time tomorrow on account of being busy stocktaking I thought rather than disappoint thee I would write this evening.

I returned from Leigh late on 3rd day night and though I almost expected thee to have returned yet I felt some little disappointment at not being able to see thee.

I have been taking tea this afternoon with T. Salthouse'salong with Sam Jesper and his sister and tomorrow evening Sam wants me and sisters to spend the evening at his house to be quite frank a Christmas party thy cousin David to be there.

Although this week I seem to have my hands full I see an announcement on walls announcing a sale a few doors from our house here in the square, I hope to meet with something to my wants and as business has been pretty good this last week I have a little spare cash ready.

I had quite intended being communicative this time but as I have but little time I must conclude and wishing thee heartily a Merry Christmas and <u>a</u> <u>happy</u> <u>New</u> <u>Year</u> I am as ever   Thine Most Affectionate
                                    Jonathan Abbatt

P.S. I presume thou will not be from home again before my next time of coming as I hope to see thee again ere long. If thou art perhaps thou will let me know.   J.

In the next few months we will hear more of Jonathan's progress with his house acquisition and furnishing, as he gives Mary periodic progress reports. However, as we shall see the information is passed on in terms of 'I have chosen and it looks good' not 'As you told me,--' or 'I hope you will like shocking purple and yellow and green', or even 'I know you like'. He never says if you do not like something I will change or replace. No doubt these furnishing matters were discussed whenever the pair met; but there is absolutely nothing to indicate that house location, acquisition and furnishing (including fine detail) was felt to be anything to do with Mary. David Dilworth marries Emma Goodall in April 1855 and in January Mary goes to Newcastle to help him, David, with his soft furnishings. Emma's diary for this period has no mention whatsoever of her own involvement in soft or any house furnishing. This sharp division of responsibility was not 'odd' for mid-Victorians, though it seems bizarre in 1988.

    To: Jonathan Abbatt
            Friargate   Preston

Calder Bridge
12 mo 28 1854 [Thursday]

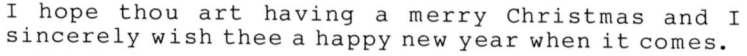

My dear Jonathan

I hope thou art having a merry Christmas and I sincerely wish thee a happy new year when it comes.

You would have a pleasant party at Jane Jespers the other evening I expect, I was to have been at Vale House that day, but my brother William being over and slight cold prevented my going. On 3rd day I met most of the Jacksons at Richards; left soon after nine and were caught in one of the heaviest of heavy showers. I should have been at James' today but I took the advice of my elders and so am staying at home - my cousin Mary is gone I think. Lee Samuel was over on first and second days. James J. of Oakenclough was very hasty telling me that was the reason I did not get to the Vale on second day he quite expected I had company etc. but I soon told his lordship he was mistaken for once in his life.

My cousin Esther and her husband have been over to Lancaster this Christmas they would return on third day morning. Mary Ann Holmes is on a visit to her sister, she is still the same merry lass. I suppose Thomas Harrison is married today and they have a fine cold day for their work. I wrote about a week since to my brother David telling him I expected to be at liberty to pay him a visit in about a fortnight from that time but perhaps he may not be able to fetch me then and I think I shall not go till he does.

I think I have now said my say for this time so must conclude remaining with affectionate esteem thine sincerely
                   Mary Dilworth

P.S. If I should hear that my brother is coming next week I will let thee know.

Identifiable people in these letters are - in Jonathan's Elizabeth A. senior and junior, Jane and Thomas A.: and in Mary's - William Dilworth, Richard and James Jackson, Mary Nichol, Robert and Esther (Pickard) Shaw, and David Dilworth.

The last 1854 letter is Jonathan's on 31st December - a fitting way to end the year. In his scepticism about the 'mere form' of Christmas greetings he sounds both modern and old. Though with his Sunday School party plus Christmas Day stocktaking he is not, after all, a modern.

   To: Mary Dilworth
           Calder Bridge   Nr. Garstang

Preston
12 mo. 31st 1854 [Sunday]

My dear Mary

Thine came duly to hand on sixth day with a wish of merry Christmas and though too often a mere form I believe we are both sincere, and so far I may say I have enjoyed it very well. Though you have been enjoying yourselves at your Christmas parties you are not alone, although I did not get to Sam Jespers party (as I was engaged stocktaking) yet I attended the school party on 6th day evening and famously it was enjoyed, we had an excellent Magic Lantern with a many comic views which pleased admirably and along with a good game of two in the Meeting house porch was a quantity of fireworks which pleased the lads well everything went off to satisfaction.

We have had a good address from Joseph Jesper this morning, referring to this closing year and reviewing the progress made heavenward, which in my

case I feel afraid is poor indeed, this is just the
period for new resolutions, for examining oneself
and endeavouring from now to enter on a different
course and now in prospect of entering on a new year
fraught as it will be with transactions of deep
interest to us both, I do indeed feel an increased
desire to live as it were to attain some great end,
I have in view the establishing of a home for myself
and thee, a home to which we may always look upon as
the sweetest spot on earth, where in sweet
retirement we can exchange thought for thought with
each other, and whilst enjoying thus each others
society may we send up our prayers hand in hand to
the source from whence all blessings flow.

I think this week may be a rather slack one and if
thou art not engaged on 3rd day I think of coming to
see thee; and as thou will review this early
tomorrow thou will have time to send me word, so
that if I dont hear from thee I shall conclude thee
to be at liberty, and as my train leaves so early I
think of coming by the train leaving here at 11.15.

If thou take in the Chronicle newspaper perhaps you
have seen what a nice notice of my Uncles death
there is, it also speaks of the shops in Leigh being
closed whilst the funeral procession was going
through the town, there were a many Manchester
friends attended, and we had a most beautiful
address from J. Crosslands wife from Bolton.

Although I have purposed coming to see thee on 3rd
day I have just bethought me I have an engagement at
the County Court so thou must not expect me till the
day following when I hope to see thee. For the
present I think I must conclude and, so once more
dear Polly I must say Farewell and remain as ever
                Thine Affectionately
                          Jonathan Abbatt

1854, for Jonathan and Mary, was the familiarisation year
between engagement in 1853 and marriage in June 1855. It
was a year of increasing confidence in, and affection
for each other - shown by the contents and length of the
letters. By the end of 1854 they are deeply and
genuinely attached to one another, which they may not
have been a year earlier. The long engagements then in
vogue were difficult for some couples, but were probably
not so for Mary and Jonathan. In 1853 they proceeded
from a ripening acquaintance with one another to an
'affaire' which by the end of 1854 has matured into what
is to become a mutual enduring and lifelong love.

VI   GLOVES and BONNETS - 1855

Mary to Newcastle - Meets Emma Goodall - A cold Winter - Jno. Skates at Penwortham - Mary Jackson Ill - Recovers - David Wilcockson Groomsman - Death of the Czar - Jane A. to Leeds - Written Marriage Consents - 'Passing the Meetings' - Mary 'Turns the Corner' - Advised by David W. - William Dilworth - Mary and Sam Married - Mary again to Lancaster - Trouble for James - M. 'Sets up House' for brother David - The Manchester Photograph - False teeth for Elizabeth - Mary a third time Bridesmaid - David and Emma married - Emma's Diary Again - Jonathan Works past Midnight - Jno. goes to Blackpool - Blackpool and Wakes Weeks - John Graham - Jane and Bonnets - Honeymoon arranged at Mrs. Gibson's in Lakes - Jonathan made Clerk to Meeting - Thomas prints 'at home' Cards - Jonathan's last Courting Letterto M. - 14 dozen pairs of Gloves - Jonathan & Mary married at Calder Bridge 27th June 1855.

In the next six months there are more and longer letters, many of them dealing with wedding preparations and with other peoples weddings. We have seen, and will continue, to see evidence of shyness and timidity on Mary's part though this diminishes as the wedding draws closer. After year's end the letters undergo a change from day to day news, chat and affection, to an increasing amount of business and 'administration'. This is due very largely to external pressures and events. Mary soon goes to Newcastle, there is family illness, followed by a second visit to David and then the domestic and bureaucratic requirements of multiple wedding arrangements.

Jonathan's plans of New Year's Eve for the next Calder Bridge visit change due to his stolen shoes 'case' 1855. His Uncle's death in Leigh is that of John Fletcher, his old master, who had died of a heart attack. Nevertheless the year begins prosaically enough as Mary writes 'by return' on Monday 1st January and after her brother David has written (the letters had crossed in the mail) postponing her visit projected visit by one week:

> Thanks for thy acceptable letter received as usual on second day [i.e. that morning]. --- so that I can be at Cousin D[avid] W[ilcockson]'s as usual during the Q[(uarterly] M[eeting] time, he seems wishful Mary N. and I should be there. --- If alls well I intend coming to Preston on 2nd day evening by the train leaving here a little after 5 o'clock. I have got to know at last when this wedding is to

> come off; Mary [Nichol] was asking me the other
> night to be her [brides]maid, and I was agreeably
> surprised to find that my worthy cousin David
> [Wilcockson] is to be the [best]man will that suit
> thee, but more of this when I see thee. Perhaps
> thou wilt be seeing Mary as she is in Preston at
> present.
>
> We are expecting Margaret Kelsall [yet another
> Jennet Cragg g.g.granddaughter from Wyresdale] on
> first day night to stay till the Quarterly Meeting.
> ---- As my brother is not coming I shall not expect
> thee this first day [Sunday], so thou will have no
> need to prepare for a walk as thou talks about.

Mary also tells of a visit with Mary Nichol to the Wilcocks' where they had talked of the formers forthcoming wedding. She had previously been mildly exasperated when rumour told her, but she did not 'know' at first hand, all the details of the wedding plans. It must be remembered that earlier there had been talk that 'Mary was too good for Sam'. However, if her admired cousin David, approved and was to be Sam's best man, then the affair was palatable and much more acceptable.

After a meeting in Preston Jno. writes on 7th January:

> Since I saw thee I have been to Leigh helping to
> take stock [after his Uncle's death] and though very
> busily engaged passed a very agreeable time amongst
> my old acquaintances, from there I went to Bolton
> and passed most of my time on 5th day with my
> brother Thomas and whilst there I purchased a nice
> little skeleton clock under a glass shade for our
> mantle piece with in 5th month [May] shall I say?'
>
> I saw little of my brother Wm. at Bolton he was
> going to Rochdale monthly meeting, they are about to
> appoint him Assistant Clerk to Marsden M. meeting
> he'll be getting to feel quite an important man
> among Friends we shall have to tell him.

The visit to Leigh to help with stocktaking is another example of Friends (and relations) helping Friends. What is more appropriate than for the old apprentice and nephew, to assist after the death of his uncle and old master John Fletcher?

Though William was the most 'public' of the brothers, all four were elders, active in their Meetings, and in the Society. Thomas and Jonathan were both Clerks to their Meeting, the latter serving several stints in Preston and was Clerk of Fylde - Preston Monthly Meeting 1871-4. His son, Dilworth A., served in the same office from 1901-1921 and his friend Sam Jesper from 1863-66. As with all organizations Friends tend to have 'magic circles'.

On Sunday 28th January after a meeting at Calder Bridge Jonathan writes to Mary at Newcastle. He had, for once, been spared a ten mile Sunday night walk by Mary's Uncle - Isaac Wilcockson Senior, Mary's Uncle, had 'married out' when he wedded Amelia Sennals. ("He was married by a priest to a woman not of our persuasion" .) He tells too of a young friends party at an older Friends house:

> I enjoyed my ride home last first day night exceedingly and had a pleasant conversation with thy uncle Isaac respecting Friends and was pleased to hear he has many pleasant remembrances of his sojurn amongst them and though he dissents in many respects he seems yet to admire them in many things.
>
> Robert Benson is ---- something more staid than many attending --- [who included] the Satterthwaites from Lancaster and a Miss Rook [later King - was a sister of the editor's Cumberland great-great-grandmother Peile, and reputed to be a great beauty].
>
> Thou has chosen a famously cold time for thy visiting --- My brother and I have been to see the skaters this afternoon at Penwortham Lodge but it looked really dangerous the ice bent so and seemed likely for breaking.
>
> I attended the sale of Isaac Grundys this last week and bought a quantity of feathers at only 8d a pound really good, and I find that when I have got the tick made and all complete I shall have a good bed for about two pounds, there is also a sale --- Bank Parades [where the Ords lived] --- which I think of going to though perhaps the Ords may see me and then Maria may have a subject to talk about ---- my brother Thomas is fussing me so much I have had a task to write thee this, he has been proposing to bind my letters if thou will forward them to him and will do it gratis and gild the edges, but says the volume will be incomplete unless I hand him thine over. What does thou say!!'

Jonathan has commented earlier on the accumulating letters as 'this valuable collection' and clearly he feels them to be worthy of preservation, but two days later, on 30th January writing from Newcastle, Mary replies with a message for Thomas. This is one of her longer letters - probably due to loneliness and illness:

> Whatever thy brother Thomas would like to do with others letters I should not like to see mine in a book even if it had gilt edges, nevertheless thou must send my kind regards and grateful thanks the next opportunity.
>
> I am quite alone this evening my brother having gone out to a party out of town. ----- arrived safe after a comfortable journey about 5 o'clock a week today since; and though I had a bad cold when I left home ---- nor has it been much better, my cough was so bad that David without letting me know brought in a doctor to see me and he tells me it is hooping cough and thought it may linger some time --- I rather object to writing about my own ailments, but thought it better to tell thee for thou might hear of it and so think me worse than I am. I was to have gone to visit my intended sister this week but as some of the family have not had my cough I must postpone my visit --- .
>
> I quite fancy thou may smile when I tell thee that Emma [Goodall] and a younger sister [Caroline] were here to spend first day [Sunday] with me, as I could not go they came down. I like her very much she is a sweet affectionate young lady and am very glad my dear brother has met with such an one.
> ---------------

Emma Goodall's 1855 diary contains some complementary information for these and future events:

Sunday 28th January:

> 'Carry and I had tea and happy with D[avid] and Polly his sister - Had a very happy day.'

Tuesday 30th January tells us where David was while Mary wrote her letter:

> 'Philip Tomlinson had tea and supper D.D. here - walked home together - very cold.'
> ---------------

On 28th January Jonathan had told Mary: 'J[oseph] Jesper [a staunch and senior older Friend] has been much worse again and there seems to be considerable doubt of his recovery, my Mother is -- again this evening to stay up with him.' --- Her reply: 'I felt exceeding sorry --- about Joseph Jespers increased illness and trust ---- .

On Sunday 4th February Jonathan writes to Newcastle but Mary has returned to Calder on that day, his letter is redirected and received on 6th, he commiserates on:

> --- thy hooping cough. My brother Wm.'s little boy has had the cough and with a very first rate receipt have cured him in little more than a week. I will write and give thy address and get him to forward it to thee, and hope it will give thee relief.
>
> Thou has no doubt heard of thy grandmother being unwell, I went yesterday to Williams [Mary's elder brother] to enquire if he had heard anything more since 5th day [Thursday] though he thought of going today in company with Isaac [Wilcockson][Isaac is "Dear David's" brother and son of John and Ann (Dilworth) W.] thy cousins so perhaps I may hear tomorrow something further.
>
> Whilst we have had so hard a frost this week I have been in company with Sam Jesper and Thos Lester a time or two to Penwortham and have had a fine time for skating we enjoyed it much, but it seems all over today being quite a soft morning and looking quite like spring, a time really pleasant to look forward to.
>
> My Mother and sister Jane have been to Bolton this week to attend the annual soiree of the Ladies O. Leaf circle, there were about 250 sat down to tea, afterwards a public meeting, and had the company of George Thomson M.P. besides many other influential gentlemen, they came home again last night. My Mother has brought me some blankets and has got me a lot of toilet covers etc. which my sisters will be making at their leisure; I intend also being at another sale or two this week so thou sees I am as busy as you are, especially as David in a great measure must have got the house furnished some time ago.
>
> I am glad to say that Joseph Jesper is again slightly convalescent and the doctors seem --- I suppose when I hear from thee again thou will have been a fortnight from home, I shall feel quite pleased to have thee in this quarter again for though I hear from and of thee regularly yet thou seems so far away --- .

Emma Goodall and her diary also tell us that the cold weather continued as seen from an entry made on the same day as Jonathan's letter above:

'Been to church once - still dreadfully cold
the snow in great drifts over some house tops.'

At this time, though doctors were consulted, and were on
the whole respectable, medicine in the modern sense had
by no means fully emerged. A good deal of self, quack
and hearsay treatment was common. Examples are: William
A.'s whooping cough cure and David Dilworth's treatment
of rabid dog bites. On one occasion David, when his
groom's hand had been bitten by a rabid dog, personally
cauterised the wound with a red hot poker from the
kitchen fire. (Emma Dilworth's brother, Dr. Ralph
Goodall, used the above method of treatment in his
practice where rabies/hydrophobia was not uncommon.)

In this letter Jonathan seems to feel a little envy for
his future brother-in-law David, whose house has been a
going concern for some time. One wonders how men who had
no mothers or sisters fared with their house furnishing.

Mary now comments on her Grandmother's desire for tea.

    To: Jonathan Abbatt
          Friargate   Preston

Calder Bridge
2 mo 8/55 [Thursday]

My dear Jonathan

Thine received from my brother on 3rd day which was
I assure thee welcome. I had a letter from home
asking me to return on second day, but I thought I
would like to be at home as soon as I could so left
on first day afternoon passing through Preston about
6 o'clock, they were surprised to see me so soon. I
am glad to tell thee that we think my Grandmother
some better tho' she will scarcely say so herself;
she has taken her food better today, but I have no
doubt feels herself weaker than she has done before
- she is still confined to her bed. My Mother is
still suffering from her cold, as for myself I think
I must have left my cough in the train as I have not
felt much of it since my return, however I can
easily dispense with it. Yesterday I received the
receipt from thy brother William I am much obliged
to him as well as to thyself.

Emma and her little sister came to the train with me
and David, as they returned D. stayed the day and as
he says spent a most delightful day so ---

I suppose Mary N[ichol] and her friend will pass the meeting next week. I should think she will wish it was over, I have not seen much of her since my return I dare say she is what some folks would call busy, and I have no time to go there.

The weather was so cold while I was with my brother, I went out only about three times, indeed it appears almost like a dream to me having been there, I can scarcely set it down as a reality.

My intended sister wants me to be one of her maids, she intends to have a cousin for her second if I will be the first; there is an old saying "three times a bridesmaid and never a bride" - dare thou venture me to fill that important post three times? I suppose thou will have no fears about it as thou had no faith in such like sayings, well be it as it may I cannot promise her anything at present.

So thou art still quite busy really what work there is which one and what another.

Oh! I thought there was something I had to tell thee, something very important thou may be sure, well it is this. I received a Valentine the other day - such a beauty, I suppose it is meant for thee as it is a cobbler in grand style, I had a good laugh at it.

Grandmother wants her tea so I must conclude for this time and hoping thou keeps clear of this bad cold or whatever it is I will remain dear J
      Thine affectionately
       Mary Dilworth

Mary has at least some domestic duties - even if they are limited to getting her convalescent Grandmother's and (occasionally) her Father's tea. The sender of Mary's Valentine later turns out to be Thomas A. perhaps making amends for himself and also gently poking fun at his more serious brother Jon.n. and 'his girl', Thomas was apparently a light and impishly gentle humorist.

Emma Goodall's diary for Sunday 4th February gives her, nearly identical, version of Mary's departure from Newcastle plus the additional information that Mary left from Whitmore Railway station. Whitmore is about 3 miles SW of Newcastle on the main north to south rail line, and David and Emma later had their summer home there:

  D[avid] and P[olly] his sister called on their way

to Whitmore - Carry and I went and them - D.D. returned with us his sister gone home.

The reference to 'Mary N(ichol) and her friend will pass the meeting next week' refers to the Friends equivalent of marriage banns or giving formal notice to the meeting of their intention to wed. In this case the Meeting referred to is Calder Bridge and this requirement and the procedures involved, which were a source of anxiety to Mary, will be heard of again in the near future. Jonathan is, as always, sympathetic in his reply:

    To: Mary Dilworth
           Calder Bridge   Nr. Garstang

Preston
2 mo 11 /55 [Sunday]

My dear Polly

Thine was to hand duly and I was much pleased to hear of thy being better again, thy cousin David quite surprised me by saying thou was at home as I was not at all expecting it, thy brother I fancy will almost want thee to go again ere the wedding this has been such a short visit.

So thou art again to be a bridesmaid if convenient at thy brothers wedding well I dont wonder and almost expected it would be so some time ago, but about "three times Bridesmaid and never a bride" thou has rightly said I have no faith in such sayings especially in some circumstances.

I am glad to hear thy Grandmother is some little [better] and though the weather is very much against a many poorly people yet I hope she will continue to improve. Thy brother would quite feel himself besieged with letters after thou left what with mine and my brothers for I fancy the Valentine thou received was from my brother Thomas, when he was so busy with his nonsense about our letters being bound - he said something about sending thee one but at the time I thought he scarcely would.

Then Mary is at last going to pass the meeting this next week I have no doubt she does wish it over as I do our own turn. I have been looking in the book of discipline for any guidance and next time I see thee I shall be prepared to <u>propose</u> the time for thy approval.

I propose if all goes well to come and see thee on
third day next but am not decided to come at 11 or 1
o'clock. I think most likely 11 o'clock though if
thou art engaged thou will have time to write and
say so.

Leaving what else I have to say till then I will
conclude and remain my dear Polly
                    Thine Affectionately
                              Jonathan Abbatt

P.S. If the frost continues perhaps I may skate
over on the canal

In the matter of 'passing the meeting' he is supportive
and he also encourages her to be a third time bridesmaid.
A large part of Mary's anxiety, in this third bridesmaid
affair at her brothers wedding, was due to David's
'marrying out' i.e. marrying Emma in a church. It seems
that the Emma's invitation/request to Mary was an offer
of a bridge so that acceptance or rejection was likely to
be of appreciable future significance to the two
families. In fact, both families became and remained very
close. Jonathan was one of David's executors being
referred to as "my lifelong friend Jonathan A."

On Sunday 18th February Jonathan writes from Bolton:

--- sister Jane is very much pleased at the prospect
of coming to see thee -- thou may expect her by
first or furthest 2nd train on third day [Tuesday]
morning but thou must not be disturbed to meet her
as she knows the way very well. I left her this
morning in bed [in Preston] with a bad cold but she
seems to think it will not prevent her coming as she
quite intends to see thee unless really unwell.

I was glad thy Grandmother [Mary [Jackson] Dilworth]
was still mending and hope she will soon be stirring
[getting about] again. Thou has no doubt heard of
Thomas Ord's fire and how careless he was.

Thou must really excuse my saying more at present as
T. Mulliner's wife has just called for a chat and it
just reminds me to tell thee that Thos. Mulliner
Senr. is deceased and is to be interred on 4th day
[Wednesday].

It was from Friend Thomas Mulliner that Jonathan had
bought his business a year earlier. In less than eighteen
months he lost his father, his old apprentice master and
the previous owner of his own shop.

On Wednesday 21st February in a brief note Jno.n retimes Jane's visit, after postponement, to the next day and Mary writes on that day telling of Jane's arrival:

    To: Jonathan Abbatt
           Friargate   Preston

Calder Bridge
22 of 2 mo 1855 [Thursday]

My dear Jonathan

Thy sister arrived safely I got only part of the way to the station to meet her, she has still a cold but hope the change will not make her worse, I should have been most sadly disappointed had she not been able to come.

We still keep my Grandmother in her bedroom, tho' I think she is almost as well as previous to her illness.

Has thou heard what a disappointment my cousin Daniel Pickard has had - he was to have been married yesterday, but on account of the illness of his lady love his marriage has had to be put off until some future time, she has been poorly five weeks or more. Mary Nichol has come in she is going to Preston this afternoon, I have packed Jane and her off to sit with Grandmother while I write to thee, but I have got hold of such a pen that I can scarcely get on. In a letter Mary had yesterday from Bessie Dixon she mentioned having seen thee in a shop, what she fancied thou was doing and so on; she seemed pleased to meet with thee I fancy thou art quite (as we used to call the lady at Ackworth) a P.G. of hers.

I have again heard from David he still wants me there, I have told him he must not expect me before I go to his wedding, he says that the 19th of 4 mo. is fixed for the important day - they have named it long enough before hand. I think he tells me quite in confidence tho'.

Well now thou must be content this time and believe me I remain as ever thine
                                    Mary Dilworth

Mary's scheme of clearing her decks when she packed off the newly arrived infectious Jane and Mary Nichol, to sit with her convalescent old Grandmother, show that the

Victorians had little idea of segregation of the
infectious. There is, of course, a suggestion that Mary
thinks that old Mary D. is perhaps 'spinning out' her
convalescence - she died, aged ninety in 1858, after
falling into the fire and suffering burns and a fracture.

Jonathan's next letter is business like and the people
mentioned:

- Cousin David is David Wilcockson.
- Aunt Amelia is wife of Isaac Wilcockson Senr.,
  proprietor of the Preston Chronicle.
- 'Mary' in para 3 is, of course, Mary Nichol and Bank
  Parade was the 'Ord' home where she was staying.
  Sarah and Maria were children of Mary Ann
  (Wilcockson) and Thomas Ord.
- Brewster and Burrows was a drapers at 5 and 6
  Fishergate - hence Jonathan's remark about his
  encounter with Bessie Dixon.
- The two weddings mentioned in para 9 are those of
  Mary Nichol and Sam Pickard and David Dilworth and
  Emma Goodall.

       To: Mary Dilworth
                Calder Bridge   Nr. Garstang

Preston
2 mo 25/55 [Sunday]

My Dear Mary

I was glad to receive thine on sixth day as usual
and was glad to hear thy Grandmother is still
improving and from sisters letter yesterday has got
downstairs again. Thy cousin David called me on
sixth day evening and told me thy Aunt Amelia was
very poorly and was ordered to be kept quiet and no
one to see her, but have not heard since though
perhaps you have.

I saw and spoke to Mary just as she was passing my
shop yesterday I presume she is a guest at Bank
Parade this time, she came to meeting this morning
with Sarah and Maria and sat with them though Mary
Ann was there, she looks very bright and lively.

So thy cousin Bessie mentioned me to Mary, I almost
thought she would notice what I was doing at
Brewster and Burrows, although we only had a short
interview she was very agreeable and shall be glad
at some future time to enjoy her company again,

perhaps when she comes on a visit to see us in <u>our own</u> comfortable home. I thought at one time of coming to see thee again on the 3rd day next but think I must defer it till the week following.

I have this last week bought a Kitchen Dresser like thy brother William's and only gave 30/- for it and intend to attend Fallows next sale on the 8th of next month (my birth day) when I hope to meet with something more useful. I shall have to take a house sometime in fourth month for I shall have to vacate the rooms where my furniture is by the 1st of 5 month [May] and from present prospects I hope to be able to get one somewhere in Chaddock Street. I was just thinking this morning it was almost time when, in 15 or 16 weeks we should be married.

It must truly have been a disappointment to thy cousin Daniel to defer his wedding especially under the circumstances but I hope she is getting better again; I made enquiry of thy cousin David who had been in Yorkshire but not having been in Leeds he had not heard.

I am thinking thou will feel thyself pretty well occupied to attend Mary's wedding next month and David's so soon after as the 19th of the fourth month [April] and then in the fifth publishing thy own wedding and 6th month making all secure.

I have just been down to meet my sisters who have just arrived well pleased with their out and Alice Ann has I hope satisfied her curiosity for she was certainly a little anxious to see thee though I scarcely thought Jane would have told thee so.

When in Bolton last first day I mentioned to my brother Thomas about having cousin David as Grooms Man and he thought with me it would be better if David will consent so in due time I suppose he must be consulted and if he agrees we will consider it fixed.

I am pretty busy now with overshoes the weather being so sloppy for it is really dirty just now.

Having almost filled my sheet I think I must once more my dear Polly say Farewell and hoping thou art no worse with thy dirty walk with my sisters to the Railway will subscribe myself
    Thine Affectionately
        Jonathan Abbatt

Jane and Alice Ann, eldest and youngest sister, have just
returned from Calder where A.A. has met Mary for the
first time, hence her curiosity. It is interesting that
Jonathan consults his brother Thomas about the
appropriateness and suitability of David Wilcockson to be
his, Jonathan's, groomsman. Otherwise, and if it had not
been for Mary's fondness for David, Thomas would probably
have been the first choice.

Jonathan's preoccupation with overshoes: 'the weather
being so sloppy', calls to mind town and country, walking
(and driving) conditions in the mid-fifties and for many
years afterwards. There was no tarmacadam or asphalt
paving in either towns or country. Preston, which was a
growing industrial cotton town, had some but not a great
deal of hard standing which consisted of either cobbles
or rectangular stone 'sets' and occasional paving stones
or 'flags'. Elsewhere there was crushed stone rammed with
mud and clay - or just mud and clay. Highways were
crushed stone and gravel rammed by the traffic; - and the
traffic was wholly horse driven. In both town and country
the numerous potholes were periodically filled with
gravel and crushed stones. The result was, particularly
in the wetter months, mud and water. In fine weather the
highways in particular were a continuing source of white
or yellow gritty dust. The Lancashire climate, which was
responsible for the cotton boom, consists of the school-
boys' four Ws.,(Warm, Wet, Westerly, Winds in Winter -
often with a preponderance of wetness) and it is not
surprising that there was a heavy demand for overshoes.

In the context of weather this is a convenient place to
imagine Jonathan's walking conditions, as they are
described above, along the road between Preston and
Calder Bridge for this was the main south to north road
from Preston to Lancaster and Scotland. The canal which
is nearly parallel to the road and railway was his one
alternative route, and here he would have had to compete
on a narrow muddy towpath with horses and bargees.

Mary's reply is short, pithy and very typical.

    To: Jonathan Abbatt
            Friargate   Preston

    Calder Bridge
    1 of 3 mo 1855 [Thursday]

    My dear Jonathan

    Thy welcome letter came to hand as usual must I tell
    thee it was I thought a nicer one than I have

received for some time, perhaps it might be that I
was in a better way than sometimes, yet so it was.
I hope Jane has got quite rid of her cold, give my
love to her and Alice Ann and also to thy Mother. I
expect Jane will have had a good deal to tell thee,
she said she should about me, I shall look for it
back again.

We had M.A. Ord came last night to this
neighbourhood I am glad Thomas is alright again, and
only wish he would keep so.

Three weeks yesterday we shall have this great event
taking place it will be a throng time.

Really Jonathan thou does make me out to be busy,
and so I am I can tell thee; my brother wants me to
be there at least a fortnight before the wedding.
Emma's brother is to be head man and my cousin Isaac
second.

I have heard this morning that Daniel's lady love is
still only poorly. I believe Robert and Esther are
coming to Mary's <u>stir</u> instead of him.

My Grandmother now goes about just the same as
before she was poorly, she and Mother are busy
talking. Jane told me thou has sometimes to write
to me during a storm of words so perhaps thou can
feel for me now, but very likely I am never as ill
troubled as thee as perhaps thou would at times be
disappointed on 6 o'clk. morning.

We are expecting Ann Wilcock to tea, she is on her
way from the Market. It is our O.L. Meeting next
third day did thou say thou was coming? But thou
will write before that time I expect. I suppose thy
Mother will be very busy with the one at Preston
today they will doubtless have a good muster.

This is I fear a poor return for thine but thou must
excuse it and allow me in true affection to remain
thine sincerely
     Mary Dilworth

Her brother David's choice of groomsmen reflects the same
type of careful 'political' choices as Jonathan's. David
has chosen his Emma's doctor brother, Ralph Goodall, as
best man and his cousin, Isaac Wilcockson, brother of
David and son of John and Jane (Dilworth) Wilcockson as
groomsman. What could be more tactful? In addition to
tact, it is another indication of acceptance - by both

families - of each other and of their different churches.

Jonathan's reply has interest because it contains one of his very few references to world affairs and their possible effects on his trade. Did other tradesmen think first of trade when they read of the Czar's death and succession?

    To: Mary Dilworth
            Calder Bridge   Nr. Garstang

Preston
3 mo 4/55 [Sunday]

My dear Polly

I must in the first place acknowledge the compliment thou has paid my last letter and presume thou has thought me getting somewhat careless latterly, but the last few I have written thee have been penned under disadvantages, either being from home or having my brothers company and not wishing to disappoint thee of thy 2nd days letter; but can assure thee it has not arisen from any lukewarmness for I can truly say the nearer the time comes when I shall have my every concern and every joy for thee to share, the more truly do I feel drawn in affection to thee and I must tell thee my dear Polly thou art more and more the subject of my thoughts and at times too when I should do well to have a thought on more important subjects.

My sister Jane left us on 6th day morning and we hope to hear from her tomorrow; poor lass she is such a home body I know it will be a trial for some time but will eventually prove beneficial to her.

Our friends O Leaf meeting for the first time was held in the friends meeting house and mustered something like 86 and after having tea for which each paid four pence there was eleven pence towards the circles funds which was quite a novelty and seemed to please very well. I understand R. Benson is so far interested as to endeavour to get them a room in the Mechanics Institution which will be better and will not look so much like a party concern - being disapproved by some as belonging exclusively to friends.

So it seems your O.L. Meeting is held on 3rd day, and perhaps as I was the cause of thy non attendance

last time I had better come on 4th day instead, I
think of coming by the 11 o'clock train as I return
so early, for thou must remember we shall have a
many things to talk of and arrange the nearer the
time comes.

How really delightful the weather is to day quite
like spring again and with its being so fine last
evening thou would be surprised how much more
business it caused me to do. Although business this
last month has been very quiet I have kept nicely on
the increase since last year and I find this last
week is about 6 pounds better than last year which
at that time I thought good, and now the Emperor of
Russia is dead and tis said his son Alexander (who
is more disposed for peace) is to be Emperor I hope
we may look again for good trade.

But I must not bore you with trade news so much for
I have a notion most women are not much interested
in trade concerns, however I can tell thee I have
just bought two nice sets of painted drawers for the
bedrooms and am really well pleased with them - they
are just to my fancy and I am rather particular in
such things however my taste suit thine when thou
comes to see them, however this too I will leave for
the present and hoping this may find thee well I
will conclude and remain as ever
                    Thine dearly
                            Jonathan Abbatt

The date of the next meeting - so as to ensure that Mary
is free to attend her Olive Leaf Meeting the day before -
may well be to diminish gossip, though it could have
indicated a genuine shared concern. It is from about
this time onwards that Jonathan begins to 'come to close
quarters' with the process of 'getting married': 'we
shall have a many things to talk of and arrange the
nearer the time comes.' -- Four days after the meeting:

    To: Mary Dilworth
         Calder Bridge   Nr. Garstang

    Preston
    3 mo 11th 1855 [Sunday]

    My dear Mary

    What a really cold and cheerless day it is, quite a
    contrast to the one I spent with thee and I feel
    myself very fortunate in having had so nice a time
    of it. I fancy thy mother would be glad to get home

200

again to her own cosy fire after her stormy journey here yesterday, I was pleased to hear thy Grandmother was better, and although Margt. Abbatt when here to tea was saying it was not yet quite decided to put Mary's wedding off another day I forgot to ask how it was settled.

Well now with regard to our own thou must remember before I can proceed any further I must have thy own and thy dear parents <u>written</u> consent with two witnesses to each and since I was with thee I have decided it might perhaps be more agreeable to solicit thy relations to be witnesses than any one else, so enclosed I have written out a form of what I think will be requisite ready for thee to make use of as thou may think fit, yet thou must remember as thou art going so soon after Mary's wedding to thy brothers thou should have it ready for me when I come next.

I suppose thou will think well thou art coming to close quarters, and it certainly does seem preparing a long time before hand yet as the discipline of our Society requires it there is no alternative.

I have again made more purchases since I saw thee and there are more sales to attend this week; I have got a very nice venetian blind and as I cant think of running away with thy chair from William's I shall buy thee one in place of it.

We have this week had a very eloquent address from George Thompson a report of which is in the newspaper on the right and wrong of war, when he advanced such arguments as noone dare oppose in condemnation of the war and the meeting dispersed I think generally satisfied.

I found on my return home on 4th day it had been an unusually quiet one for business but since that time it has brightened up and last night was very good and on comparing with last year I find I have an increased income of about 12/- per week clear above last year which considering the state of trade is very satisfactory.

I have great cause to feel thankful and feel there is truly an almighty care extended to me, from these considerations my dearest Polly I experience at times an indescribable glow of pleasure at the prospect of a union with thee and am persuaded we may live very comfortable, and still I hope to be able to pay off yearly about 50 pounds besides towards the 350 I have borrowed money, each 50 pounds paid will lessen my expenses 2 pounds 10 shillings per year, and with my business still increasing I hope soon to do more, from these statements thou will be able to realize my motives in wishing <u>at least</u> for a time to do without a servant, yet I will at the same time have thee to understand I dont wish my dear Polly to be "any mans slave" as thy worthy cousin said, for I hope by engaging some one each week to do the washing and rough cleaning so to arrange as to leave thee comparatively speaking at ease.

Thou will fancy me entering somewhat into details this time yet as they so much concern thee perhaps it may not be uninteresting, but having almost filled my sheet I must defer saying more till some future time so will conclude and in the mean time remain as ever   Thine affectionately
                                    Jonathan Abbatt

This letter, Mary's reply on Thursday 15th March and several of the subsequent ones give a good idea of the responsibility of the individual Friend for his own arrangements - and disposition. He, (in this context for 'he' read 'he or she'), could and did consult their friends and relations such as David Wilcockson or even Elders, but they were first and last responsible and accountable for themselves; there is no priest to guide, or blame. In the next three months, both Jonathan and Mary give clear evidence of their awareness of this responsibility, and also evidence of some of the associated strain. It is well to constantly remember that both were still young and not only very self-conscious but also genuinely anxious to do the correct and the 'good' thing.

In his letter of 3rd Jonathan leaves Mary in no doubt about their future financial state when married. It is interesting, too, that Jonathan had borrowed his money from the late John Fletcher at 5% interest and is more than conscious that the sooner this is reduced the better for his budget. Mary was left under no delusions about an early 'living in' help, though she was assured at the same time that there would be provision for someone 'do the rough'. It was not common for Victorian women to know anything of their husband's business and financial affairs so that the clear and relatively frequent passing and sharing of information is some evidence of the relatively great degree of sexual equality. In this Friends were different, and always had been, in regarding women as responsible and more or less equal people. The women of Jonathan's world not only knew about their menfolk's affairs, but expected to know. This state of sharing, while being the desired one, was not necessarily representative of all English Friends, spiritual equality did not by always carry over to the rest of life.

The "written consent" statement was, in Jonathan and Mary's case, needed by both parties because they were members of different Meetings.

Copy of draft provided by Jonathan to Mary in his letter of first day, 11th 3rd month 1855:

    1.   To the Preston Monthly Meeting of Friends.

    Dear Friends,

        It is with my consent that my friend Jonathan Abbatt lays before you his intention of marriage with me

                              Mary Dilworth

                Witnesses -------------
                          ----

    2.   To the Preston Monthly Meeting of Friends.

    Dear Friends,

        It is with our consent that Jonathan Abbatt lays before you his intention of marriage with our daughter Mary Dilworth

                            John J. Dilworth
                            Ann Dilworth

                Witnesses -----------

I think that the foregoing is all that will be necessary but to make certain of the exact form thou will perhaps have the opportunity of seeing thy cousin D. Wilcockson who will no doubt be able to tell thee to a certainty.   Thine etc.

                                                J.A.

Friends marriages had been recognised by the State, as being valid towards the end of the Commonwealth and there had been few changes in format or requirements. Personal appearance at each Meeting was necessary and if the parents, whose consent was obligatory whatever the age of the couple, were not present, then written permission was necessary. After this procedure, which is the equivalent of the Anglican publication of Banns of marriage, each Meeting appointed a committee to determine freedom from entanglements, and whether anyone had objections to the proposed union. Later we shall hear of Jonathan's committee and of some of the other steps involved.

Mary's response to the request for permission now follows. This letter is serious in tone and content, asking as it does for 'thy encouraging sympathy' which she receives in good measure the following Sunday:

> To: Jonathan Abbatt
> Friargate   Preston

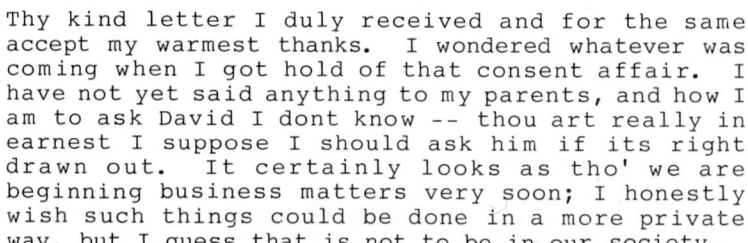

> Calder Bridge
> 3 mo 15th 1855 [Thursday]
>
> My dear Jonathan
>
> Thy kind letter I duly received and for the same accept my warmest thanks. I wondered whatever was coming when I got hold of that consent affair. I have not yet said anything to my parents, and how I am to ask David I dont know -- thou art really in earnest I suppose I should ask him if its right drawn out. It certainly looks as tho' we are beginning business matters very soon; I honestly wish such things could be done in a more private way, but I guess that is not to be in our society.
>
> A week yesterday and we shall have this grand stir on I suppose. Mary tells me they are thinking of driving Northward for their out, she is in famous spirits - for my part I dont see how she keeps up as she does. Now Jonathan dont thee say anything but I must once more tell thee I do at times feel as tho' I stood in need of thy encouraging sympathy, yet I would not for a moment have thee think I doubt thy love for me; no my dear Jonathan thine I have good reason to hope and believe will be a lasting affection, truly married people have need of an affectionate and loving heart - but I will have done with that subject or perhaps I shall almost frighten thee as thou did me on 2nd day morning.

I hope you have good accounts from Jane, Mary had a
letter from Esther the other day she said she had
<u>seen</u> Jane and sat in her company some time before
she knew she was such a near relation to Jonathan, I
fancy they will get quite good friends.

We still hear but a poor account of Daniel's lady
love - that she is able to leave her bed only a
short time each day, last first day but one he was
over to see her he thought her looking a little
better, I do hope she will get out again.

We were indeed favoured with the fine weather the
day thou spent here. I hope next 4th day will be as
fine, how cold and damp we have it today.

Father and Mother were at Lancaster M.M yesterday so
I had the time to myself, I suppose William Waitham
is to be disowned.

George Satterthwaite and his wife from Manchester
are in this neighbourhood, they called on us this
morning - they are Joseph Jacksons guests. We are
going to have tea soon and then I am going over to
see if I can render any assistance to my dear worthy
cousin, poor lass she will be quite throng at this
interesting and important time. I am well pleased
to hear thy business is still pretty good, and tho'
I seldom say much about such things to thee do not
fear that such information is lost on me.

Well now I must take an affectionate leave of my
dear friend and will remain his ever faithfull

               Mary

The people and events in Mary's letter are:

- David Wilcockson - about consent.
- 'this grand stir' is Mary Nichol's wedding to Sam Pickard.
- Jane Abbatt now in Leeds, Mary N. hears from Esther (Pickard) Shaw.
- Unfortunately we do not know what Wm. W. had done to be disowned - nor who he was.

Jonathan's Sunday letter is a clear and helpful response
to Mary's request for support. He is clear, light in
touch - 'induced to wish I had been concealed in some sly
corner --- '; and later supportive, and understandingly
kind and forward looking.

To: Mary Dilworth
Calder Bridge Nr. Garstang

Preston
3 month 18 '55 [Sunday]

My dear Polly

My turn soon comes round again to address thee and with pleasure I sit down to acknowledge the receipt of thine in which thou tells me I almost frightened thee in my last about this <u>consent affair</u> as thou calls it. I was induced to wish I had been concealed in some sly corner just in sight of thee when thou was reading it and then to come out on thee all at once, perhaps I may follow my letter, sometime and try it on, but about this consent affair, I endeavour to persuade myself thou does not <u>really dread</u> our coming wedding so much as thou would have me believe. I readily believe thou feels very weightily the undertaking but I trust not more than I do, and yet it is a source of deep joy to me though at times from a sense of its importance I may be rendered thoughtful. Yet when I reflect on thy disposition and a many of thy inestimable qualities which seem so peculiarly adapted to render me happy I can but feel I have every reason for joy, and though thou expresses confidence in my affection thou truly remarks that married people have need of loving hearts, I have endeavoured all in my power to view what our future positions may be, and I can truly say there is nothing in that view otherwise than to produce a gladness of heart, I do not truly confine myself to view the bright side only I can scarcely expect to push through life without trials and yet I trust we may with endeavours to do right and a trust in him who reigns above be so prepared that such trials as he may in his inscrutable wisdom see fit to [try] us with as to prepare us for an inheritance to come where we may be united for ever in bliss, and join in heavens holy throng in singing praises to the lamb.

I little thought on second reading of thy last I should be led thus to express myself, and though I can fully sympathize with thee and feel to realize <u>thy</u> feelings in this important engagement yet I may venture to tell thee that it is a blank at times to me when I see thee thus backward and fearful, and although at times it may seem hard to leave a comfortable home where every want is amply provided, for one where thou may have to practice economy and where we may have to live on 100 pounds a year yet with our trust in God and in each others love, and with steadiness and perseverance I feel bound to say we may realize more of happiness and true enjoyment than a many in more exalted circumstances.

Oh my dearest Mary I think I cannot convey to thee how much I have felt on this account, often have I asked myself was it right to draw thee from home and its comforts to share one with me as yet uncertain; even though it increase my happiness ever so much, and were it not that I have a trust in a supreme power, in an Almighty care taker, together with my own ability and diligence with brightening prospects, I think I think I should have been faint hearted in asking thee to be my wife.

Thou must not think thou has frightened me at what thou has said although it has led me to write so much more than I thought, yet having a desire thou should fairly understand me I have written the above for thy encouragement and do sincerely trust as the time approaches thou may feel more and more confidence but perhaps I ought hardly to say confidence as I think the thoughts of leaving thy parents is the most trying, and whilst it is pleasant to witness so sincere an attachment it is desirable thou should endeavour to prepare thyself for the coming change.

This morning Jane Gornall was interred at our Meeting house her poor sister in such a condition as is expected soon to follow and Richard Gornall poor man under his heavy trials looks cast down and dispirited. I saw Mary yesterday and spoke to her just as she was passing the shop.

We have heard again from Jane who writes in famous spirits but nothing about seeing thy cousin Esther. I suppose thou will be at home next 3rd day but one and if disengaged propose coming then. I might have come on the humiliation day but as the wedding is at that time thou will be so engaged as to have not the time to look even on me so that is out of the question.

I bring my letter to rather an abrupt close but as Saml. Cragg is awaiting to have a walk thou must excuse more at the present from
    Thine very affectionate
      Jonathan Abbatt

Samuel Cragg who was waiting to go for a walk with Jonathan was another descendant of Jennet Cragg.

Mary Nichol's wedding passes off well, and is responsible for a shorter than usual 'Mary' letter on Thursday 22nd March telling Jno. that she had even resolved:

> --- this "consent affair", well I got David [Wilcockson] into a quiet corner and he told me they are near right, but we can talk --- .

Well and this great grand day is at last here, and I am happy to tell thee everything passed off in first class order. I think not one of the party could miss being pleased with the proceedings throughout the day, everyone seemed to be quite at home, and made their minds up to enjoy themselves. Our bride and bridegroom said their say well, and Mary poor lass kept up wonderfully, tho' as she said was ready for a good cry and I doubt not longed for some quiet corner as did most of us at times, the ladies I mean. They left a little before 6 o'clock.   --- thou does not need to think I forgot thee yesterday even. I had good reason for that I wonder how many times I was told my turn would be next and asked "whats to do Jonathans not here", and the like.

Mary had now 'turned her corner' and does not again indulge in doubts and questioning. The example of her friend and cousin had no doubt cheered and encouraged her in what was a near dress rehearsal, both with place and people, for her own wedding in three months' time.

As a boy in the early nineteen thirties the editor was present and signed the marriage certificate of Mary (Nichol) Pickard and James and Elizabeth Labrey Jackson's grandchildren. The wedding was that of the editor's cousin James Pickard with Janet Rowlandson. James was the son of Clement and Christine Labrey (Jackson) Pickard. Clement being Mary Nichol's son and Christine, daughter of James and Elizabeth (Labrey) Jackson of Oakenclough. This Jackson/Pickard wedding at Calder Bridge was the last of the 'Families' weddings to take place at the Friends Meeting House Calder Bridge.

Both Jonathan and Mary have affection but also an obvious 'aweful' regard for and were regardful of their parents. There was little, if any, true communication between generations, with no sharing of innermost feelings. The next letter illustrates this when Jonathan tells Mary (parafive) of a conversation with David Wilcockson in which: ' --- he said on fourth day [Wednesday] thou had not mentioned my proceedings to thy parents, but was glad he had advised thee -- '. The letter follows:

To: Mary Dilworth
    Calder Bridge   Nr. Garstang

Preston
3 mo 25/55   [Sunday]

My dear Polly

Thine was duly to hand and though short was quite as long as expected considering the bustle you must have had, indeed I almost thought thou would miss this time but was agreeably disappointed.

We had my brothers [Thomas'] company on 4th day with his wife and little one and had Jane Thomas staying till sixth day night when Alice Ann returned with her to spend a few days in Bolton, and this afternoon being so temptingly fine my Mother, brother and myself have had a nice out to Longridge where we enjoyed ourselves much.

I was much pleased on 5th day to have a visit from thy cousins Bessy and Frank who were exceedingly warm hearted and pleasant, Bessy gave me the piece of bride cake which I suppose you suggested between you for which I am obliged. I have not seen thy cousin Sarah but perhaps will ere long. I was glad you had so fine a day though cold and windy and was pleased all passed off so nicely, I have heard pretty much of your proceedings both from Bessy and William.

Thy cousin David called on me yesterday and we had a good chat together of various things concerning ourselves and about the house I have engaged etc. but as I did not sit down with the intention of writing thee a long letter this time (hoping to see thee so soon). I will defer entering into particulars until then, he said on fourth day thou had not mentioned my proceedings to thy parents, but was glad he advised thee to do so, and though I believe thou finds it a trial to begin yet I hope thou will find a relief when thou obtains their approval and trust thou will then my dear Polly begin to look forward with less faltering and more firmness to the coming change.

But I must for this time stay my pen or I shall be going to greater lengths than I intended and defer saying more until 3rd day when I hope to leave here at 11 o'clock and can then talk over our affairs and must also have a talk with thy dear parents to whom I have said little yet relating to ourselves.

Hoping we may again have a fine day when we can enjoy our accustomed walk I will once more my dear Polly take an affectionate farewell and remain as ever   Thine
                                    Jon.n Abbatt

Thomas and Jane A. were making their first visit, with their new baby, to grandmother Elizabeth A.'s Preston home, and, no doubt, Thomas was able to see The House that Jonathan had 'engaged' (rented) at Number 4 Chaddock Street where they first lived. Numbers 1-5 Chaddock Street have been demolished and replaced with a small factory and Trade Union stand.

Before Mary's letter arrived Jonathan had already heard about the Pickard Calder Bridge wedding from her cousins, Bessie and Frank Dixon. He had too received a piece of the 'bride cake' from William Dilworth, her elder brother. In earlier times Friends did not have wedding cakes, as such, though there was usually a meal associated with the wedding. This was provided primarily for those who had travelled some distance.

WILLIAM DILWORTH (1822-1901)

William, Mary's eldest brother, was born at Caton Green shortly before his parents moved to Ortner in Wyresdale. After attending the Friends school in Wyresdale he was sent to Ackworth for three years, which was intended to be a prelude to joining his father on the farm. However, after a very few years William went to Preston where he became a moderately successful grocer and later a farmer. Like his brother David, William left Friends shortly before his marriage (4/V/1856) to Alice Bibby of Condor Green. They had eight children, of whom seven were girls. The only boy - John Jackson - died at the age of six and his Dilworth name died with him. (One of Alice's sisters Betty (Elizabeth) married Thomas Kelsall of Wyresdale.) William's Wyresdale roots proved strong and he retired to his parents old home at Ortner where he died aged eighty. His nephew, Dilworth A., remembered him as a kindly, diffident, remote and a lonely old man.

On 31st March Mary writes from Sam and Mary (Nichol) Pickard's new home in Lancaster. In 150 words Mary alludes to six people and also to others as 'my cousins', clearly showing the profusion of people in her world.

--- thought I might as well inform thee of my safe arrival at my cousins new home: they got into the house about 1/4 hr before me so they tell me I was a pretty bridesmaid to be just too late to receive the bride, we are to have David's company before long, he will be staying over --- . Shall I receive my usual letter on second day? thou must address Lune Terrace [Samuel Pickard Senior's home] if thou should write. My father has been here ---

Jno. now shows that he, too, can be brief and to the point. Samuel Pickard's home at Lune Terrace was in Skerton, Lancaster and was demolished in the nineteen sixties to be replaced by apartments/flats:

>To: Mary Dilworth
>Samuel Pickard
>Lune Terrace   Nr. Lancaster

Preston
4 mo 1 /55 [Sunday]

My dear Polly

I must once again beg thy excuse for a short letter as this one may be, although an important one. I have been to Bolton along with my brother James today to see my brothers on an important piece of business of which I will tell thee when next we meet. I find our preparative meeting was held <u>today</u> and our Monthly meeting to be on 5th day <u>next</u>, being held a week earlier on account of the Quarterly meeting so that I shall after all require thy written consent as well as thy parents, ready for <u>fifth day</u> so I purpose being at Calder Bridge on the 4th day afternoon instead of Good Friday by train leaving here at 1 o'clock. I shall be sorry to take thee from amidst thy Lancaster friends but we must give our attention to this interesting piece of business and thinking thy dear parents would like to know early I shall just drop them a few lines to acquaint them of my requirements this afternoon.

Well now Polly dont this rather surprise thee that we have to make a beginning earlier than usual, I must confess when first I heard I almost thought I had made a blunder and began to calculate whether we should have to put off a month longer or not, but hoping thou and thy parents can have the needful all

ready when I come we shall be alright yet, and being
your meeting day perhaps we can get someone to sign
as witnesses; but really how needless the
regulations of our society are in this matter,
however there is no alternative.

Hoping thou will excuse more at present I will
conclude and remain   Thine as ever
                                    Jonathan Abbatt

Mary responds - with a change of plan and the request:
' -- thou must please write by return -- .'!

    To: Jonathan Abbatt
           Friargate   Preston

Lune Terrace
4 mo 2/55 [Monday]

My dear Jonathan

Thy letter of this morning would have surprised me
very much (at least the contents would) had not my
cousin David told me yesterday that your M.M. was to
be held this week, so that I was somewhat prepared
for it. I am very glad thou has written to my
parents, and if thou has quite made up thy mind to
present this M.M. I suppose I must write my consents
out here and get Samuel and Mary to sign it, and I
have been thinking if thou could come to C.B. by the
4 o'clock train on the 4th day and stay over night
(as thou would be in plenty of time for Meeting the
next morning) I would return by the 1/4 after 4
o'clock train from Lancaster: so that we shall
almost meet at the station - or perhaps thou may get
there a short time before me: we might then write
these consents out and perhaps Joseph and Lucy
Jackson might sign it. I shall have some shopping
to do on 4th day morning so that I cannot leave
before afternoon. We have had to sit in state today
only nine friends have been to call upon us yet,
tomorrow must pass in the like manner.

Thou dost not say if thou has received my shabby
note yesterday or not but suppose thou has not. This
consent work really I do wish that we could do
without it.

Well thou must please write by return post and say
if my plans suit thee; and at the same time perhaps
thou will have time to tell me what thou has been to

Bolton about or did thou do it to make me wonder? what thy business could be there!!! Sarah and Jane have come to see what I am doing, they will have it that I am writing to thee, well as it happens they are not far wrong tho' they do not know it. I have enjoyed my visits very much indeed only sometimes I have been almost wild, we have not had much quietness I can assure thee.

Hoping this may find thee well and expecting to have a line on 4th day morning. I am thine truly
Mary Dilworth

It is interesting to see that Mary invites Jonathan to spend the night at C.B. so that he may 'present this M(onthly) M(eeting)'. Why, if it is so easy, has he not been invited to stay before instead of being seen off to trudge home to Preston in the rain and snow?

When Mary and her Cousin: 'sat in state today, only nine friends came' - they were part of the "calling" and "Morning visits" system which welcomed the new bride in her home. These visits were always made in the afternoon, never at meal times and were accompanied by the leaving of calling cards. Etiquette demanded that the bride return the calls within a set time, failing which there would be no further communion between caller and callee. Though the system was rigid, by the mid-fifties, "friendship" as opposed to "visits of congratulation, condolence" or "ceremony" were made with less formality.

Jonathan replies as requested 'by return post':

> --- fully approve of thy plans and will make it my business to come by the 4 o'clock train and will wait till thy train --- .
> --- about my journey to Bolton --- was in consequence of a report we had heard of Sam Jespers intended treatment to my brother James and as he has seen indications of its truth in Sam's behaviour to him for the past few weeks we concluded it best for James to leave, and he has accordingly given notice, so what I wrote surrounded with such mystery is soon unravelled and I can explain more when we meet --- .

James did leave 'Jesper and Wilson's' and we soon hear more of the Sam Jesper/James affair. This conflict of brother and best friend was very difficult for Jonathan.

The consents were duly signed and Jonathan made his personal appearance at his own Monthly Meeting on the Thursday as we hear from his letter on the Friday. His

Preston appearance over, Jonathan is anxious to deal quickly with Mary's own Monthly Meeting - Calder Bridge.

To: Mary Dilworth
      Calder Bridge   Nr. Garstang

Preston
4 mo 6 1855 [Friday]

My dear Polly

I just sit down to scribble thee a few lines and inform thee of the impression my <u>speech</u> made yesterday, I can assure thee it was received with eclat and gave universal satisfaction!!!! Insomuch that <u>I</u> am pointed at as a young man worthy of imitation. What does thou say? well done thee, well but I must give thee an instance, thy cousin David was coming down Chaddock Street this afternoon along with Isaac Fearon when he was told it was hoped both himself and R. Veevers would look to me as an example and take courage thereby to commence at once a change in their way of life. Oh just whilst I think on, David was asking about his likeness and wishes thee to bring it when thee comes.

Thou sees I have not been to Penketh or anywhere else but the shop today, but though stopping at home hope I have not spent my time unprofitably. I have had a very long and confidential talk with Sam Jesper and find on <u>both</u> sides there has been quite a misunderstanding of each other and some misrepresentations which I have cleared up to satisfaction and there is now a prospect of James staying in his place and having a comfortable situation which is very pleasing to us all.

Although Sam has been somewhat injudicious yet on the whole he has acted as I should have done myself and am happy to inform thee my <u>previous good</u> opinion is not only renewed but thoroughly improved and T. Lester I also hold in high esteem, and yet after all James has had a very good seeming reason for his surmises which Sam honestly admits.

Charles Wilson has made out my certificate for thy Monthly M. and handed it me last night what if thou stops at home and we attend your next M.Meeting next week? Having seen thee so recently and hoping to see thee then so soon again thou must excuse more this time from   Thine ever Affectionate
                                                 Jonathan

Mary writing on Sunday 8th April salutes her friend:

'My dearest Jonathan' --- --- on the able manner in which thou got through with thy say, I often thought of thee on that day in particular. --- My cousin [David Wilcockson] is going at 1/2 past 5 so I must be off and make tea ready. I intend him to take this to Preston to post and then it will save me or someone else a walk to Garstang. I intend to be in Preston on third day day morning by the first train, and go on at 1/2 after 10, my brother will meet me at Whitmore, I had a note from him this morning.

Mary is on her way to Newcastle for her brother David's wedding having 'got this consent business' out of the way. She is happy and pleased with life, with Jonathan and herself, and dashes off a short cheerful note more or less commanding Jonathan to meet her for an hour at Preston Station as she passes through. In his usual Sunday reply Jonathan is equally happy and despite 'I dont seem to have much to say' - tells of many things:

    To: Mary Dilworth
            David Dilworth
            Newcastle-under-line   Staffordshire

Preston
4 Month 15 /55 [Sunday]

My dearest Polly

I am glad once more of my turn to write to thee though I dont seem to have much to say this time, yet as this will bring from thee a reply I shall be well pleased, for when our usual course of writing is interupted it seems so long before I hear from thee when a sixth day is omitted and no word from thee.

I shall perhaps not hear from thee before the wedding as thou will be so busy, when perhaps thou will let me know how thou got to thy destination, and what probable time thou has fixed for thy return with a history of your proceedings; for though not so full of information myself I am quite inquisitive and interested in your proceedings. I have again had a nice business week though not quite so brisk as last year though more profitable, and am also quite busy getting furniture and shall I expect have workmen in the house this week. I seem to have almost all my furniture but shall still have a many things to buy when I get in possession of the house. I got this week a very nice rocking chair for thee - cane seat and back. I have got some nice crimson damask to recover the best chairs with and think they will look really elegant.

We have had the company of Henry Fletcher this afternoon on his way to Longridge and as it is the fair there tomorrow he was in hopes of seeing thy Father there who he seems quite wishful to see again.

I purpose being at the Quarterly meeting on the 4th day and having some business to transact hope to pay my expenses at the same time, and in passing through Bolton intend stopping to see my brothers so shall make it an out of pleasure as well, and as a first rate friends coat maker lives there shall leave an order for my <u>wedding</u> <u>coat</u>.

Dear me Jonathan what a letter writer thou art!! did any one see such a mixed medley of matters before!! Thou seems determined to spin a long yarn out of something even though it <u>bothers</u> me to read it!! If these be thy exclamations I shall have to remind thee of what thou said when I wrote a few shabby short letters some time ago, but to have done with nonsense I may tell thee Joseph Jesper is still rapidly improving and can now sit up for some 5 to 6 hours at a time and a good deal of this they attribute to the homeopathic doctors skill who seems to be much in favour with our Preston friends.

Mother had tea on 5th day with Isabella Benson who seems quite pleased to talk about our coming wedding; and in remarking to my Mother how busy she would be said - and then there will be brides visiting etc. - so thou sees our friends are chalking out our course for us. I can just fancy I. Benson talking about us in great glee for I have heard she is considered by some quite a match maker isnt it queer that some such ladies should delight so much in this sport may I call it.

Well not wanting to disappoint thee of this in the morning I must conclude before post time and hoping to hear from thee when thou has convenience will remain as ever   Thine Truly
                                      Jonathan Abbatt
P.S. Enclosed I forward the penny I borrowed with thanks.

Henry Fletcher, brother of Jno.'s dead Master John, was a friend of Mary's father. See Chapter III page 45.

A Quaker wedding coat necessitated a Quaker tailor or coat maker. Jonathan, naturally generous but frugal where frugality and high standards were possible, obviously felt that he would do better in Bolton than with his friend Sam Jesper! A Quaker coat was very simple, being completely without ornamentation. There were no lapels, no unnecessary pockets or buttons, indeed, it was without "Buttons and Bows". Mary, as we shall soon hear, was to be married in a Quaker bonnet and their wedding was one of the last at Calder Bridge where the bride, the groom and many of the guests were in full Quaker garb.

In his next letter Jonathan thanks Mary for a letter now lost; and this, to judge from his almost ecstatic first paragraph, must have been one of her most affectionate. This letter is a real loss, too, because it described David and Emma D.'s wedding.

    To: Mary Dilworth   David Dilworth
           Newcastle   Staffordshire

Preston
4 mo 23rd 1855 [Monday]

My dearest Polly

Thy <u>welcome</u> letter was to hand this morning, doubly so in not having heard from thee for so long and am delighted to notice the more expressive form of endearment used in thy two last which are extremely agreeable the more so as in thy case I truly believe is sincerely heartfelt I dont know whether it is a weakness in me or not to feel such inexpressible satisfaction at these much prized expressions of thy fond affection yet during our acquaintance it has been a true source of pleasure to me to watch the gradual development of thy love for me, and to address me as in thy last two as dearest seems to have been the summit of my wishes and may tell thee it has not gone unlooked for; perhaps thou will consider me weak on this point well I am ready to admit it. For a little tenderness from one I love does seem to soften and humble me astonishingly. The above I have written out of a full heart and are intended for thy eyes alone.

I am glad to hear of thy intention of returning home though perhaps not in accordance with thy brothers and <u>sisters</u> wish, what a delightful time they must have had and it so fine, and pleasant it must have been on the wedding day tending to make you all feel light hearted and happy. Leamington was the resort of my brother William and his bride after their wedding which is I suppose considered a very nice place.

I enjoyed myself in Manchester on 4th day along with my brothers, we all got our likeness in a group to send to my Uncle in America who has not seen any of the family for 12 years wont he see a fine lot of lads!!! I also have got a copy for our own mantle piece to hang along side my sisters, and should dearly like the different members of thy own family either singly or in a group including conspicuously thy venerable Grandmother I should prize it much.

Workmen have got in the house and are making a very satisfactory job of it I have made the choice of the papers and think thou will [be] pleased with my choice, the landlady seems to spare no expense to make us comfortable and in the course of the next few weeks hope to have a nice looking home for thee to come to.

We have good accounts of Jane yet but she is quite wishingto be at home again and my mother is quite intending her a surprise when she comes. I went with my mother on sixth day to get a model of her mouth taken for a new set of teeth and intend meeting Jane without letting her know previously and see how she finds it out, she felt quite desirous to have teeth before our wedding took place and I feel glad she is going to get them she looks so much better and younger.

Henry Fletcher met thy Father in Longridge last 2nd day and had a rare chat with him and seems quite inclined to slip over to Calder Bridge some time to see you again. He also met other North acquaintances and enjoyed (with his little son) his out very much.

William Wood was at Quarterly Meeting and made enquiry of thee and Mary Pickard as also did George and Ellen Glover they seem quite Q.M. friends so regular in attending them. Well now I think I must bring my letter to a close and whilst wishing thou may feel no worse for thy <u>midnight</u> <u>revels</u> (of which with a long string of other news I hope to hear on seeing thee) I will remain my dear Polly
        Thy loving Friend   Jonathan Abbatt

THE MANCHESTER PHOTOGRAPH – Wednesday 18th April 1855
Left to right: William, James, Thomas and JONATHAN Abbatt.
'A fine lot of lads.'

THE OLD FRIENDS' MEETING HOUSE, FRIARGATE, PRESTON.
This was JONATHAN's Meeting, built in 1782 and rebuilt 1847.

JONATHAN and MARY's 'AT HOME' WEDDING CARD
Printed by Thomas Abbatt of Bolton – 1855.

A 1903 JACKSON WEDDING at WOODLANDS, GARSTANG
The 'new' home of Richard Jackson of Oakenclough was occupied by his nephew Frederic and Florence (Dilworth) until her death in 1943. This wedding was that of Ernest and Bertha Jackson – the guests in addition to Jacksons, include Dilworths, Pickards, Satterthwaites and Simpsons.

The Manchester photograph was prominent for many years in the Abbatt children's homes. It is interesting that the four brothers all show signs of early baldness. This inherited phenomenon has occurred in some members of four succeeding generations.

False teeth for Elizabeth A. senior were very much a family concern, since her health had been poor for some time, even before Benjamin's death in 1853. Jonathan notes the beginning of a dramatic improvement in her health which followed the extraction. At this time, though false teeth were by no means 'new', they were far from common, and their fitting and use was frequently accompanied by a great deal of pain and discomfort. The cosmetic result was only fair and the observer was never in doubt as to who wore 'artificials' or 'pot uns'.

My Mother has got her new teeth in this last week and although they are tolerably easy she scarcely looks natural in them yet, but improves with use.

Emma Goodall's diary entries for the same period read:

10th April Tuesday: 'Mary [Dilworth] and D[avid] D[ilworth] came, met her at Whitmore -- Had my dress tried on. D. drove us up again. Cake came.'

As planned David met his sister at Whitmore Station, Emma had the final fitting for her dress - probably in Newcastle - and David drove her home again. There can be little doubt about the nature of the cake and the dress, but unlike Mary's they were not home made - at home!

12th April Thursday 'D.D. came'.

15th Sunday: 'Mary Dilworth and D.D. here to tea and supper with us.'

19th Thursday: 'Our Wedding Day and may God's Blessings rest on us'.

20th Friday: 'Spent a very pleasant day at Leamington'.

Emma's diary tells us that on subsequent days they went to Warwick Castle, Guy's Cliff, Kenilworth and then on Monday 23rd April to Stratford on Avon where she bought a piece of muslin at Shakespeare's House.

Mary's last letter from Newcastle needs no explanation, again it shows faith in the speed and reliability of the mail. Mr. North periodically took tea at the Goodalls.

    To: Jonathan Abbatt
            Friargate
            Preston, Lancashire.

Newcastle
4/25/55 [Wednesday]

My Dearest Jonathan

I just drop thee a line to say tomorrow I leave about 2 o'clock so shall be in Preston somewhere towards 5 o'c so wilt thou have time to come to the station, I wrote to David W. this morning but did not then know the time I would start. I intend being over night in Preston of course I cannot get back now. It will be nice to be home again. I have been spending the day with Mr. North and have to make another call late as it is.

Hoping this will find thee well I will say goodnight remaining as ever thine,
                    Mary Dilworth

At their 'reunion' in Preston on Thursday and Friday the couple plan a Calder meeting the following Tuesday and Jonathan writes on Sunday 29th to confirm the time:

    Thou must not expect much from me this time as I hope to see thee so soon again, and feel rather idle today, yesterday I was very busy and kept serving customers until 1/2 past 12 last night. My Mother almost began to get uneasy about me as it was near 1 o'clock when I got home. I have had a real good week again.

    Thy cousin David went with me from the railway when we had seen thee off, to look through <u>our</u> house so thou canst fish from him for his opinions about it when thou sees him, tomorrow I expect will see most of the furniture in the house and every day I expect to see it look more to my mind.

    Thy cousin Mary Ann was at Meeting this morning but not Thomas, we were favoured too with one of Sarah Ord's solemn sermons, quite a revival again she has been rather silent for some time past. ----

    P.S. I had almost forgot thou would receive this on thy birth day, though I have thought of it

previously and though I forward nothing tangible more than this I tender thee my dear Polly my sincere wishes for a many happy returns.
J.A.

Mid-Victorian tradespeople were clearly willing to keep their shops open literally 'until all hours' if there were business to be done. It is not at all surprising that Elizabeth A. was becoming uneasy about her son, most mothers of other ages would have sent out search parties long before midnight. The next paragraph of the same letter clearly shows that Jonathan was already proud of his new, though still unfinished home. But in all the excitement of reunions, furnishing and business, Jonathan has forgotten Mary's birthday and all he can do is add a Postscript to his letter!

Though the 'consent business' is nearly finished there still remains the personal appearance of the pair at Mary's own Monthly Meeting. This was a serious and important occasion as can be seen from Jonathan's letter telling of visitors likely to attend Calder Bridge M. M.

    To: Mary Dilworth
           Calder Bridge   Nr. Garstang

Preston
5 mo 6th 1855 [Sunday]

My dearest Polly

Will thou expect a long letter from me this time when I see thee so soon again, when I hope we shall manage our business comfortably although I find we shall have a many visitors curious to hear us, Sam Jesper talks of attending your Monthly Meeting, and I suppose the Pickards will be there as Emma Veevers talks of being over on that day. I have written to my brother Thomas to have his company and I think he intends coming and should not be surprised to see William too, he has business in Preston and think it likely he will go on so far.

I gave your kind invitation to my Mother which pleased her much but having again heard from poor Jane who intends returning on 5th day next she begs to decline your kindness for the present at least, being quite wishful to be at home to receive her and hear all the news etc. but she may be better able to decide ere she sees you.

My Mother has got her new teeth in this last week and although they are tolerable easy she scarcely looks natural with them yet, but improves with use.

Our meeting commences to be held in the evenings today and although Sam Jesper is renewing his old custom of engaging me to walk with him I must not let it interfere with my writing to thee. Our preparative meeting was held today and an appointment made to select a fresh clerk in place of Sam who has been in that Post for five years and although I am one on that appointment I fear they are about aiming at me though I hope not - I should really like to be excused such an honour.

How smart and trim thy cousin David was today at meeting with his new hat etc. He and Robert Benson fulfilled their mission to me this morning in ascertaining if I have any other engagement on hand in the matrimonial way, what a nonsense it seem to ask such questions when all is so clear beforehand, however it may have had its uses.

I was excedingly busy yesterday and have had a really good week once more and amidst all complaints can still report a comfortable increase on last years receipts having made a gross profit this past week of 7 pounds or more so I feel tolerably well satisfied.

I hope when thy dear Mother comes to Preston we may have some of her company here, I should just like her to see what I have got, for my Mother I think has now made all except short curtains and intends this week to begin with carpets though we have not bought them yet.

I have a washstand and about 1/2 dozen chairs to get yet and then I calculate after we have laid the carpets the house will begin to look finished for a house really does not look home when there are no carpets down. I have got two good quilts that I think will suit thee well, they are not the knotted ones but I dont know what they call them though after thy Mother has seen them she can explain to thee.

I mentioned to Jane about thy things from D. Pickard and she will be glad to bring anything thou may have to come and as thy Mother will perhaps be in Preston she can bring them with her when she returns.

> Well now Polly I hope when I see thee on fourth day to find thee in good spirits, thou must cast all fears to the winds and as we have not much to say we can surely manage such a bit easily and in hopes we may have a fine day which will add to the pleasure of all I will remain as ever
>
> Thine Truly
>
> Jonathan Abbatt

Though William A. (a probable) had business in Preston, Thomas travelled from Bolton and back specifically to support his brother. The paragraph referring to David Wilcockson and Robert Bensons ' mission ' --- in ascertaining if I had any other engagements on hand in the matrimonial way -- ' refers the their joint function as the committee appointed by Preston Meeting after Jonathan's notice of intention to marry. The committee's function was to enquire into Jonathan's freedom from entanglements, both by general enquiry and by personal interview, and then to report back to the Meeting.

The mention of ' --- a washstand and about 1/2 dozen chairs to get yet --- ' are only the latest in a long list of acquisitions for 4 Chaddock Street, which tells us that young peoples' methods of acquisition of furniture and belongings have changed little. During the last six months or more of the letters, Jonathan's activites have been a long succession of sales, and refurbishings. Young people now furnish in exactly the same manner after acquiring their belongings at the 20th century counterparts of his sales i.e. in 'modern' flea markets, garage sales and sale rooms.

Jonathan writes a brief note on returning from Calder Bridge M.M. on Tuesday 8th May. He is clearly pleased:

> --- just arrived home again all pleased with the days out ---- and for myself feels like having done a good days work. ---- I find my sister had still got the pattern and forthwith enclose it --- looks rather dark yet I think it will make up nicely --- .

The material referred to above is of great importance as it is for Mary's bonnet.

On Tuesday 15th May Jonathan writes after seeing Mary the previous day in Preston where she has been shopping:

> I hope thou got nicely home last night though thou would have rather a dark walk. [The walk from Garstang and Catterall Station to Calder Bridge would take about 15 minutes.] Jane has heard from

> --- thy cousin Esther (Pickard) Shaw along with the dress piece she ordered, but was sorry to hear they consider Robert (Shaw) no better and for a change is gone to live in Meeting house yard. Esther herself thinks the doctor looked a little alarmed yet. I have got something like 50 names down to send cards to but must compare with thine to see if I have got any of thine down, perhaps when I come over ---- .

Later on 27th May after discussing 'cards and lists' with Mary he says:

> --- writing to my brother Thomas about our cards I dont know that I can find a nicer plan than Sam and Mary Pickard adopted, that is, to have the name on the envelope, and the address on the card, I just enclose thee a sample of the type I like best, which I think very neat. I am intending to order 150.

> --- given in <u>my</u> [To the registrar of Births Marriages and Deaths] notice and have got this blank notice filled up ready for thee, all except date and signature, and although it is a <u>Preston</u> notice yet with the correction made I think it will answer --- for registering which perhaps thou will attend to tomorrow as thou knows we cant be liberated unless the Registrars certificate be produced at <u>your</u> <u>next</u> Monthly Meeting ---- best to do it soon for fear there <u>might</u> be some unforseen delay.

> P.S. I am sorry to tell thee my dear Mother is quite poorly today with sick head ache, she stayed too late at the house last night, she seems so interested and anxious to get all nice that I can't prevail on her to take it easily.

It was necessary for Friends to file notices in advance with the Registrar, to comply with the legal requirements to ensure civil registration of their marriages.

Jonathan - a methodical man who endeavoured to leave nothing to chance - was meticulous in matters of detail. This trait may be another family characteristic as it has been frequently observed. (Consequently Abbatts may sometimes miss a wider view of life.) The letter's postscript is yet another indicator of the amount of female family labour involved in the wedding preparations.

Mary reports in a short letter that she has duly dealt with 'that precious piece of paper' at the Registrar's office in Garstang; she reassures her fiance that all is well. She is too clearly pleased with her bonnet.

To: Jonathan Abbatt
      Friargate   Preston

Calder Bridge
18 of 5 mo /55 [Friday]

My dearest Jonathan

It seems to me a long time since I wrote to thee and now I must cut thee somewhat short as the postman will be here before long.

That precious piece of paper I sent to Garstang and three weeks today it will be ready for us and as our M.M. is not till the 26 of next month it is all in good time.

I had a letter from my cousin David this morning, he seems to think Robert in rather a critical state; but I hope that with rest he may come round again; Esther poor lass I feel very sorry for her, D. says she is better than can be expected.

Mother has been to Lancaster this week and in the morning if alls well she intends coming to Preston to stay with William.

Thou may tell Jane that Mary's bonnet suits her.

Hast thou found out the sad mistake thou made in thy last? I suppose thou has finished thy letter on a half sheet and has enclosed the wrong half - now this is most sad for me as there is sometimes a <u>tit bit</u> at the end of a love letter; - thou may be sure I had a good laugh; but I will excuse thee if thou wilt send the other part in thine on first day. I must not forget to tell thee to come on 4th day instead of 3rd as we are going out to tea if Mother gets home again in time.

Hoping this may find thee well with love and I will conclude as ever thine,
                                        Mary Dilworth

Jonathan replies enclosing the missing 'fragment' and from his letter it is clear too that both mothers - Elizabeth A. and Ann Dilworth - were hard at work. Ann was probably using the opportunity of helping her son, William, with his house to inspect No.4 Chaddock Street together with her niece Mary Ann (Wilcockson) Ord.

To: Mary Dilworth
      Calder Bridge   Nr. Garstang

Preston
5 mo 20 /55 [Sunday]

My dear Polly

Thine was to hand yesterday morning and famously amused I was at the blunder I have made of which I was entirely ignorant until I read thine so thou may judge how engrossed with <u>care</u> I was, I fancy thou <u>would</u> be amused but to make my last complete I will include the recreant slip [The 'fragment' has been preserved with the letters!] and am glad to correct the portion about my Mother who was just as usual the day before.

I called to see thy Mother yesterday at Williams and found her unpacking a parcel from David enclosing with other matters a present for thee, a most beautiful quilt, thy cousin Mary Ann was there and expect she along with thy. Mother go to peep through the house tomorrow. My Mother has got the carpets made all except the front parlour and one I have yet to get for the back bedroom and kitchen which will soon be done and then we may begin to make things straight.

I was very busy again yesterday and hope this week to do more than ever being our busiest time in the year.

I am still going to endeavour to persuade thy cousin D. to be Groom's Man he can surely manage to spare one day for such an occasion and for <u>such</u> a <u>cousin</u> or else we must consider him shabby when he can <u>make</u> time to be at a Quaker Meeting so if possible we must make no excuse for him, he and we can talk this over along with other matters on fourth day.

If I dont intend to disappoint thee I must close this for the evening having just returned from a very pleasant out to Blackpool so hoping to see thee on 4 day I will once more say to thee an affectionate farewell and am my dearest Mary
           Thine Affectionately   Jonathan Abbatt
                                       17 minutes to 10

Jon.n's day trip was in what became the grand tradition of a 'day out' to Blackpool. Such trips were then in their infancy and a pale shadow of what was to come. By the eighteen sixties the railways were running frequent 'specials' for days out to Blackpool - and other resorts. The Great Exhibition of 1851 had generated many special trains and short outings to London from all over the country and this served as an effective demonstration and incentive, both to railways and customers, to provide trains and day excursions to all sorts of destinations.

Blackpool, as a resort, was unique in that it was a large Victorian town devoted wholly to visitors and the holiday industry. Initially it had vied with Fleetwood before establishing itself as the first Holiday Resort in the country. In the future it was to be compared with Coney Island, and acquired its first pier 1863, to be followed later by two more piers, The Tower, The Wheel, The Pleasure Beach, many theatres and enormous dance halls.

Lancashire Wakes Weeks were cotton town holidays and were the main, early and continuing, source of Blackpool's 'customers', - for that is what the people were. Each Lancashire town had a 'time slot' or week, to avoid saturation of tranportation and of the objective resorts. Victorian Blackpool, for many, typified Victorian Lancashire, in that it was new and always up to date, it gave value for money, had an endless variety of the 'biggest' entertainments while at the same time it was brash and vulgar. For all of this, and from all, it sought money. It came to be called the 'Northern Playground' and achieved and was at its peak, in the years before and after the 1914-1918 war. During Wakes Weeks in these years, fifteen to twenty fully laden special trains per hour arrived in the resort.

The late twentieth century collapse of industry in the North of England, massive unemployment, overseas holidays, and differences in taste and expectations have forced changes in all resort towns including Blackpool.

After Mary's Lancaster visit Jonathan writes on 27th May:

> --- has thou persuaded Ann Jackson to stay with thee as thou was intending and has thou heard from Leeds how Robert Shaw is I hope getting better.
>
> Does thou know I feel quite in high spirits since yesterday we were busy, more so than ever before, I took during the day 36 pounds and altogether in the week almost 53 pounds and when I consider the state of trade generally and find my business still increasing I can assure thee it gives me great satisfaction.

Tomorrow morning we open shop early I think about 6
o'clock as there is often good business done till
noon on Whit Monday although so many are pleasure
seeking and this time there seems to be an unusual
provision to a great extent of Old English Sports
revived such as running in sacks and grinning
through horse collars, and ever so much nonsense of
this kind.

My Mother has now finished making our carpets and is
this week making window blinds and valances and then
next week or soon after they are intending to clean
down again and put all in order, I quite long to see
how all looks when finished.

This afternoon although so very dusty I am engaged
to go out with John Graham; Sam Jesper, and Thos.
Lester being gone to see J. Jesper so I must begin
to fish up an excuse for bringing my scribblings---

An indication of dry, as opposed to wet, road conditions
is given in Jonathan's above concluding paragraph about
his proposed 'dusty' outing. John Graham, with his
brother Michael from Cumberland, had arrived in Preston
in the early eighteen fifties and they and their children
became and remained friends of the Abbatt family. John
Graham junr. and Dilworth Abbatt were also lifelong
friends and in their older age in 1931 John G., then a
distinguished man of letters, wrote the Foreword to one
of D. A.'s books.

Mary writes on the last day in May and is beginning to
worry whether David Wilcockson will be a 'grooms man':

    To: Jonathan Abbatt
           Friargate   Preston

Calder Bridge
31/5/55 [Thursday]

My dearest Jonathan

Many thanks for thy kind letter, as thou supposed I
returned from Lancaster on first day night, after
spending the time very pleasantly with my cousin, we
were at Williams on fourth day and at Aunt's on 7th
day so not much of my time has been spent at Sams.
Ann Jackson could not stay on first day so we have
concluded for her to stay next until 4th day and as
we are already engaged out for tea on 3rd day thou
will perhaps like to defer thy visit till 4th but I

shall hear from thee again before that time. Now
dont thee say, I am always going out remember thou
art not master yet, so I shall do just as I like.

I have not heard again from Leeds so we hope that
Robert is no worse indeed I trust he may be better.

We are busy dressmaking etc. so for that reason thou
must not look for a long letter this time; we have
the dress in hand that I am to be happy in; dear me!
how some folks can come out in their wishing cant
they. I am glad to hear that thou art in good
spirits and that thou hast been busy.

Thy mother and Jane are I hope well. I shall not be
in Preston before I see thee again. We had David
here the other day, and he expects to be with us on
first day, hast thou seen him yet, and what does he
say? I had not any talk with him it was the O.L.
Meeting here that day and we had Ann Jackson. I
think he quite enjoyed our company, we managed to
get 2/6 of him for our dress.

But, I must now say farewell to my dearest friend
and remain his faithfully ·
                                              Mary D.

We hear of the completion of her first (i.e. the second)
visit to Lancaster. Here she had stayed with Mary
(Nichol) and Sam Pickard but had moved around among the
relations seeing William Pickard - Sam's elder brother
and husband of Mary Ann (Walker) on Wednesday and his
mother Jane (Satterthwaite) on the Sunday. N.B. The
Satterthwaite and Walker relations are more than usually
confusing since the families not only were large and
intermarried but often duplicated the same christian
names in each and in succeeding generations.

The editor's fourth great grandmother, Mary Jane (Walker)
Peile, daughter of Isabella (Pickard) Peile and John
Walker has documented remembering Mary Dilworth as
'coming to tea before her marriage'. Mary Jane was then
a girl of eleven.

Unlike her-sister-in-law Emma, Mary's dress 'that I am to
be made happy in' was made at home.

Jonathan's next letter was mostly written in Preston but
completed in Bolton. He sets Mary's fears at rest about
David W. as groomsman; but clearly he D. did not think
highly of Jonathan's waistcoat ideas! Among other wedding
talk we hear of Jane A. as bonnet maker extraordinaire.

Preston
6 mo 2 /55 [Saturday]

My dearest Mary

I purpose being in Bolton and Leigh tomorrow and as it would interfere with my writing I thought I would pen thee a few lines today instead, I hope to ascertain who intend to be at our wedding and shall perhaps be able to say when I see thee on fourth day.

Thou will no doubt see thy cousin David tomorrow when he can no doubt tell thee what we have been talking about, he consents I am glad to say to be Groomsman if he is at the wedding and when I told him I thought of having a white quilted waistcoat he advised me different, so Wilson and Jespers or someone else must find me a silk one more to my mind than any Wood had in stock when I last saw them.

Jane has made Ann Swithinbanks bonnet and for for thy mother as well, and purposes bringing them all when I come on 4th day, I quite think she will soon be a <u>nobby</u> bonnetmaker, but perhaps thou may ask what <u>I</u> know about bonnets? well I must say I am rather presumtious in so freely giving my opinion of an article of ladies dress yet thou sees what ones self esteem leads to for I am so conceited as to think I know when I see a nice bonnet even a friends bonnet.

I got some information from D.W. in reference to our course to pursue in the Lake district and instead of lodging at an Inn he suggests our engaging private lodgings (just the thing I myself thought of) and suggests Mrs. Gibsons with whom the Jacksons stayed as a suitable and comfortable place and engaged to write and ascertain their terms, he will also kindly lend me a guide to the lakes and by adopting this plan (the place being so central) we may make a many delightful excursions all around. These plans meet my views so nicely yet if thou has had any other plan to propose nothing will give me more pleasure than to fall in with it.

I have just taken a cup and saucer to Williams to pack with the other things thy Father has to take, I should have brought them with me on 4th day but I thought thou might want them to show to Ann Jackson etc. I regretted I had not brought them the last time I was over but thou must excuse my negligence.

We are expecting my sister Jane Thomas over here on the 2nd day she is at present at Southport also Maria, the train being so convenient she intends coming around and calling here.

I have been down to the house today and find the seeds are nicely up and in course of another month expect to see the garden looking well filled.

6 mo 3/55 - I had this part written yesterday intending to send by thy father but was prevent[ed] finishing on time and could not get time to post last night.

Thou will be somewhat in astonishment at seeing so smart an envelope [lost] and address too not quite familiar, I am just beginning now at my brother Williams and it is the only one to hand.

We are just about setting out to Leigh so thou must excuse more at present from thy ever Affectionate
            Jonathan Abbatt

A Lake District honeymoon was becoming popular at this time and the Jackson family favoured it, including as we see James and Elizabeth (Labrey) J. of Oakenclough. We soon hear more of the boarding house arrangements.

Jonathan writes again the following Sunday to tell Mary of his appointment as Clerk to his Meeting, of his waistcoat - and of other things:

  To: Mary Dilworth
      Calder Bridge Nr. Garstang

Preston
6 mo 10 1855 [Sunday]

My dearest Mary

Does thou know, today our friends here have appointed me clerk to the meeting I must say they have displayed bad taste and should like to have been excused for I am afraid I shall be a blundering hand at my post.

I went yesterday to the Registrar and obtained the <u>important</u> and <u>precious</u> document I now enclose so I presume we shall be liberated at your monthly meeting on 5th day.

I have been again to Wilson and Jespers and have selected as a wais[t]coat a piece of the pattern enclosed which I thought most suitable and think it will look very well. I have had a letter from my two cousins (not friends) accepting my invitation and well pleased they seem at the prospect never having been I believe to a Quaker wedding.

We have had the company of Joseph Jesper and more at meeting this morning and friends do indeed seem glad to have him amongst us again, we had too a nice address from him this evening and it it really is pleasant to see him looking nicely since his illness, he called in my shop yesterday and was quite chatty, asking about our wedding and indeed they all here seem quite interested, thy cousin David seems again in some <u>little</u> doubt whether he shall be at the wedding or not owing to his engagments but I think he will if possible.

Lizzy Jackson called yesterday and suppose by this thou has got the small parcel which I hope suits thee.

Sam Jesper, James and I ·have been to see the new cemetery this afternoon and were well repaid for our walk there, the grounds are laid out most beautifully with nice gravelled walksinterspersed and seems already quite attractive to the townspeople and how much more so when so many and loved ones are laid low, it is nicely situate, and commands a good view both of town and country for miles around.

I am just about writing to my brother Thomas to ask him how he is getting on with the cards and as I have some other things coming from Bolton to send them at same time so thou will perhaps again be hearkening for my old excuse for coming to a finish.

I hardly know whether I shall come again till next week especially as thou was talking of coming to Preston so soon but perhaps I may hear from thee once thee has some time soon.
I think now Polly I have acquited myself <u>manfully</u> in writing thee <u>so</u> <u>much</u> this evening and feeling I can fully rely on the dear little womans generosity I must once more conclude and with my dear love remain
      Thine truly attached
          Jonathan Abbatt

For three young men in their mid-twenties a casual visit

to a brand new cemetery may seems an odd place to go for a walk. However it was not in the least odd because Victorians, who had immense pride in their towns and cities, were intensely interested in every new civic addition and amenity. Moreover, particularly after the Great Exhibition, they were convinced that everything was getting 'better and better' - and always would do. Fifty years later in December 1905 Jonathan was to be buried with Mary in grave # A 251 of the non-conformist section of this same cemetery.

Mary's last letter follows and it portrays a happy, busy girl - who despite being rushed off her feet - writes an excellent letter in which she remembers everyone.

       To: Jonathan Abbatt
              Friargate   Preston

Calder Bridge
13 of 6 mo /55 [Wednesday]

My dearest Jonathan

Thy truly welcome letter I duly received along with the important paper, which I suppose will set us at liberty, so proceed. I like thy waistcoat very much and have no doubt thou will look very taking but perhaps I shall have so much to think about I may not see it. I am very much obliged for the parcel and note received from Jane, I have been from home or I should have written her a line to thank her for her kindness but she will perhaps excuse me seeing it is rather a busy time just now, the braids suit me very well. I went to Oakenclough on first day and came back the day after, yesterday we were at Thomas Marsdens to tea, Elizabeth and her husband are going to their own home today. I do not hear from Leeds yet I think I must drop them a line again - I think they might one of them write.

I hope if all goes well to be in Preston on 6th day morning by the first train. I may perhaps stay overnight.

What a beautiful morning this is, it is not often I get a letter written before 8 o'clock this however will be the case this morning, Mother is busy in the garden. I am expecting to go to the [Calder] Vale after Meeting to attend the book meeting, I feel as though I should like to be excused but Ann made me promise to be there some time since, it will be rather warm I fancy.

I had almost forgot to wish thee joy of thy new appointment, and hope thou will try to fill it with all order and exactness, thou will begin to feel quite an important young man, indeed one thing and another there will be no coming up to thee after a while.

As I have some little matters to attend to before making ready for meeting I must bring this letter to a close and after sending my love to Jane and thy Mother and the rest I will remain with the same to thy dear self thine in fondest affection

                    Mary Dilworth

P.S. I have forgot to deliver a message to thee from my cousin Mary Pickard she will be glad to see any one of you to dinner on Q. meeting day, or any time during the day.   Art thou thinking of going?

                    <u>Fare thee well</u>

The invitation from her Lancaster Pickard cousins is an indication of acceptance of a 'new' family (the Abbatts) by some of Mary's more staid Quaker relations - and she almost forgot!

Jonathan writes his last courting letter on his normal Sunday, three days before their wedding. It is a happy letter and provides fascinating glimpses of many things - including his past week's business report!

    To: Mary Dilworth
            Calder Bridge   Nr. Garstang

Preston
6 mo 24/55 [Sunday]

My dearest Mary

Well now I suppose thou will look on this as about the last of my courting letters, but not love letters, for I hope these will always continue when we do write, and perhaps too thou may be expecting a good long one from me this time but fear thou will be disappointed for I hope to see thee so soon again I must leave my joy till then.

I was glad to see thy Father again yesterday but he was too much loaded to bring thy collars and so thinking thou might not require them <u>at least</u> before 3rd day I thought I could then bring them. J. Standing thought it best we should have plenty of gloves to choose from so has actually sent 14 doz. and of course all returned that are not wanted; thy Father has perhaps told thee what Isaac and T. Ord think about bringing drivers, and all things considered I think we had better have them and be on the safe side.

Thy cousin David has heard again from Mrs. Gibson who does not seem to make a practice of boarding her lodgers but simply makes a charge of 1 pound for bedroom and parlour and lets them provide for themselves, this I suppose includes cooking and waiting etc. and may suit us well as we may often be from home at meal times.

What a party they are going to get up from Lancaster on 5th day next to Windermere, perhaps we may be seeing some of them, Emma Veevers wants Jane to go but she is already engaged to go with my cousins to Longridge though a trip to Windermere would suit her better I fancy.

I had a first rate week again this past week much more so than ever for this time of year, I took 20 pounds on seventh day alone, and still find some indications of a comfortable and increasing trade which is very satisfactory.

I have almost completed my arrangements to set me at liberty this ensueing week and have got my clothes all ready which suit me well and my waistcoat as <u>ladies</u> would say is a <u>love</u> of a vest so thou may expect to see a rather <u>nobby</u> looking <u>chap</u> to set claim to thee on <u>Wednesday</u> when I hope to see thee all cheerful and gay and as Bessie says with all tears dried up though I have no doubt my dear one feels somewhat anxious getting as the time approaches but thou must bear up well and remember what David says "when thou gets used to it".

I had a call from Wm. Jackson this last week and received from him a most elegant paper machine portfolio or writing case which when stocked with some nice views of lake scenery etc. which we may get when we go there will make a handsome ornament for our <u>drawing room</u> table. I have not yet got my Brothers Report but intend doing so ere I come.

Our cards are now all ready and stamped etc. and Harrison says he is engaged <u>this</u> <u>afternoon</u> with our certificate think perhaps "better the day better the deed".

And so you have been talking over our arrangements with C. Marsden etc about accommodating your company, and have no doubt begun to find yourselves very busy for the coming <u>kick</u> <u>up</u> and will I am sure all rejoice when things have once more resumed their wonted aspect, but as <u>thou</u> <u>would</u> be married it cannot be helped so we must make the best of it. I am in a rather frolicksome mood and if I continue writing more I am afraid thou will think it nonsense so will once more say a short farewell, and hoping to find thee all bright and lively
    I will subscribe myself
        Thine Most affectionately
                      Jon.n Abbatt

Victorians liked people and even on the second day of their honeymoon in Windermere Mary and Jonathan had visitors - 'What a party --- from Lancaster --- ' - who in addition to 'all' of Mary's cousins might well have included Jonathan's sister Jane.

The 'certificate' upon which Harrison was engaged was the marriage certificate which was signed by the witnesses at Calder Bridge. Quaker wedding certificates, which were sometimes works of art, can be invaluable in providing information as to 'who was where when', because it is/was customary for virtually everyone at the wedding to sign.

Jonathan in one of his 'frolicksome' moods gives us a new expression in his last paragraph, namely a 'kickup' for the 'stir' of their wedding.

The provision of gloves for guests, both at weddings and funerals, was an interesting and curious custom. It seems to have originated when shaking hands was the **only** form of body contact at social functions, presumably originally as a hygiene measure. It later became - as at Jonathan and Mary's wedding - a 'favour' for guests, and sometimes one they treasured but did not wear. It was not uncommon for new unworn gloves to be found among the belongings of 'old' Victorians. The custom seems to have died out before the end of the century. Dilworth Abbatt remembered, as a boy, seeing large numbers of pairs of gloves in a bedroom at Calder House before John Jackson Dilworth's funeral in 1870. The guests chose suitable ones and fitted themselves.

The wedding took place at Calder Bridge Meeting House on Wednesday 27th June 1955 - a beautiful, fine clear day.

Unfortunately we know little of the wedding and associated 'stir'. The following partial extract from Paul Beswick's diary is our only source, apart from the list of witnesses who signed the marriage certificate. Paul Beswick (who described Benjamin Abbatt's funeral), because he was a Churchman and not a Friend, would have been a valuable historical witness.

<u>Extract from Paul Beswick's Diary 1855</u>

Entry in right margin reads:
'Jonathan Abbatt's wedding June 27 1855'

26 (June) Tuesday - Fine - This evening went over to Preston Mary and I to Jonathan Abbatt's wedding - company Wm. Abbatt, Thos. A, their wives, Alice and Mary Abbatt with Eliz. and Mary Fletcher got to Preston at 9 3/4 took supper at Mrs. Abbatt's, after which the gentlemen went down to Jonathan's new home at Chaddock St. to sleep - he has it very well furnished everything very complete.

27 (June) Wednesday - 6 Thomas A. and I walked it on Avenue walk - Breakfast at Mrs. Abbatts after which 3 carriages with pairs to Calder Brook [Bridge] the place where the lady lived, the drive was most pleasant, a beautiful agricultural country, fields green and waving trees decked out in their happiest hues, hedges white with good old English hawthorn blossom and the morning clear and fresh whilst our errand itself lent an additional zest for our enjoyment of all, ---

----

'good old English hawthorn blossom' (it must have been a late spring) is the best note on which to leave Jonathan, Mary and their Letters ---

Witnesses* who signed the Marriage Certificate of

JONATHAN ABBATT and MARY DILWORTH

at Calder Bridge Meeting House 27th of 6th mo. 1855

Close Relatives	Friends and Relations
Elizabeth Abbatt	Margaret Kelsall
John Jackson Dilworth	Margaret Rawcliffe
Ann Dilworth	S. Armstrong
Ann Morrow	E. Rooking
John Wilcockson	R. Kelsall
William Abbatt	James Jackson
Jane Nichol	Elizabeth Jackson Junr.
Thomas Abbatt	Elizabeth Arminson
James Abbatt	Margaret Boys
Maria Abbatt	Ann Lewis
Jane Abbatt	Ann Ibison
Jane T. Abbatt	Mary Ibison
Alice Ann Abbatt	Alice Boys
William Dilworth	Jonathan Jackson Junr.
David Dilworth	Margaret Kelsall
Emma Dilworth	John Barrow (Reg. officer)
Alice Abbatt	Sarah Barrow
Mary Abbatt	Sarah Alice Chapman
Ann Fletcher	Ann Wilcock
Elizabeth Fletcher	Jane Atkinson
William B. Fletcher	Alice Altham
Mary Jackson	John Jackson
Elizabeth Jackson	James Paul Beswick
David Wilcockson	Mary Beswick
Elizabeth Dixon	Mary Jackson
Isaac Wilcockson	Ann Jackson
Thomas Ord	William Robinson
Mary Ann Ord	Sarah Ann Jackson
Samuel Pickard	Elizabeth Holmes
Mary Pickard	John Wadkin
Ann Swithenbank	John King
Mary Holmes	Eleanor King
Charles Holmes	Martha Singleton
Jonathan Jackson	Jonathan Jackson Senr.
Lucy Jackson	Maria Atkinson
Mary Ann Holmes	George Mason
Richard Jackson	
Mary Jackson	

----

* Only six of the names above do **not** appear in the letters.

VII MARRIAGE and HEAVEN

Chaddock and Latham Street homes - Final home 'The Poplars', Fulwood - Introduces Annie and Caroline the eldest children - Beatrix Potter - Fortunes of business and 'The Golden Boot' - Eldest son Dilworth succeeds Jonathan - Extracts from Annie's diaries - Dilworth and Frank - Ackworth letters home - Frank 'put in the bank' - Visits with relations - Newcastle Dilworths - Visits to Ackworth - A family Comedietta - 1901 Mary's death - Jonathan's stroke and later death - Mary in Heaven.

After Jonathan's and Mary's marriage there are no more letters. These are replaced by other sources of information such as diaries, letters, many photographs and some personal recorded memories of their close family. In this context 'close family' means - children, nephews, nieces and the odd grandchild!

Perhaps the most valuable source are the papers given to the author by Mary's and Jonathan's eldest son, Dilworth. The nature of this material is documented in the preface and bibliography and it is the author's very strong impression that everything that Dil wrote was accurate, - he had a passion for accuracy and fairness. This adds variety and perspective, and as there are no conflicts, it almost certainly provides a true picture.

The letters tell us of Jonathan's preparations to provide the first home in Preston at 4 Chaddock Street; here they began married life after their honeymoon in the Lake District. This must have left happy memories since they often returned for day trips. The family soon expanded, two girls born quickly - being Annie in 1856 and Caroline in 1857. Despite Jonathan's preparations of the nest it lacked bedrooms and rapidly became too small and the tenancy was short. (The house has now been demolished and the site occupied by a warehouse/Trade Union office).

In 1859 the family moved nearby to a much larger house at 11 Latham Street where Dilworth was born in 1861. (This house still stands though it and the neighbourhood are badly run down). They were very happy at No. 11 but the final move soon followed to an to an even happier house in Fulwood. Here the last child, Frank, was born in 1866.

In 1861 the Freehold Land Society had opened up and developed land in Fulwood, which was then still open country on the outskirts of Preston. (One of the objectives of this development was to qualify more people to vote in Parliamentary elections). In 1865 Jonathan bought a large building plot on the 'Fulwood Estate' and 'The Poplars' (later to become 1 Albert Road, Fulwood) was built. It was here that Jonathan and Mary lived with their family until the ends of their very happy lives in 1901 and 1905. This house was continuously Abbatt owned and occupied (apart from a brief rental in 1916) until the death in the nineteen fifties of Dilworth's widow.

The Poplars, now an office of the U.K. Social Services, is a typical Victorian red brick house; and in the author's youth was a favourite and happy place to 'go to tea'. Both house and garden were free from restrictions and the contents of the house were solid and very Victorian, though in retrospect, simple and operational. There were innumerable books, photographs, albums, papers and in the left front room, a truly enormous Bible. There was also a very large stock of games for children. The prevailing colour downstairs was dark red! Upstairs there were two spare rooms - one believed to have been Jonathan's and Mary's bedroom - with very old decoration in the most delicate lavenders, blues and pale yellows. Whether these were Mary's choice is not known but the probability that it was is high.

Jonathan's and Mary's final commitment to Ackworth was total and all four of their children went early to 'the Hereditary School'. The two eldest, Annie and Carrie, after dame schools in Latham Street (for Annie) and later Higher Bank Road, were sent to Ackworth together at the ages of 12 and 10 respectively. Their time in Yorkshire was happy, particularly for Annie, who later, with Dil, wrote an Ackworth playlet. On leaving Ackworth they were sent to a finishing school run by a Friend - Hannah Wallis - in Southport.

About this time the 1871 census gives us a glimpse of the menage where Jonathan is recorded as a shoe dealer employing in his shop 4 men, 1 woman and 1 boy. There were five members of the household (Jno. (42), Mary (42), Dilworth (9, a scholar), Frank (5) and Sarah Ann Dickenson (20) a domestic servant). The return also gives places of origin (birth), Sarah Ann coming from Bleasdale (near Oakenclough) which suggests on the thin evidence of one sample that Mary preferred country servant girls and that she still obtained them from her own area. We do know, however, that she had 'living-in help'. Annie Elizabeth's and Caroline (Carrie) A.'s absence was due to them being away at Ackworth.

After Southport, Annie and Carrie returned to 'The

Poplars' where they remained for the rest of their lives. They then assumed a common Victorian responsibility for the rest of their parent's lives', looking after them, running the house, entertaining and visiting. At this time domestic help was plentiful, the shop was prosperous and there were many visits and exchange visits to and by friends and relations from Bolton, the Lake District and Staffordshire.

Annie, named Ann Elizabeth after her grandmothers, and always known as Annie, was a prolific, if spasmodic, diarist and letter writer. Prominent among her entries are records of visits with and by her Dilworth and Jackson cousins and their children, including Annie Crichton with Nell, Fred D., Lucy Jackson.

> Jan. 9 1877 Going to Bolton tomorrow, it is jolly to think about it, I always look forward to our visits there, the folks [William and Thomas and their wives and families] are so nice and kind , and make a good deal of us.
>
> Jan. 19 1877 Quarterly Meeting here. Aunt and Uncle Thomas [Abbatt] came to dinner, we numbered fifteen in all. Cousin Willie and B. came, they stayed overnight and some jolly fun we had! I almost feel in love with B. J.A. asked me for my photo.
>
> Jan. 24 1877 had a horrid morning - I told Mamma that Little Aunts [Alice Ann and Elizabeth A.] were not made as welcome as they might be; it made her grieved and I was very sorry and have asked for forgiveness - Carrie and I had been talking about it before. We are perhaps wrong, she is a precious Mother and I wish I had been more thoughtful.
>
> Jan. 26 1877 Uncle William has returned from the continent and has brought six brooches - I wonder if Carrie and I are to have one each. I hope so!
>
> Feb. 19 1877 Mamma had a good night and is much better, thank God. I do pray for her very often. I hope not in vain - I think not sometimes, but I long for more faith. Papa very cross with me, simply for nothing; I felt vexed and went off to bed, I forgive him heartily.

Annie's 21st birthday was on 17th and since there was a clash with Quarterly Meeting the celebration was postponed:

> April. 18 1877 At Manchester Q.M. - saw lots of old

School-fellows. Rufus King, an American Friend, gave a splendid sermon. Had tea at Uncle William's and stayed overnight. Aunt Jane [Abbatt] Adair [from the Lake District] has come and is staying over my birthday celebration.

April. 25 1877 the great celebration of my birthday. Uncles William and Thomas (A) - Little Aunts arrived in afternoon. [her cousins Annie and Fred Dilworth from Newcastle-under-Lyme had arrived the day before]. - 21 sat down to a very excellent tea after which speeches were made and three cheers given; this was too much for me and I broke down completely! Had 'Prisoners Base' and 'Fursey' (? games) in Boothman's field, then came in and had games etc. All except Uncle Thomas stayed overnight - some of us slept five in a room, others went to Uncle James' [A] and to Rockland very enjoyable day.

April. 26 1877 Sat down 12 to breakfast: had a dance afterwards which was great fun.

May. 11 1877 The house almost feels like a hospital and myself as head nurse. Mother and Carrie both in bed and I have a bad cold. Papa cross with me because I filled the tea pot too full.

One of Annie's more interesting diaries is that for 1912 and records a three month stay in Bordighera in the south of France, with her cousin Annie (Dilworth) Crichton and the latter's daughter, Nell. (Annie (D) C. was the eldest child of Mary's brother, David and his wife, Emma.)

Both Annie and Caroline were able, pleasant and entirely adequate women. Like many Victorian girls they never married or left home but instead helped their Mother, (and Father), entertained, visited and did 'good works'.

Caroline, was extremely good looking, vivacious, and 'great fun', she had at least two serious proposals of marriage; but later suffered 'a nervous breakdown' after her parents' death. She recovered and led a normal life being an outstanding cook and dressmaker. She spent much time making Quaker dressed models, and framed collages for considerable profit.

Annie was no less able, but was more energetic, preferring spring cleaning to housework! She was not as pretty - just good looking as we see! She had an immense sense of humour - a 'people person' - was almost universally popular often not knowing whether to laugh or cry. She was an Elder of Preston Meeting, and was for

THE POPLARS – now 1 ALBERT ROAD, FULWOOD, PRESTON, 1987
Built by Jonathan on a 'Fulwood Estate' plot in 1865, this house then became Mary and Jonathan's home for the rest of their lives. (The porch is a recent addition.)

JONATHAN and MARY ABBATT AND FAMILY c.1871
Left to right: Carrie, JONATHAN, Frank, Annie, MARY, Dilworth. (Photo by 'J. Monk, photographic artist, Church Street – opposite the Parish Church – Preston. Negatives kept, copies can be had'.)

THE GOLDEN BOOT
154 FRIARGATE, PRESTON c.1930

A REASONABLE BILL of 1871

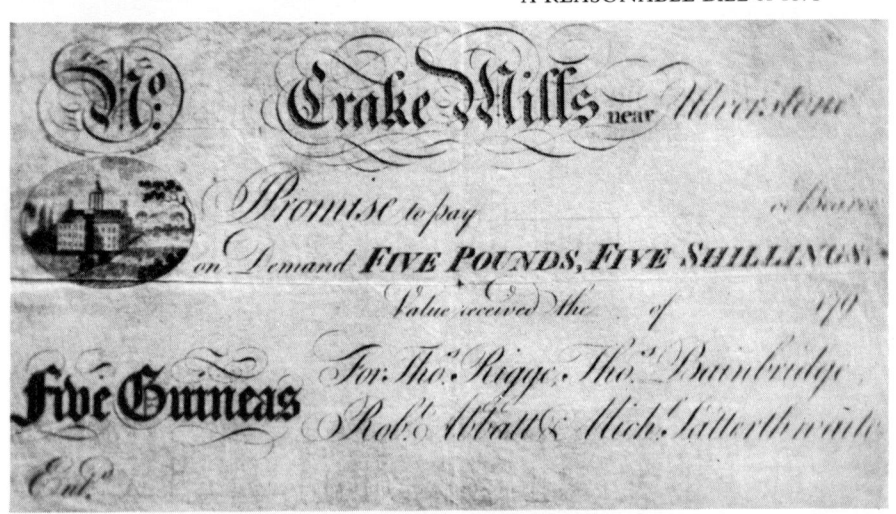

CRAKE MILLS FIVE GUINEA BANKNOTE

The Crake Mills Bank was one of the enterprises which included the Crake Corn Mills near Lowick. Those involved in the enterprises, in addition to Robert Abbatt the Younger – page 12 – were: Thomas Rigge (Robert's brother-in-law), Thomas Bainbridge and Michael Satterthwaite of The Wood, Hawkshead – see Satterthwaite family tree, page 64.

long an active Sunday School teacher.

Annie often stayed with Lilly Satterthwaite near Sawrey, and there she formed a friendship with Beatrix Potter with whom she shared a great concern for poor children. In 1917 - in return for a pincushion - Beatrix sent Annie an autographed copy of her "Appley Dappley's Nursery Rhymes". (This is now in the editor's possession.)

After his marriage Jonathan was in business, as a tenant, at 158 Friargate until 1874. In the early days the business was very prosperous, though in the middle and early eighteen eighties trade began to increase more slowly. This diminution was attributed, by Dilworth A. (by then in the business), in part to hard times and in part to the advent in Preston of the first 'multiple' shoe shop. By this time the family were growing up and the struggle to become established was over. However, he was much concerned by the decline in business and he feared (briefly) for his eldest son's financial future. Nevertheless under Dil's management the business was prosperous until it was sold in 1935.

In 1874 Jonathan built two shops - 154a and 154b Friargate. 154a was occupied initially - until 1880 - by his brother, James and his tailoring business. James' heart was never really in business and his departure, though regretted, was in many ways a relief for those at 'The Poplars'. For Jonathan it meant that his efforts to help his brother were now finally over (as were those of William in the cane business twenty years before). When James left the two premises were merged into one shop. This business known as "The Golden Boot" - complete with a large golden boot above the shop - was continued without interruption until 1935 when it was sold on Dil's retirement. (As a boy the author was often supplied by Dil with his earliest clogs and shoes!)

In 1890 Jonathan largely retired and, in his son Dil's words, 'kindly turned over' the business. For many years thereafter, Jonathan, travelling by horse drawn tram, continued to visit the shop twice a day to chat with old customers and, as he put it, "just to have a smell at the leather". This is not surprising since for so many years the shop, home and Meeting had been nearly his entire life. Indeed, bearing in mind his loquacious nature and the fact that so many of the customers were 'Friends and Relations' this is not surprising, though it must have been irritating for Dil.

After the succession, Dil, who had already worked for twelve years, ran the business for another forty-five bringing his total service in the same shop to over fifty-seven years. In this connection it is interesting to read Dil's own words written near the end of his life:

> Close though my attendance at business was, I do not think I was at any time really happy in it. The business of buying and selling anything I was never fitted for. Still I must not growl for I have been able to keep my end up, and even to save money, though I often feel that many a young man who had had the same advantages which have been mine would have made better out in a material way.

Dil, who should have been a formal academic, was born on 19/11/1861, the day and time of Prince Albert's funeral and this latter event was marked by the firing of an artillery salute in Avenham Park. The salute can have done nothing to delay the birth, and was vividly remembered by, and became one of, Mary's family reminiscences. (She was under an erroneous impression that the guns used were captured from the Russians at Sevastapol). Dil was a healthy boy who initially went to the Preparatory Section and then the main Preston Grammar School before going to Ackworth for three years in 1874. In later life he wrote of himself that he left Ackworth:

> --- at the age of fifteen and half, just when I was beginning to like study: I often regret that I was not sent on to Bootham or elsewhere for I possessed neither the 'nous' nor the inclination to pursue study on my own account.

This latter opinion of himself was unnecessarily self-deprecating, since like his father Jonathan, he was a well read and an exceptionally cultivated man.

The youngest child, Frank, born at 'The Poplars' in 1866, was initially a sickly child and received much of his early schooling from his eldest sister, Annie, before being sent to a private Academy in Great Avenham Street, Preston. At the age of 13 Frank went to Ackworth and was there for the Ackworth Centenary in 1879. The family penchant for letter writing is well demonstrated by a collection of about seventy of Frank's Ackworth letters written to his home, together with a few from Annie and Dil. The following small selection is intended to give a flavour of changes at Ackworth since Mary and Jonathan's time, see Chapter III, and to show a loving affectionate family. The contrast with Jonathan's home is marked; Mary's softer and perhaps more human influence, was of enormous importance and had very largely prevailed. It is interesting, to see the flavour of another generation in the following 'snippets' from 'the children'.

Annie Abbatt aged 13 to Jonathan and Mary.

Ackworth School
5mo 1869

My very dear Parents,

I must now write my weekly letter and I hope it may find you all very well.

On 4th day we had a lecture on India and it was very nice it was given by Thomas Captain Lidbetter* he told us about the plain of Crocodiles and about a monkey that had a chain round its body and it fell into the water about 8 o'clock in the morning, and after a while they saw a whale and they got a harpoon into it and pulled it on board and as a sailor was cutting it open to his great surprise he saw the little monkey's skeleton and Thomas Captain Lidbetter brought it home and put it in the Kendle [Kendal] Museum "poor little monkey".

Sarah R Geldard thinks my writing very nice in my books but I am in a hurry to get this finished so I cannot write very well, she also says my reading is better.

George Satterthwaite has gone to London for a little time.

I am sorry to tell you that M. King has had the face-ache very bad but I think it is a little better today.

Hope you are all very well and I think I have no more to say but with very dear love to you all
    I remain Your loving daughter
                    Annie E. Abbatt

* Thomas Lidbetter (1823-) Sea Captain and Manager of Huntley and Palmer was great great uncle of E. M. (Lidbetter) Sessions - a publisher of this book!

Frank aged 8 to his brother Dil (at Ackworth) then aged 13. Written in a good 'copperplate' with purple ink.

The Poplars
2 mo 6 /74

My dear Brother
I am writing this letter in school-time, [Normal School, Great Avenham Street, Preston] much obliged

for thine received this morning. Last night we had
a toffee joining it was such a long time in boiling
after Alfred went this morning, Carrie got it and
hid his share of toffee.

I found both the guinea-pig that wore lost down the
grate.
            I am
     Thy loving Brother - Frank

                               Ackworth School
                               4 mo 26/79
Dear all

I have got permission to write to you in this class-
room from I. Parsey if I will write four sides of
this sheet full as he was asking me how much I
generally filled, I meant before I asked him to
write more than I did before, but to begin

I think I am doing very well here at school, we are
going to be examined by the committee on Tuesday in
reading.

Now as to my friends, I generally go about with E.
Benson on week days and on Sundays, I walk with a
set composed of A. Binyon, (alias) "Pussy",
Hutchinson (alias) "Hutchy", two Taylors, E.
Benson, (alias) "Badger" and another fellow whose
name I have at present forgotten (but I will tell
you it next time I write if I remember) who, with
all the other fellows agreeing with him says I talk
exactly like Dil and the same fellow says, "I
remember Dil Abbatt well, he used to besock me
awfully when I sat next to him which I did for 2 or
3 years", and another says "his brother says, "his
brother was Dil Abbatt - a jolly fellow Dil".

Joseph Walker is the top of the school. The kite
which Badger and myself made took an awful pitch
down the back of the girls wing and nothing was
saved but the lathes and tassels but we have now got
it rigged up properly again, Badger getting R.
Fields to cut out for him the letters "Hercules" and
such it is christened. It is Pussys birthday to-day
they made a subscription for him, to which I gave
2d, and think they are going to get him a pair of
cricketing-shoes. Would you mind sending a piece of
elastic sewed into something the shape of a garter
as I have lost one of mine.

I had a bad night on Thursday last, first being

broiling hot and next shivering, I had a bad headache next morning and stayed a good part of recess in Matron's room and had a jolly good tea there with Badger though the tea was rather weak.

I find the lessons pretty hard as the boys in the 3rd class have just gone through some roots, and nearly know them off by heart, we are repeating, a lot of roots at once. Has Fred got his summons yet and how is Dil getting on with his Bicycle.
I received your letters last week also a letter from N. Connell.

----

6 mo. 20/79

Dear Parents,

I think this will be the last letter of mine you will get for some weeks to come for which I am very glad, not only for the sake of writing the letters but for coming home which will take place in 12 days and in 4 more I shall expect to see you all here. We have just finished examinations but I do not think I shall get up (many at any rate). Though after the vacation I expect I shall be pushed up a good many places.

I hope we shall have fine weather at the centenary (as we shall) according to predictions which can't be depended upon.

The cause of my not getting up many (as I think I shall) is because I have not been in the clafs [class] long and so have not as much chance as the other boys who have been in longer. If any news comes after I have posted this letter, (which I perhaps shall do so to-night Friday) I shall be able to tell it you <u>verbatim</u> on Tuesday.

One subject Latin, which I expected to do pritty well in got me down pritty well getting only 45 out 100, but my worst subject so far, is arithmetic for which I got 19 out of 100 but our papers have not all been examined and the bottom chaps have not had reading yet.

M. Brunne and Joe Parsey were, one wet Saturday carrying on most cracked in the Gym, both being good athletes and made us soar [sore] and another wet Saturday he drilled a few of us, teaching us to "form a square" which we did in no mistake, for he told us that if the officers or superintendant were to pass by he should like us to stand well, so he told us to 'form a square' which we did not being suspecting when he quietly "hooked it" and left us standing, did we think the officers etc would thing we looked nice but as soon as we found it out we quickly "broke a square" and followed, unsuccessfully, in pursuit. I think I have no more to say so with much love to all, hoping to see you on tuesday, I remain Your Affect. Son

FRANK

The following brief Ackworth letter miscellany are extracts from some of Franks letters to J. and M.

4 mo 26/79

Dear All

Please send me some stamps. I daresay you will think this rather a curious beginning, but I put it now for fear I should forget to put it at the end. --- I joined the workshop yesterday and so shall try to make something though you cant expect anything very 'spert'. I had a very good offer of half a garden --- for 2/3 which we could sell altogether in Autumn for 5/- or even 7/- -----

Your loving son, brother and c. FRANK.

June 15/79
[**N.B.** June not 6mo.]

Dear omnibus
I think when I sit down to write this letter that it is very nearly the last (being the last but one) that I shall write to you.

It was the essay excursion on Tuesday and we had a whole holiday ----.

It was the York match on Friday and we had a half holiday to watch it. I saw Walter there and did not know him when he was in he has grown so, he made a score so that only Coleman equalled him but we beat them after all (wern't we just glad)!

In the morning meeting a lady had a fit (epeleptic I think) and it was very disturbed. we are just in the thick of the Exam. ------

No more so with dear love to omnibus I remain your affectionate Son   FRANK

                                              Ackworth
                                              Aug 9/79
Dear Parents-

I found on going to my boot number to clean my
Sunday boots that you had not packed them and the
shoe-maker told me that J. Airey had given special
orders to bring 3 pairs back though I did not hear
him so that I have only one pair here do you think
it would be worth while sending my sunday boots
soon? If you do would you mind putting one or two
books in that I have not read such as "Pilgrim St."
and "Sturdy Jack" and if you see that red pencil
case of Carries would you mind sending me that
sponge that is in it. if so I would be much
obligated as ------- I now will tell you that I
have got pushed up about 30 in size order and also
to 3rd in my class where I am school sweep. -----

------- The Boys Own paper is not now allowed so
would you mind getting it me in monthly parts from
Aug. to keep until I come home? ----- J. Airey says
that books will cost 3d sending, have I to send it?

Frank's hand writing is now mature. It is interesting to
note the change from the use of numbered date months to
named months and days which begins in 1879 and is
consistent by 1881. The big change however, is that
there are now both summer and Christmas vacations, the
latter were only introduced during Dil's time at school.
This is a dramatic contrast with the NO vacations regime
of Jonathan and Mary's time.
                                              Ackworth
                                              Oct. 30th 1881

Dear Carrie

Tho' I did not forget that thy birthday was today, I
could not well write on Saturday as they were
cleaning out the school room, and so please excuse
it if it comes a little late and accept best wishes
for "many happy Returns". I have very little to
say, but will say what I can and then think that
will be enough.

We had an examination in literature against the
girls on Friday, we for once, beat them. I suppose
I shd have said the second time, because they have
been beaten once before.

They seemed rather bad about it and only gave us a
half hearted clap when the numbers were read out.

J. A. Barranger has given us leave to go walks again so yesterday I went towards Featherstone but only succeeded in getting very wet.

On Tuesday night we had a very jolly lecture from Wm. Johnson who has just come over from Madagascar, he shewed us a lot of things he had brought over, I think it was liked very much by all of us.

As I said I went to Q.M. at Leeds last Wednesday. I enjoyed it a great deal more than usual, because, though the other part of the proceedings was the same, instead of going to the musuem, wh. was getting stale; we went over Kitson's iron works. it was splendid!

We first went through the fitting-rooms, immense places, where we saw the iron parts of engines etc. being planed, turned etc. After going through two or three large rooms of this kind we went into a similar one where brass was worked. Altogether I should think we went through about 12 or 15 rooms each were very large. The most interesting I think was the molding room and the room where the steam hammers were at work. Before we went into those, we saw some Railway engines being put together and some that were going to Japan.

We saw many fly-wheels being made - they did ring under the tremendous blows of the sledge-hammer!

The molding room looked very grimy and black except where they were pouring the iron out of great caldrons and carrying it about in small things between two men.

When they were carrying it or pouring it out of anywhere there was a great shower of sparks wh. fell all about the men who were attending to it - when the iron was under the steam hammer.

As I have no more to say, I will conclude.
      Thy Affect. Bro.
          Frank.

P.S. I suppose this letter will do for all?
P.S.S. Annie B. says that Annie better look out for her cutting her acquaintance if she does not write,
        F.

One of Jonathan's friends, Thomas Mason, was manager of

ACKWORTH COUSINS

A sketch by Dilworth, Marie (and Annie anonymously) first played at Ackworth 1897. The right hand silhouette is Esther (Satterthwaite) Wilcockson, mother of Ann D. and MARY's grandmother, the sketch left by Annie is anonymous.

ANNIE ABBATT c. 1898
In Quaker Dress for her part in 'The Ackworth Cousins'.

THREE GENERATIONS IN THE POPLARS GARDEN c.1900
Front: Geoffrey Peile, Salley (Sarah Maria) [Peile], Philip Dilworth, MARY, Annie Elizabeth, Mary Dilworth, Mary Ann [Enoch], Ruth Enoch.
Rear: Frank, JONATHAN, Carrie (Caroline), Dilworth.

CONEY GROVE, WHITMORE, STAFFORDSHIRE
David and Emma Dilworth's country home – sketch by George Crichton 1883.

the local branch of the Lancaster Banking Company; and after much consultation, which included Frank, it was arranged that the latter should be 'put into the Bank.' He became a bank clerk immediately after leaving Ackworth and due to a mixture of ability, good luck and good timing had rapid promotion. The luck arose from a series of bank amalgamations and the 'timing' was due to the unexpected and early deaths of several of his seniors. He was appointed manager of his first bank at Dalton-in-Furness in 1901 and after Barrow-in-Furness, Ansdell and Preston he retired as a Senior Manager (of the Preston branch) of the (then) District Bank. In 1916 Frank and Sallie went to live at Bruna Croft, Calder Bridge where they remained until their deaths.

In appearance and manner, Frank resembled Jonathan's favourite brother, Thomas. He was a rather fussy, meticulously neat, dapper little man who, like Dil, had a marked and dry sense of humour. Like his Father he delighted in recitations and could, and frequently did, mimic Stanley Holloway's and similar Lancashire stories. Also like his Father and brother and he was a lifelong Liberal and 'The Manchester Guardian' was a mainstay. Despite his humour and basic generosity, Frank followed strict banker's practices with his family and material assistance (e.g. a loan or a house) always had an associated interest rate. Frank remained an active lifelong Friend, and he and Sallie (Sarah Maria [Peile]) always used 'Thee' and 'Thou' at home with their family.

Jonathan and Mary's daily married lives have not been consistently described - though there are many snippets of others' views and remarks, occasional diary comments, and letters. The resulting overall picture is clear.

Visits to friends and relations were common, and judged by the incidence of photographs there was constant interchange and visiting between Newcastle/Whitmore, Bolton and Preston. In the later years of Newcastle, until David Dilworth's retirement to Low Abbey, Wyresdale, this involved primarily the younger generation of cousins. It is interesting in this connection, to observe the very rapid spread of the (initially penny farthing) bicycle and its influence on the young. This influence was probably comparable with the introduction of cheap motor cars in the earlier part of our own century. Young men no longer had to walk from Preston to Garstang and back to do their courting!

An idea of these interchanges can be obtained from the notes and diaries of the participants, i.e. the younger generation. Annie, Dil, Frank, and Sallie in particular,

DAVID and EMMA DILWORTH and FAMILY c.1873
Left to right: Frederic, Ada, Annie, Emma, John Jackson, David, Lillian Emma, Florence.

DAVID DILWORTH'S WYRESDALE HOME – LOW ABBEY, ELLEL 1890
David and Emma retired to Low Abbey from Staffordshire in 1884 and left for 'Hillside', Bowgreave on Emma's death.

STARTING OUT FOR A VISIT FROM LOW ABBEY c.1890
Left to right: David, Florence (Dilworth) Jackson, Lillian (Dillworth) Simpson, Emma, John Jackson.

MARY (NICHOL) PICKARD and her son CLEMENT 1900
Clement married Christine Jackson of Oakenclough. Photograph at Edenbreck, Lancaster.

frequently mention their cousins and others, either as visitors, visitees or as travelling companions. Examples include Annie A.'s three months in France with Annie Crichton (Dilworth) and Nell, and Dil's cycle tours to Scotland and Cornwall with Fred Dilworth and his brother-in-law (Ada's husband) John Crichton. (Fred and Ada were two of David and Emma Dilworth's children).

Though the young people moved about more, Jonathan and Mary remained very close to the the Newcastle Dilworth family and Emma's death in Blackpool in 1894 was very much felt by Mary - as was David's, by Jonathan in 1902, occurring as it did, only a year after Mary's. (One of Jonathan's last duties before his first stroke was to act as one of the executors of David's Will).

Mary retained virtually all of her old friends; and an attractive picture is the photograph taken by Clement Pickard of 'The three Marys' of The Letters. 'Jane Thomas' A. became and remained a close and trusted friend, and there was always, of course, her cousin 'dear David' (Wilcockson). All of these, who were very close, and many more, were shared with Jonathan.

They made many short - perhaps 'day excursions' - to the Lake District of which they were very fond; but probably their favourite outings were to Ackworth. Despite the introduction of Summer and Christmas School holidays they made regular visits to see their children. Doubtless, an important additional motivation was the certainty of reunions with other 'friends and relations' and old schoolfellows, making these 'outs' at their old school doubly nostalgic and attractive.

Towards the end of their lives Mary and Jonathan were particularly and quietly proud of the 'Friendly Comedietta in two Scenes' entitled "Ackworth Cousins" by Dilworth and his (then new) first wife Marie (Enock) of Sibford. This comedy playlet was performed by the authors and Dil's sister Annie (a cooperating author), at Ackworth (and in Preston) on a number of occasions in the later nineties. The upper silhouette is that of Esther Shaw's mother (Ann (Wilcockson) Dilworth's sister and Mary's Aunt).

Jonathan and Mary were both strong characters, and both had strengths and imperfections; they were, however, complementary to one another and when parted by Mary's death Jonathan never fully recovered. As will have been seen in this chapter, an effort has been made to allow their married lives to be portrayed largely through the eyes of others and this necessarily give an indirect and

THE THREE MARYS c.1884
MARY (Dilworth) Abbatt, Mary Ann (Wilcockson) Ord, Mary (Nichol) Pickard. (Photo: Clement Pickard, Edenbreck Lancaster.)

TENNIS PARTY at OAKENCLOUGH 1891
Popular gatherings of this nature preceded the Weddings.

WEDDING of FLORENCE (D) and FRED JACKSON 2nd June 1892
Frederic J. of Oakenclough and 'Flo.' lived at Woodlands. The group in addition to bride and groom includes David and Emma Dilworth, JONATHAN and MARY ABBATT, Mary (N.) Pickard, and the bride and grooms siblings including John Jackson Dilworth. Photograph taken at Low Abbey.

MARY and JONATHAN c.1893.

inferential view compared with the letters which are direct 'first person'. The picture which emerges from this type of treatment is less wooden; it is hopefully liable to many more interpretations by the reader.

Of the two, Mary, though apparently quieter, was much the stronger and more demanding of performance in life and in others. In some things she may well have been a little extreme and near the end of her life Dil said of her:

> --- the early bright, merry disposition of her youthful days at Calder Bridge matured and continued to express itself as cheerful optimism; her own likes and dislikes we sometimes thought were rather pronounced.

Knowing Dil, the author suspects that what he really meant was that there were some people she could not abide at any price. Pretension and pomposity were her particular betes noires. Less creditably perhaps, she preferred 'her own family' (or families), to the Abbatts - but perhaps the Abbatts as in-laws were truly less likeable.

In politics she was apparently (and surprisingly to the editor) mildly conservative; she was always very tolerant of the religious beliefs of others. Mary herself, though a Friend by conviction as well as by birth, was never a particularly active worker in the Society.

Again in Dil's words:

> Like her Mother she was an excellent cook and excelled in housekeeping; many a half sovereign saved from the weekly amount allotted her, she contrived to hand over to her children. Our Father was meticulous to the farthing in money matters and I do not think any of us knew that some in the world were dishonest until we went from home.
>
> He felt that it was demeaning for weekly housekeeping to be passed by hand; instead a weekly envelope was left by Mamma's bed and he insisted that there be a reserve emergency housekeeping purse, containing one hundred sovereigns. This was kept with her keys and diary.

Mary did not have good health in the latter part of her life, though the asthma which had troubled her for so long disappeared after removal of her teeth in her late fifties. She died at the age of 72 in 1905 following an unsuccessful operation for colitis. She is buried with

Jonathan in Preston Cemetery.

The descriptions of Jonathan are shorter and less direct than those of Mary, but the clear picture is that of a staunch Friend concerned almost exclusively with his faith, his family and his business. The virtually total lack of involvement outside the Society is marked - but not unusual in his family - and he was devoted to this family and to his friends. Later in life he became a gardener but this may well have been makework occupation, since reading and letter writing seems to have been his only real outside interest. He had a keen, dry sense of humour, was kind and patient but possessed of a rare but explosive temper; this being apparently reserved exclusively for his nearest and dearest! In 1987 his grandson Philip Dilworth described him as a genial, welcoming old man with a short beard and a 'bristly' kiss. His lunchtime remark to the same grandson was "A little beer to make him feel queer". He remains to the end the Jonathan of the letters.

Jonathan was an Elder of his Monthly Meeting for many years and its Clerk from 1871-74. Throughout his life he was a diligent attender and was always active in furthering the concerns of his Meeting.

In 1905 Jonathan died following a stroke; he was aged 77 and had survived Mary by four years, as well as all of his brothers and sisters. At his funeral, attended by about sixty people, there were Friends from London, Cumberland and Scotland as well as those from Bolton, Preston and nearby. He and Mary are buried in the same grave in the Friends (non-conformist) part of the (then new) Preston Cemetery that he had visited and described in a courting letter to Mary in 1855.

A few days before his death he was asked by one of his daughters:

"Would thou like to see Mother?" Whereupon he used his non- paralysed right hand, in a traditional way that he had learnt at Ackworth, to spell out **'Heaven'**.

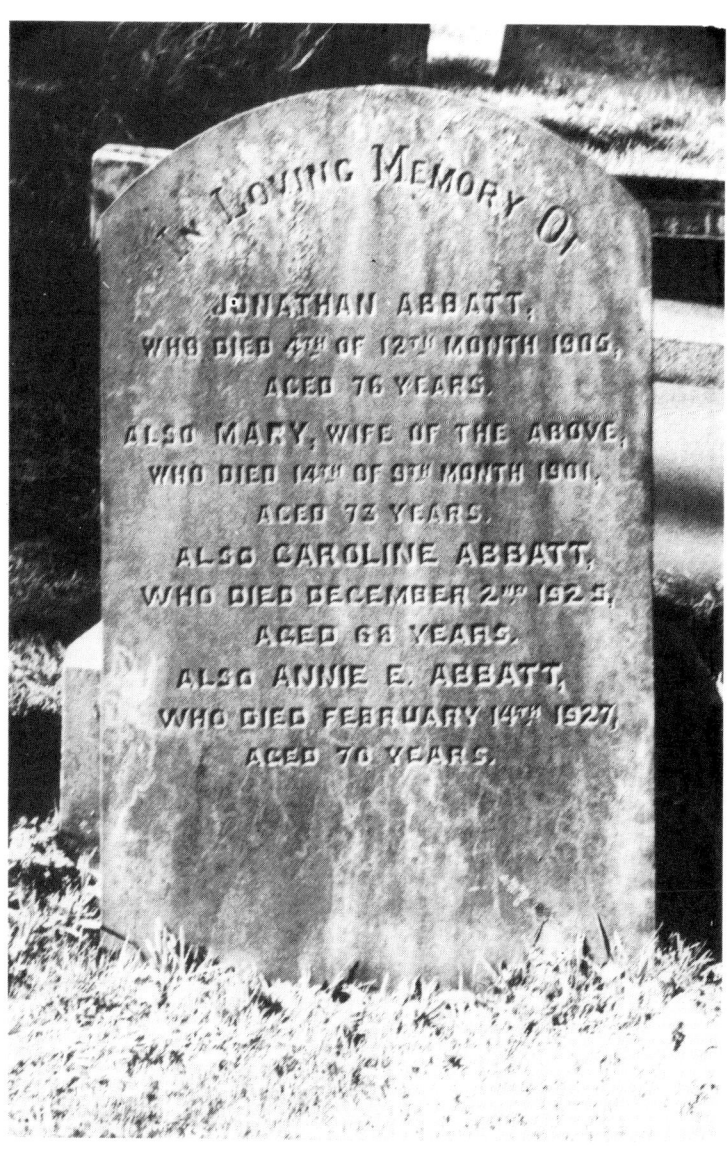

IN THE NON-CONFORMIST SECTION OF PRESTON CEMETERY 1987

EPILOGUE - WHERE THEY ARE

Jonathan and Mary's story ended with their deaths, as does this book; but they, and perhaps the reader, would have wanted to know what became of their families and the places from which they began.

In this century there have been profound changes in society and hence in people, though it can be argued, as do the French, that the more there is change the less is changed. None of the present generations of 'the families' are nailers, flaxmen, hatters or cordwainers, though several including a grandson, a great, a great great, and a great great great grandson are, or have been, farmers. Others have included bankers, journalists, soldiers, sailors, airmen, members of the Friends Ambulance Unit, teachers, doctors, civil servants, engineers, physiotherapists, transport drivers, scientists and academics. As far as is known none has been convicted of major crime, and none has been appreciably decorated, - or appeared in any National Dictionary of Biography. They were and they are Everyman. (Or everyperson).

Dilworth Abbatt married twice, and his two daughters (by his first wife) never married. Both are now dead. Frank had two sons, the elder of these, Geoffrey, who was the author's father, also had two sons, both still living. Of the two, only one is married with issue - two daughters and a son, Jonathan Paul Dilworth. Frank's younger son - Philip Dilworth - is still living in this year of 1987 and has one son and one daughter. There are male and female issue and issue of this issue.

Mary and Jonathan's grandchildren were all educated as Friends, one going to Ackworth and two (Frank's boys) to Bootham. Of their great-grandchildren only the eldest, the author, went to a Friends' school - Bootham - and none married Friends. None of the g.g. grandchildren are Friends. None now live in Lancashire.

Benjamin Abbatt's Bolton cane factory was sold in the nineteen seventies, and a few Abbatts still live in Bolton. William A., who married twice, and Thomas A. have descendants in the South of England, Lancashire and Yorkshire. Many have been to Ackworth, some very recently, and some are still Friends.

The Dilworth family still exists though it is now much attenuated. David and William (Mary's brothers) both 'married out' and both had moderately large families none of whom went to Ackworth. Nothing is known, to the author, of William's issue in the second generation. David's family of seven (three male and four female) is now extinct in the male line - grandson, Robert, died unmarried c.1950. Issue of three of the female families still live. The author is one and through his mother, Millicent, daughter of Florence (Dilworth) Jackson, he has Mary and Jonathan and David and Emma as his great grandparents.

In Canada and the United States the families of James and Ann (Waln) Dilworth, and of Nicholas Waln are numerous and continue to flourish; a few are still Friends. They live in sixty U.S. States and all the Canadian provinces. Many still live in Pennsylvania and some in Philadelphia.

Two of the Jacksons of Wyresdale still live there, though they no longer own the cotton and paper mills in Oakenclough and Calder Vale. Of these two, one family, with issue, now live within sight of Calder Bank or Oakenclough and both are engaged in rural pursuits. Other Jacksons have left the area and Lancashire, many, long ago, and one large and flourishing set of families are Australians. Few, if any, are members of the Society of Friends. While very few Wilcocksons remain, the Kelsalls are still numerous and 'local'.

The Meeting House at Calder Bridge is unchanged. It is in good repair, and remains peaceful and picturesque. It is a now a very small Meeting and many of the attenders are not Friends. The Burial Ground, where graves have recently been rearranged, is now nearly full and it, too, is trim and well kept. In spring the ground is still covered by Mary's carpet of multicoloured crocus and Lent Lilies (wild miniature daffodils). Physically, there are few changes, either here or at Calder House. Many of Mary's contemporaries of the letters were buried here, as were her parents, grandparents, a son, his wife and a grandson and his Jackson/Dilworth wife.

Mary, and Jonathan too, would still feel physically very much at home in 'her country'. There has been major construction of the M6 Motorway, changes in Garstang and the closure of Garstang and Catterall railway station; but all of Mary's country of the Fells, Wyresdale, Barnacre and Scorton are virtually unchanged. In addition to her own home, Calder House, all the houses of her 'friends and relations' not only exist but are little changed.

The fells are unchanged. The grouse, heather and the peewits (plover) are unchanged; the curlews still call.

APPENDIX i.

JONATHAN'S APPRENTICESHIP INDENTURE

BENJAMIN ABBATT and SON

to

JOHN FLETCHER

INDENTURE of APPRENTICESHIP for 7 YEARS.

THIS INDENTURE made the third day of April in the year of our Lord one thousand eight hundred and forty three BETWEEN Benjamin Abbatt of Bolton le Moors in the County of Lancaster, Skip and Basket maker and Jonathan Abbatt his son of the one part and John Fletcher of Leigh in the said County Clogger of the other part WITNESS that for the consideration herinafter mentioned the said Jonathan Abbatt of his own free Will and desires and by and with the consent of his Father the said Benjamin Abbatt testified by his being made a party to and executing these present DOTH place and bind himself Apprentice to and with the said John Fletcher and with him to remain and be after the manner of an Apprentice from the day of the date hereof for and during and unto the full and term of seven years. During all which said term the said Apprentice shall faithfully serve his said Master his secrets keep his lawful and reasonable commands everywhere and at all times obey, hurt or damage to his said master he shall not do or knowingly suffer the same to be done by others but immediately on his privity thereto shall give notice of the Same to his said Master, he shall not embezzle or purloin and of his said Master's Goods or Chattels nor absent himself from his said Masters services without his consent during the said term but on the contrary shall and will behave and demean himself as a true faithfull and diligent apprentice ought to do towards his said Master and all his family during the said term AND the said Benjamin Abbatt doth hereby for himself his heirs executors and adminstrators covenant promise and agree to and with the said John Fletcher his executors administrators and assigns that the said Apprentice shall and will faithfully and diligently in manner aforesaid serve him the said John Fletcher for and during and unto the full end and term of Seven Years next ensuing the date hereof AND ALSO the said Benjamin Abbatt shall and will find and provide the said Apprentice with all sorts of wearing apparel suitable for a person in his degree and station during the aforesaid term AND the said John Fletcher for the considerations aforesaid doth hereby for himself his heirs executors and administrators Covenant promise and agree to and with the said Benjamin Abbatt and as a separate Convenant to and with the said Apprentice to be well and sufficiently taught and instructed in the Art Trade or business of a Clogger in the best manner he or they can during the said term <u>and</u> <u>also</u> shall and will proved the said Apprentice with good wholesome and sufficient meat drink washing and lodging during the said term. In Witness whereof the said parties to these presents have hereunto set their hands and seals the day and year the first before written

Signed sealed and delivered   Benjamin Abbatt
by the said Benjamin Abbatt
on paper they duly stamped   Jonathan Abbatt
in the presence of
                                           John Fletcher
    Henry Glover
    Robt. Bolton

Signed Sealed and delivered by these within named Jonathan Abbatt and John Fletcher in the presence of

                                           Thomas Mulliner

THE PENNSYLVANIA DILWORTHS
Of Thornley and Bradley Hall, Chipping, Lancashire.

```
                    JAMES DILWORTH = Wife
                       Chipping.

        JAMES DILLWORTH(E) (1577-    ) = ISABEL (    -1649)
           Christened. 15/07/1577 Chipping as were all his family.

  John      (1609-    )                Jane      (1617-    )
  Isabel    (1611-1655)                Aveline   (1620-    )
  Alice     (1613-    )                James     (1623-1678)*
  Thomas    (1615-1669)

  AND

        WILLIAM DILWORTH* (1618-1689) = ALICE (    -29/1/1683)
    Yeoman of Thornley; children all Christened at Chipping.  A. a Friend?

  John    (1651-1690) = i    1675 Ellin (HADWEN) m. Ed. Cummings Ho. Arnside.
                      = ii   1689 Jennet (RAINGILL) m. in John D.'s own Ho.
  Ellin   (1653-    ) =           Richard BRACEWELL of Settle Monthly Mtg.
  JAMES   (1654-1699) =      1680 ANN (WALN) (15/08/1654-1710)
  Isabel  (1655-    )
  Alice   (1656-1659)
  Thomas  (1660-1726) = i    1680 Sarah (PEARSON)(1660-1687) A Cumbrian.
                                  m. John Read's ho. Langthwaite, Wigton.
                                  Issue: Two females died young.
                      = ii   1689 Mary (TOWNSON)(1664-1769) of Moorehead.
                                  Sister to Jennet Cragg. m. in Jennet Bond's
                                  House, Woodacre, Wyrsdle. Issue: Dilworths
                                  of Lancaster and Yealand Conyers.
                      = iii 1705 Ann (CORLESS)(DRIVER)(    -1/11/1759)
                                  m. John Bond's House, Dunnishaw, Wyresdale.
                                  ---------------------
```

<u>John Dilworth</u> (1651-1690) - Thornley & Goose Lane, Chipping. Cordwainer.

JAMES DILWORTH (1654-1699) and ANN (WALN) (1654-1710)
James was a Flaxman of Thornley and Bradley Hall, Lancs. Ann, daughter of James and Ann W., born Burrholme, Nr. Whitewell, Lancs. James and Ann married 9/05/1680 in her brother, Nicholas Waln's house, 'Chapel Croft', Newton-in-Bowland. Emigrated to Pennsylvania 1682. Both became prominent Friends (Quakers) travelling extensively in the New and Old Worlds. James died of yellow fever at Bristol, Bucks. Penn. Ann's second husband was Christopher SIBTHORPE by whom she had issue. She died in Philadelphia.

<u>Thomas Dilworth</u> (1660-1726) Carrier of Thornley, Bradley Hall, Chipping and Farmer of Moorhead, Wyresdale, Lancashire.
----

* See page vi. for issue of James (1623-1678) and William (1618-1689), the latter's family were all early Friends. The three Quaker brothers are mentioned in Chapter II.

JAMES DILWORTH (1564-1699) = 9/5/1680 **ANN (WALN) (1654-1710)**

- **WILLIAM (24/5/1681-   )** = **SARAH (WEBB)(1690-   )**
  William b. Thornley, England and died Birmingham, Chester. Pa.

- Richard (8/7/1683-8/8/1749) = Elizabeth (WORRALL)
  Richard b. Middleton, Bucks. Pa., d. Philadelphia

- Jane (18/3/1684-8/5/1701) = Thomas HODGES
  Jane b. Middleton, d. Bristol, Bucks Pa.

- Hannah (25/12/1688-9/6/1709) = John WORRALL
  Hannah b. Middleton, Bucks.

- Jennet (20/3/1690-   ) = 24/3/1710 Samuel BOLTON
  Jennet b. Middleton, Bucks.

- Ann (1692-1692)   b. and d. Middleton, Bucks.

- Rebecca (c.1693-   ) = 31/12/1711 George SHOEMAKER
  Rebecca b. Abington, Montgomery, Pa.

- James (3/11/1695-6/8/1749) = 1718 Sarah (WORRALL)
  James b. Abington, Montgomery, Pa.

WILLIAM DILWORTH = **SARAH (WEBB)**
Sarah b. Gloucester. All children b. Birmingham, Chester, Pa.

- Richard (c.1718-   ) = 1744 Susanna (HOUSE)

- **JAMES (1720-?/8/1769)** = 28/2/1744 **LYDIA (MARTIN)**

- John (1722-c1753)
  = i. Hannah (NAGLE)
  = ii. Hannah* (WOODWARD)(1733-1749)
           *John Woodward's daughter.

- William (1724-1788) = 17/8/1762 Ruth (WHITE)(1748-   )

- Hannah (1726-17/9/1814)
  = i. John MARTIN
    ii. 16/3/1763 John WOODWARD

JAMES DILWORTH = 28/2/1745 **LYDIA (MARTIN)**
James built the first log hut in Dilworthtown.
Charles and Joseph born Concord and all other issue Birmingham, Pa.

- Charles (5/9/1745-11/10/1811) = Mary (TAYLOR)

- Joseph (15/11/1746-   ) = 6/7/1774 Mary (GUEST)

- Sarah (28/6/1748-1812)   Unmarried

- William (1749-   )

- **JAMES (1751-   )**
  = i. Sarah (   )
  = ii. **MARY (BURNSWORTH)**

```
├─ Caleb     (1753-29/9/1835)        = 17/11/1791 Ann (RANKIN)
├─ Hannah    (1755-       )          = 4/11/1775 John PARRY
├─ Lydia     (30/3/1757-  )          = James PYLE
│                                         Lydia a twin.
├─ Letitia   (30/3/1757-1832)        = Edward BRINTON
│                                         Letitia a twin.
├─ Mary      (1760-       )          = i.  William JONES
│                                      ii. John MORRIS
└─ George    (1762-       )
```

JAMES DILWORTH = MARY (BURNSWORTH)
All of their children born Dilworthtown, Pa.

```
├─ Ruth      (1788-1855)             = 1809 Henry MERSHON
├─ THOMAS    (1789-17/9/1873)        = ANN (BLUEGLESS) (8/2/1809-5/10/1852)
├─ Hannah    (1792-       )          = i.  Aaron BAKER
│                                      ii. Jesse PARRY
├─ Ann       (1794-       )          = Isaiah DYSON
├─ Rachel    (1798-       )          = 28/11/1822 Joseph R. BAKER
├─ Ziba      (3/4/1804-13/1/1866)    = 7/1/1829 Deborah Brinton (LEWIS)
└─ Norris    (19/4/1807-7/5/1851)    = 29/3/1836 Martha R. CHARLES
```

THOMAS DILWORTH = ANN (BLUEGLESS)
All of their children born Birmingham Pa.

```
├─ Theodosia M.   (30/10/1828-8/12/1888)    = 1847 Nathaniel E. MORRIS
├─ JOSEPH WALTER  (18/7/1831-25/3/1891)     = i.  5/2/1847 REBECCA L.(PIERCE)
│                                             ii. 9/9.1868 Emmeline (PIERCE) Issue
└─ Sarah          (1833-       ) unmarried.
```

JOSEPH WALTER DILWORTH = REBECCA L. (PIERCE)(22/11/1836-30/11/1865)
All of their children born Dilworthtown Pa.

```
├─ Thomas Howard  (10/9/1857-11/7/1923)    = 20/7/1882 Mary (HOSCH)(1864-1948)
│                                              Issue.
├─ Wilson Pierce  (30/9/1859-18/1/1918)    = 25/5/1886 Rosa Matilda (SIMONS)
│                                              Issue.
└─ Anna Emma      (4/12/1861-24/3/1957)    = 18/12/1884 Mifflin S. HICKMAN
                                               Issue.
```

Note. The spelling of Dilworth varied until the early part of C.19, spelling seems to have been determined by whim. James (1654-1669) John and Thomas all used single and double ls indiscriminately.

LANCASHIRE ORIGINS of the U.S. WALN FAMILY
Burholme and Newton-in-Bowland, Lancashire.

WALN

— Nicholas   Of Heyhead Nr. Newton.

— Edward   Signed James and Ann Dilworths' marriage certificate.

AND

                   RICHARD WALN (1620-   ) = JANE (   )
                   R. of Burholme

— Isabel   = 1666 JONATHAN SCOTT of Newton. M. at 'Widow Waln's House'.

— Jane   i. =   Edward RUDD of Stainmerrow.
            ii = 1677 William BIRKETT of Stainmerrow. M. at R. Wallbank's Hse.

— Ann   i. = 1680 James DILWORTH. m. Nicholas W.'s Hse. Chapel Croft.
            ii = 1702 Christopher SIBTHORPE.

AND

                   NICHOLAS WALN = 1673 JANE (TURNER)
           N. of Chappel Croft, Newton. J. of Windyeats, Newton.
        Married at Wm. Birketts's House Stainmerrow, Nr. Bentham.
       Emigrated to Pennsylvania in 1682 with Penn in the 'Welcome'.

— Jane W.   (1675-   )   B. Chappel Croft, Newton-in-Bowland Lancs.

— Margaret W. (1676-1676)   B. Chappel Croft.

— Margaret W. (1677-   )   B. Chappel Croft.

— Richard W. (1678-   )   B. Chappel Croft.

AND

                NICHOLAS WALN II (168?4-1750) = MARY (   )
                 N. born Neshiminy, Bucks-County, Pennsylvania

              NICHOLAS WALN III (1742-1813) = 1770   (   )
              Nicholas born Fairhill Nr. Philadelphia,
              was a Lawyer, Man of Letters and a Religious.

Nicholas III who has many descendants, some of whom are Friends, once said to an eminent minister who was always late to speak in Meeting:
              Arthur Howell, what's the reason
              Thou art always out of season?
              For when its time to go away
              Thou must always preach and pray!

THE JACKSONS of WYRESDALE

WILLIAM JACKSON (C1630-   ) = 1672 **DEBORAH (CROWTHER)**
Of Brighouse, Yorkshire.
or
JOHN JACKSON ᵧ **ALICE (   )**
Of Northwich, Cheshire.

    JOSEPH JACKSON (1680-1728) = **ANN JAINE (   )(-1717)**
    Of Lanegill, Catterall. Joseph buried Little Eccleston.

    Ann   (-1720)

    Elizabeth (-1720)

    Dorothy (-1723)

    Mary   (-1719)

    and   **JAMES JACKSON (1701-1788)** ᵧ 1723 **ISABELLA (ECCLES)**
    Married T. Edmundson's Ho. Hothersall. Died Spout Ho. Wyresdale.

    JOHN JACKSON (-1795) = **ANN (KELSALL)**
    Issue:**MARY(JACKSON)(1768-1858)**=8/3/1785 **WILLIAM DILWORTH** *

    RICHARD JACKSON (1733-1818) ᵧ 1776 **MARY (PARSONS)** (-1838)
    R. owned Byerworth, b. & d. Spout Ho., b. Lancaster,
                                                      M. bur. Calder Bdge.

    James   (1776-1812)

    Joseph   (1778-   )   = 1817 Deborah (BUTLER)

    Mary   (1782-1806)   Unmarried.

    RICHARD JACKSON (1783-1846) = i. 1817 **ELIZABETH (LABREY)**(-1818) *
                                         No issue.   ii. 1820 **MARY (WILCOCKSON) (1780-1853)** *

    Isabella (1785-1807)   Unmarried.

    William (1786-1787)

    William (1788-1852)   d. Brow Top Quernmore.

    JOHN   (1789-1845)   = **MARGARET (WILCOCK) (1800-   )**   *

    Isaac   (1792-1792)

    JONATHAN (1794-1886)   = **ELIZABETH (ROBINSON)**   *

                    JOHN JACKSON = MARGARET WILCOCK
J. b. at Spout House, d. Calder Bank (Oakenclough).   M. of Old Holly.

Mary   (1826-   )   = Joseph HARLOCK   Issue   *

Elizabeth (1828-1901)   = Richard JACKSON - Her first cousin.   **
                                                   Issue.
Richard   (1830-1889)   Of Woodlands.   No issue.   *

JAMES JACKSON (1832-1890)   = 1854 ELIZABETH (LABREY)(1835-1875)   **

Margaret   (1833-1847)

William   (1835-1836)

William   (1837-   )   = Jane (GARDNER)   Issue.   **

Sarah Ann (1839-1899) = Albert SIMPSON Of Elmhurst. Issue.   *
Albert's 2nd wife = LILLIAN EMMA (DILWORTH) niece of Mary (D) Abbatt.

John   (1841-1843)

                    JAMES JACKSON = ELIZABETH (LABREY)
                        Of Oakenclough (Calder Bank).

Margaret   (1858-1912)   An artist.   Unmarried.

Elizabeth   (1859-1947) =   James William ASHBY.   Issue.

John James (1861-1932) = i. Margueretta (CHAPMAN)   Issue   *
                         ii. Rhoda (   )

Ann   (1863-1933)   An early woman doctor. Unmarried. *

FREDERIC JACKSON (1864-1926) = 1892 FLORENCE (DILWORTH)(1868-1943) **
Florence daughter of David & Emma & Mary (D) Abbatt's niece. Issue.

Harold   (1866-1947)   = 1897 Beatrice (MALLEY) Issue.

Christine Labrey (1873-1938) = Clement PICKARD   Issue.

                    FREDERIC JACKSON = FLORENCE (DILWORTH)
                            Of Woodlands.

MILLICENT (1893-1968) = 1921 GEOFFREY PEILE ABBATT (1895-1978) **
M. and G. were grandchildren of David & Mary Dilworth.   Issue.

JAMES ERIC (1900-1953) = MARY (BLACKHURST)(-1985)   Issue Twin boys.
     Eric of New York and London. Mary of Preston.

JONATHAN JACKSON (1794-1886) ⊤ ELIZABETH (ROBINSON)   *
                Of Spout House and Vale House

- Mary   (1821-1884)   Unmarried.   *
- Richard   (1822-1899)   = Elizabeth (JACKSON) of Oakenclough. Issue. *
- Eleanor   (1824-   )   = Charles J. HOLMES of Warrington.   Issue. *
- James   (1826-1903)   = Martha (LABREY)   The 'Dimples'.   Issue. *
- Joseph   (1828-1894)   = Lucy (HOLMES) once of Calder House.   *
- Ann   (1830-   )   = John HODGKINSON.   Issue.
- John   (1832-1885)   = Hannah Maria (JESPER)   Issue. *
- Elizabeth   (1834-   )
- Jonathan   (1837-   )   = Eliza (WOOD)   Byerworth   Issue.

Notes:

i. The origins and exact identity of the first generation of the Jacksons are not definite. A very strong family 'legend' says they came from Yorkshire before settling in Lanegill, Catterall and Spout House, Wyresdale. They arrived in Wyresdale two to three generations later than the Dilworths.

ii. Richard, John and Jonathan Jackson left Spout House in c1820. Richard and Jonathan built the Calder Vale cotton mill (though Richard soon retired in favour of his younger brother) and John built the Oakenclough paper mill. Both operations were initially combined with farming. The descendants of both are indicated above, those of John being shown more fully than those of Jonathan, as there are more links with the Dilworth and Abbatt families.

iii. Calder Bridge Meeting (situated in Bonds) was always small. The Meeting House was built in 1828 by Richard Jackson assisted by his brothers John and Jonathan. Heavy type above. (Minor modifications were carried out in 1890.)

iv. Asterisks *>** indicate the frequency of mention in the text.

Appendix v.

THE LIFE of TIMOTHY CRAGG, WRITTEN by HIMSELF

I was born at the Chapel House in Wyresdale and was the son of Thomas and Jennet Cragg; on the 2nd day of the 10th month 1658. My parents were of the Protestant religion and I was educated in the same by them, my great grandfather John Cragg came out of some part of Cumberland and was one called a clerk, being one that did the office of a priest, according as it was practiced at that day and time. My Mother's name was Townson of the Townsons of Moorhead who came from Greenbank. My Father died when I was about nine years of age or something more, my Mother married again when I was something past 12. I was, my age considered, desperately bent against her marriage, for he who was her husband was a sort of rough man and one called a Quaker and that was all a cross to me, but now, to look back at my early days, I can well remember both before and after my Father's decease, that my Mother was very careful of me and the rest of her children, that we should live in the fear of God and that we should not swear nor lie nor talk idly and I can well remember when the great Plague was in London and I heard people tell sorrowful tales of it, I being then short of 7 years of age and had so little scholarship, to the best of my memory we had a book called "Creams of Comfort" that had a prayer in it that was to be read in times of pestilence. I suppose so ordered by the Church of England, for it is many a year since I saw the book, I was at that time sore concerned for the for the people of London, so that (as I remember) I read that prayer over many a time.

But O! as I grew in years I grew in wildness and sometimes met with reproof in my bosom, and as I grew older I fell into company with those that spent the first day afternoon playing at pinny prick or shooting with bows and arrows and in the winter evenings playing cards, sometimes all or most of the night long, although my using such games was more for sport than money, but be sure an idle course of life it was, and sometimes we met at the alehouse and ranted and sang there, alas, not thinking of our last end; and though I was preserved from swearing, yet in my young days I had an ill practise of swearing at things that grieved me. I was wonderfully preserved from having any unlawful doings with any woman, and when I have taken a view of my past life I have wondered and admired that I was preserved clear in that matter considering the temptations and opportunities I had to act in that kind of wickedness, I must say this was altogether a mercy, and I have great cause to be truly thankful to the Lord of the same.

One thing I think not to omit and that is about tobacco. When I was about 22 years of age I began to smoke. I may say I was reproved about it in the sense of my bosom many a time and several years, but it being used by my companions and I had got a custom of it, it was a hard thing to leave it tho I met with abundance of exercise about it, at last I would and did give up the use of it extravagantly and used but a little every day, sometimes smoking, sometimes chewing but after a time in a great measure I was forced to give that up too. I ought not to be unthankful that there was so long a day of mercy holden out to me, tho by the way of judgement, for of judgement had not been poured down upon me, I believe I had not left that extravagant use of smoking and chewing tobacco, and many other beloved lusts beside that, yet I think tobacco may be lawfully taken as physic. But to return; about the 26th year of my life I married with Agnes Jackson, daughter of Peter Jackson of Haythornthwaite (died 1692). Her mother's name was Croft of Tongue Moor in Littledale and through marriage we have thus far lived a loving life together, for when my soul has come to praise the Lord, though we met with exercise. We having 11 children and of several of them my wife was, as we thought, likely to lose her life. We have 7 sons and 4 daughters, 2 of these sons were born dead and one daughter died when about 13 weeks old. The rest of them at the time of writing here being through mercy all alive. My eldest son Thomas lived while he was about 30 and 3 months old.

But to return again and take a view of my life past, When I was about 22 years of age I was put on for a Trainland soldier, or one of the Militia, which certainly led to more jollity, joking drinking and such like idleness there was to be seen and heard. We met to be trained yearly for some years and an abundance of idleness there was, tho' through mercy I was preserved from swearing tho' I heard abundance of it. The same year I was married, King James 2nd then ruling, him that was called the Duke of Monmouth came into the southern parts of the Nation and got a considerable army together and then was the Militia called up to meet at Lancaster and being one, must go, for there was at that time there was no hiring or getting off for me, tho' I endeavured it but in vain. But the thing I most feared at that time came upon me and that was taking the oaths of allegiance and supremacy as they were called, for I remember yet, tho' it be many years since, when the greater sort of officers came down to us on the Green Area with the books to swear us, and one of the Officers said to this effect "Now lads, for your oaths" it struck to my heart like a dart. O, then I was strangely down but so cowardly that I did not deny to take the oaths nor any man in the whole regiment that I heard of or can remember but one and he was of our company, yet our hearts were for the Duke, for when the news came that he was taken, there was but a poor shout, for tho' we were so slavish as to swear, yet we could not many of us be so hypocritical as to shout when the poor man was taken and his army routed.

The taking of an oath was sometimes by me shunned when I could well do it, it was so against me, but I was so slavish as to take an oath; then this about Monmouth being over, there passed on about 2 years when I was put on for church warden as they are called, and in that year which was 1687, I came to convinced of many things, and one thing I like here to mention, it was this, we had at that time many workmen, both wrights, masons and some others who were employed in building. They and we were many of us young people and a light and airy course of life we led, some telling great stories and others laughing at them, I was at that time struck in my mind that the course of life we led was not right and often that year, I being a warden, was amongst the priests and saw so much jarring and quarreling when they met with one another, and the covetousness of some of them, that it set me against them, nor was I satisfied with the formality of their worship. Sometimes I went to hear the Presbyterians but it was not very often, but to go when I should have gone to the Bishop's court to be sworn and take the office, and when I went out at the year end, I denied to swear in the open court and the registrar threatened me because I would not swear and there were 2 priests there, one of them would have persuaded me to have sworn, I told them of that Scripture in Mathew about swearing but one of the Priests said it was about vain swearing but to that I could'nt agree. I was likewise strangely alarmed about playing at cards and one night, being at a neighbours house carding (as I remember) for apples and a considerable number of people playing, it happened that the wind rose very terrible and roared extremely, I was struck with this thought that if the house should be blown down upon our heads what would become of our souls (or to this effect) so away out of the house I went and got soundly wet but (as I remember) never carded more.

I was convinced of several things I was addicted to before I left the Church of England. I may say that I was one that was convinced and was driven out by inward judgement for here was a cross to be taken up and tho I had a loving wife yet it was a cross to her for me to become a Quaker, and she had then her Father and one Uncle, who was dead, who in his time had been a great preacher and put forth 2 books, and for one to learn to become a Quaker was much against my wife's relations. I began to frequent the meetings of the people called Quakers in the year 1688, for before that year I had been at but few meetings. A little time after came the Priest to discourse with me (whose name was James Fenton) and abundance of discourse we had about swearing, baptizing infants, abuse in the Bishop's courts and such like things, but when he saw he could not prevail on me to bring me back, he was ever after very bitter against me.

That year came in the Prince of Orange, and I, being a trainland soldier must go, for the Militia was called to meet at Lancaster; so to the head of the company I went, to which I formerly belonged, but did not put on either the red coat or took with me any arms, and when they called the list over, I appeared but was not free to carry arms any longer, and so was freed just there and then. But as I had been baited as I may say with Fenton and some other Priests, so at that time it was my lot to be in discourse with soldiers, as I had been a merry blade amongst them and they were loth to part with me, and abundance of discourse I was forced to have both with relations and neighbours, but all these were small matters to me compared to the inward exercises which I met with.

This is certainly true which I think here to write, that weights and burdens I have at times met with, have been such that when it was evening I could have wished it morning and would need to be persuaded many a time that no man's lot was like mine nor ever man trod the steps I trod. Alas! I am persuaded disobedience was the cause of these things, for want of giving up my too well loved lusts. I wish that those who who may read these lines may give up freely; things were ever so with me that I have thought I could be willing, if it were lawful to have been in the forest part of China in my working clothes and clogs so that these burdens and sorrows I lay under might be removed and that I might have been freed of these terrors that seemed daily to take hold of me. And I often though I could have been willing to have gone found this nation like a poor pilgrim in want and poverty so that I could but have witness peace with the Lord.
 And O! I was so brought down at times that there was nothing I could set my mind upon that would bring comfort to me, for if I had vast quantities of gold or silver or of the most valuable things on earth I could have been willing to have given them all so that I might have peace with the Lord, and that my strength might have been so

renewed that I might have served and worshiped him that is worship and adoration worthy forever.

Now that he or she that may read these lines may not be cast down as I was at times, for I could needs be thinking my condition worse than any man's, Yet I was in and under these judgements brought into such a condition that I had a real love to the sons and daughters of men, and that (w)hole I shall still enjoy and retain the same mind, for when I have heard of evil deeds and actions done by any of the sons of men, let their profession be what it would, I was very sorry for them, for O! it was well done that I travailed for both myself and others and after a mourning time I did at times meet with brokeness of heart and have been a witness of showers of love which have been showered down upon me and a hope raised in my soul that I should continue to the end, and O! it is is the travail of my soul that I may be so assisted that I may continue faithfully to the winding up of all, and the time that my eye must close, this is what I tenderly breathe for.

But some may think it strange that I went through so many difficult passages, I shall answer what I believe was a cause, to wit, disobedience to the call and invitation of the blessed truth in my bosom, and it is my desire if these lines (in time) come to be read by any of the sons of men and especially those that are young in years, that when they are sensible of the movings of the spirit of truth in their bosoms against their vanities of evil deeds, that they join it against these enormities and with practices to which the children of men are too much subject, for I believe if I had faithfully given up my well loved lusts, I had never met with half the exercises that I did meet with, and am further persuaded that if I had met with exercise in order to bring me out of these things, that were contrary to the truth, I could not have loved and pitied the sons of men to the degree that I have done and do desire to do, for though I cannot nor ought not to love a mans bad actions, yet I ought to love and pity the man. So far as I yet see I may draw to conclusion of this piece of work desiring it may not be torn or consumed but read by those into whose hands it may fall and it is the sincere travail of my soul that I may be preserved in hope, fidelity and true fear and in a holy awe while here I may have a day, and the same I wish to other mortal men.

                                                    Timothy Cragg

---

Timothy Cragg, a Minister in the Society of Friends, died aged 84 and according to his nephew, John Kelsall, he: "was in great peace saying death was no terror to him."

APPENDIX vi.

LORD DERBY and the QUAKER

The author has always been amused by this childhood story told to him, (and published), by Dilworth Abbatt.
Lord Derby, who once hospitably entertained Joseph John Gurney and Elizabeth Fry, went to Preston Grammar School with one John Danson of Woodplumpton and Preston. The latter, described as a 'whimmy' (character) by nature was once in financial difficulties and sought help from his old schoolfellow and landlord:
On arriving by foot at Knowsley Hall John rang the bell and asked the footman:
"Is Edward in?" the reply being "Edward, what Edward do you mean?" "Edward Stanley thy master is he in? - for I want to see him". "Go away", said the footman and shut the door. The procedure was repeated and John said: "I want to see Edward very particularly and I can tell thee another thing - I won't go away till I have seen him - so now thou knows" When the Earl heard his name he was admitted and the following ensued:
"Well Edward how art thou getting on?"
"Very well thank you John" - and a warm handshake.
"It is a long time since thee and me went to Preston Grammar School together" - from the Quaker.
It is indeed, John, a very long time," --- "I am very glad to see you, and how are you getting on? And what has brought you over to Knowsley?"
"I am sorry to say" - said John - "I've been getting on vast badly lately, for I cannot raise my rent and that man of thine at Preston says if I don't pay up by next Thursday I'se have to turn out. And so I've come to ask thee to give me a bit longer time to pay up in."
"Well John", said his Lordship, "I suppose you've been a bit unfortunate lately, so I'll forgive you the rent altogether."
"I'm sure I'm very much obliged to thee Edward", - said the delighted Quaker.
"And", Lord Derby added, "I'll tell you what I'll do further. You may live in your cottage, rent free, as long as you do live."
Some time later during Preston Race Weeks the two met again, in Stoneygate, while Lord Derby was on his way to the Cock Pit for his favourite sport. After mutual salutations John said:
"I see, Edward, thou has'nt given up thy silly sinful practices yet!"
To which the Earl replied:
"No, John, I have not, but if all my tenants paid their rents as you do I should very soon have to give up altogether."

BIBLIOGRAPHY and MANUSCRIPT SOURCES

ABBATT, Dilworth.: Quaker Annals of Preston and the Fylde. Headley Brothers, London 1931.
ABBATT, Dilworth.: Assorted mss. and personal papers.
ABBATT, Dilworth, and Marie, [+Annie]: Ackworth Cousins - A Friendly Comedietta in Two Scenes by D. and M., Swarthmore Press, London 1898.
ABBATT, James.: Miscellaneous family and personal papers.
ABBATT, Jonathan.: Personal papers.
ABBATT, Jonathan and DILWORTH, Mary.: Courtship Letters. 1853-1855.
BESSE, Joseph.: The Sufferings of Quakers, 1733.
Burt, Struthers.: Philadelphia: Holy Experiment. Doubleday, Doran and Co. Inc. New York, 1945.
FOX, R. Hingston.: Dr. John Fothergill and his Friends.
FOX, George: The Journal of -- . Editor. John L. Nickalls.: Religious Society of Friends, London 1975. Macmillan, London 1938.
FISHER, Sydney G.: The Quaker Colonies. Yale University Press, New Haven 1920.
HEWITSON, Anthony.: Country Churches and Chapels. Preston 1872.
HEWITSON, Anthony.: Northward. Geo. Toulmin and Sons, Preston 1900.
HOWITT, William.: Description of a walk at Ackworth c.1824. Description dated 1861.
TAYLOR E. A.: The Valiant Sixty. The Bannisdale Press. London 1947.
TREVELYAN G.M.: The Life of John Bright. Constable and Co. 1913.
THOMSON, Henry: A History of Ackworth School. Harris and Co. London, 1879.
THURSFIELD, Rebecca.: Letters from Evesham describing Ackworth in the eighteen twenties. 1878.
VIPONT, Elfrida.: the Story of Quakerism 1652-1952. The Bannisdale Press. London 1954.
WALKDEN, The Rev. Peter: Transcribed/Edited W. Dobson. Preston Chronicle, 1866.
WRIGHT, Maria.: Jennet Cragg: A story of the time of the Plague. S. W. Partridge and Co. London 1877.
WHITTEN, Wilfred.: Between the Cupolas - A 'Light and Airy' record by W. Headley Bros. London 1905.

INDEX

Abbat, 1
Abbat, Robert d.1587, 2
Abbatt and Jesper - Preston, 140
Abbatt Clerks to Fylde Meeting, 12,187,233
Abbatt Family Tree, x.,xi.
Abbatt, Alice Ann 1838-1914, 55,140,196-197
Abbatt, Annie Elizabeth, 241-2, 244,249,255,260
Abbatt, Benjamin 1799-1853, 29, 51,55,60,92,93,95,268-9
Abbatt, Caroline, 120,137, 241,244,250,253,256
Abbatt, Dilworth, 17,71,241, 247-249,256,260,263
Abbatt, Dr. Philip Dilworth, 127,256,264,266
Abbatt, Elizabeth 1840-1886, 139-140
Abbatt, Frank, 117,142,241, 248-254,256-257
Abbatt, Geoffrey Peile, 117, 256,266
Abbatt, George 1685-1761, 7
Abbatt, George d.1631, 2
Abbatt, Henry, 4
Abbatt, Isabel, 2
Abbatt, James 1796-1868, 14, 33,96,155,218,
Abbatt, James 1831-1895, 46, 153-155,213-214,219,234
Abbatt, James of Longridge, 12
Abbatt, James The Weaver, 4
Abbatt, Jane - later Adair, 53, 56,74,80,99,137,149,198-9, 205,224-227,231-232
Abbatt, John I, 2
Abbatt, Jonathan - pictures: xvi.,219,245,256,262
Abbatt, Jonathan Paul Dilworth, 266
Abbatt, Margaret, 23,201
Abbatt, Mary Dilworth, 256
Abbatt, Robert the Elder, 7,11
Abbatt, Robert the Younger, 12,19
Abbatt, Ruth Mary, 256
Abbatt, Thomas I of Alston, 6,7

Abbatt, Thomas, 1827-1897, 68 80,141-3,156,171,209,226, 234,243
Abbatt, Thomas The Dyer, 4
Abbatt, Thomas, 1767-1836, 14
Abbatt, William, 93,103, 135-7,186,218,243
Abbatts in 20th Century, 266
Abboott, 1
Abbott, Geo., 1635-1662, 5
Abote, 1
Ackworth - Beginnings, 34
Ackworth - Admission Bills,35
Ackworth - Dress in 1820-40, 40
Ackworth - Fund Raising, 34
Ackworth - Examinations, 36
Ackworth - Early Curricula, 35
Ackworth - 19C Travel to, 46
Ackworth - Punishments, 37,38
Ackworth - Rules, 36
Ackworth - School Food, 40,41
Ackworth - Societies/Leisure, 38
Ackworth Cousins - Comedietta, 255,260
Ackworth School, 29-46,72,120, 136,140,154,178,194,248-55, 260,264,266
Ackworth Travel Subsidy, 45
Ackworth's Life Preparation, 47
Adair, Gilbert, 67
Adair, Harold of Egremont, 67
Adair, Lucy later Beswick, 67
Adair, Wm. of Cockermouth, 54,55,74
Address - Friends Mode of, 51
Airey, J., 253
Albert, Prince - funeral, 248
American Abbatts - Founder, 6
Ansdell, 257
Anti-Slavery Bazaars, 103, 165-167
Appley Dappley's Rhymes, 247
Apprenticeship Indenture, 268
Apprenticeship Indntre. Jno. A, 47,268-9
Arsenic Poisoning, 154
Aunt Harding, 65,157,167, 172-4,
B.W.T.A. - Womens Temperance, 55

INDEX

Baines, Edward, 65
Baldness of Abbatt men, 221
Barranger, J.A., 254
Barrow-in-Furness, 257
Bay Horse Railway Station, 61
Bear and Staff, Lancaster, 69
Benjamin Abbatt's:
- Death and funeral, 91-94
- Approval Letter, 61
- Letter of Queries, 60,
- Fatal Illness 90-92,
Benson, E., 250
Benson, Isabella, 216
Benson, Robert, 72,225
Beswick, Ewart, 67
Beswick, Paul of Bolton, 92, 93,96,143,239
Bibby, Alice later Dilworth, 152,210
Bicycle and Penny Farthing, 257
Bill - Reasonable of 1871, 246
Bill of Fare at Ackworth, 41
Binyon, A., 250
Birkett, Emmanuel, 92
Bissbrowne, Chris, 6
Blackburn, 126
Blackpool, 152,228-9
Bolton, 54,103-105
Bolton Education Board, 136
Bolton Town Council, 136
Bolton, Robt., 269
Bond, James, 16
Bond, Thomas, 17
Book Meetings, 135,137,168-9, 180,235
Bootham School, York, 67,136, 178
Bordighera, France, 244
Bradbury, J. of Bolton, 142
Bradley Hall, 9,17,18
Bradshaws Railway Guide, 142
Brewster & Burrows, Preston, 195
Bridesmaids, 186,191-193
Brighouse, Yorkshire, 72
Bright, John, 176,178
Bristol, Bucks. Penn., 21,22
Brock Valley - Snape Rake, 47
Brockholes Arms, Garstang, 49
Brown, Mary, 44,47,103,109-110

Brown, Elizabeth 1803-1873, 29, 55,68,92,95,108,132,139, 171,177,180,218,224
Brown, Sarah later Cameron, 82
Bruna Croft, Garstang, 117,121, 257
Brunne, M., 251
Burrow, Richard, 6
Calder Bank see Oakenclough
Calder Bridge F.M.H., 32,33,267
Calder Bridge, Garstang., 1, & everywhere
Calder House, Nr. Garstang, 30-33,112,267
Calder, River, 102
Caldervale - Vale House, 53,54, 67,113,182,235,267
Calling & C. Cards - see Cards
Cameron, William, 82
Cards - Calling and Morning, 213,220,226,234
Carr House, Garstang, 18
Carrick, Margaret, 71,134
Cartmel, Ann of Liscoe, 11
Caton Green, Lancaster, 71
Cemetery - New at Preston, 234,265
Chaddock Street, Preston, 210
Chambers Journal, 54,83,142
Chapel House, Wyresdale, 10, 120,163,277
Chapmen - Lancashire, 9
Charles I, 3
Children of the Light, 3
Cistercians in Wyresdale, 70
Cock Pit - Preston, 282
Collages, 244
Colthouse F.M.H., 12,75
Comedietta - Ackworth Cousins, 255,260
Concern for Privacy, 52
Coney Grove, Whitmore, Staffs., 256
Coney Island, 229
Connel, N., 251
Consent Affair, 201,203-208, 211-214,223,225
Conventicle Act, 20
Coppul, Lancashire, 8
Cousins, 66

285

INDEX

Cragg, Elizabeth (Kelsall), 24
Cragg, Jennet (Townson), 18, 23-6,277
Cragg, Samuel, 207
Cragg, T., Lancaster, 14
Cragg, Thomas, Chapel House, 277
Cragg, Timothy, 24,277-281
Crake Corn Mills, Greenodd, 12
Crake Mills Bank 5 Guinea Note, 246
Crimean War, 119
Croasdale, John, 16
Cromwell, Oliver & 'Seekers', 3
Crossland, Jane of Preston, 164
Czar, 199-200
Dachshunds and Beswicks, 67
Dalton-in-Furness, 257
Danson, John, Woodplumpton, 282
Dates - Quaker, 48
Dates of 100 Years, ix.,
Day Trips, 72,143-145,260
Derby, 154
Derby, Lord, 282
Dialect - English, 101
Dilke Riots in Bolton, 136
Dillworth, Isabel of Thornley, 15
Dillworth, John of Newton, 16
Dillworth, William 1716-1789, 19
Dillworths - Lancaster/Yealand, 18-9
Dilworth Bank of Lancaster, 19
Dilworth Family Tree, xii.,xiii.
Dilworth, Annie later Crichton, 243
Dilworth, David: 30,65,73,86, 120-121,126-133,188-190, 217-218,221,256-258
Dilworth, Florence > Jackson, 117,262,267
Dilworth, Frederic, 120,243
Dilworth, James 1654-1699, 17, 18,20,22,23,267
Dilworth, James of Thornley, 15
Dilworth, Jane > Wilcockson, 71,140,170
Dilworth, John 1651-1690, 6,20

Dilworth, John Jackson, 1,29, 30,33,52,71-72,75,134, 162-3,218,237
Dilworth, John Jackson II, 120
Dilworth, Lillian Emma>Simpson, 73,258
Dilworth, Mary > Abbatt, xvi., 245,256,261,262 - Pictures
Dilworth, Thomas 1660-1726, 17, 18,19,20
Dilworth, William 1618-1689, 15
Dilworth, William 1822-1901, 86,121,133-4,141,189,210, 228,
Dilworth, Wm. 1756-1833-Will:28
Dilworths of U.S.- Family Tree, 267,270-272
Dilworthtown Pennsylvania, 96
Dimples, Garstang, 157
Disastrous Abbatt Generation,13
Disownment by Society of F., 65
Disownment of James A., 12
Disraeli, Benjamin, 59
District Bank, 257
Dixon, Bessie, 111,135,194, 209-210
Dixon, Frank, 84,209-210
Dockray, Thomas, 6
Dolphinholme, 19,61,69-70
Driver, Ann (Corless), 19
Drury, Thomas of Fleetwood, 100
Education and Wm. Abbatt, 136
Enock, Anna Mary > Abbatt, 155, 256,260
Escaped Black Slave, 147,153,
Eskin Lodge, Keswick, 55
Everyman, 2
Excursions - Railway, 149
F.M.H. Wyresdale, 70
False teeth - Elizabeth Abbatt, 218,221,224
Family Tree - Abbatt, x.,xi.
Family Tree- Dilworth, xii., xiii
Family Tree - U.S. Walns, 273
Family Tree - Satterthwaite, 64
Family Tree - U.S. Dilworths, 270,271,272
Family Tree - Jackson/Wyresdale 274,275,276

INDEX

Family Tree - Wilcockson, 63
Fearon, Isaac and Ann, 139,214
Fell, Judge Thomas, Swarthmoor, 8
Fell, Ruth, Langtree Standish, 8
Fellows, Edith, 160
Fields, R., 250
Fleetwood, 98,100,149,152
Fletcher, Ann, 137
Fletcher, Henry, 44,47,117, 216,218
Fletcher, John (1802-1854), 44, 47,92,108-110,177-178, 184-185,268-269
Flounders Institute, 136
Fothergill, Dr. John, 33
Fothergill, Samuel, 11
Fox, George, 2,3,4,16,76
Franklin, Benjamin, 33
Friends School, Wyresdale, 70
Frith, Thomas, 39
Fulwood Estate, 242
Fulwood Freehold Land Society, 241
Funeral of a Friend, 93
Furness Abbey, 70
Furnishing - Acquisition etc., 182,196,215-216,224-225
Fylde Plain, 70
Garstang, 215,226-227
Garstang & Catterall Rly. Stn, 61,102,267
General Meeting at Ackworth, 42-43
Generations - Three Abbatt, 256
Gibson, Mrs. of Windermere, 232,237
Gillworth, Peter - Printer/Pubs, 120
Glover, George, 62,79
Glover, Henry, 269
Glover, Margaret, 161
Gloves - see Wedding, 237-238
Golden Boot, The, 246-247
Goodall, Caroline, 188
Goodall, Dr. Ralph, 190
Goodall, Emma > Dilworth, 73, 110,121,130,188-189,217,221, 258-259

Gornall Family, Preston, 207
Gough, J.B. - TT advocate, 126
Graham, John G., 230
Graham, John Senr., 230
Graham, Michael, 230
Great Bolton, 29
Green, The - at Ackworth, 42,46
Groomsman, 197-198
Grundy, Isaac of Preston, 187
Gurney, Joseph John, 42
Hadwen, Ellin - Arnside, 19
Hadwen, Mary of Arnside, 5
Halley, 2
Harlock, Joseph, 131
Haworth, Jane > Abbatt, 62, 141-2,156,171,209,233,243, 260
Haydock, John of Bogburn Hall, 8
Hayhurst, Cuthburt, 16
Haythornthwaite, Wyresdale, 70
Hessle Common Outing, 39
Hillside, Bowgreave, 120
Holloway, Stanley, 257
Holmes, Lucy > Jackson, 53,54, 56,83,89,111,149
Holmes, Charles 1784-1858, 24
Hope, Barque foundering: 152
Hope, Samuel of Fleetwood, 150
Hothersall, 1
Howitt, William, 39
Hutchinson "Hutchy", 250
Interest/Costs 1853-5, 109-110, 112
Jackson, Agnes later Cragg, 278
Jackson, Ann, 78
Jackson, Christine > Pickard, 208
Jackson, Dr. Annie, 23,78,154, 156
Jackson, Elizabeth, 66,78
Jackson, Frederic, 117,120,262
Jackson, Harold, 117
Jackson, James of Dimples,164-5
Jackson, James of Oakenclough, 70,117,124,129,133,208,235
Jackson, John 1789-1845, 30
Jackson, John, 'Honest Miller', 71
Jackson, Jonathan - Vale House, 30,53-54,77,161

INDEX

Jackson, John James, 70
Jackson, Joseph, 53-54,149,205
Jackson, Mary, 66,77,127, 135,137,161
Jackson, Mary, 1768-1858, 23, 71-72,117,147,189-190,218
Jackson, Millicent > Abbatt, 117,267
Jackson, Peter, of Haythornthwaite., 278
Jackson, Richard, 1743-1846, 30
Jackson, Richard, 1830-1889, 62,108,117,125,160,182
Jackson, Sarah Ann > Simpson, 73
Jackson, William, 113,115,132, 134,137,158,169,237
Jacksons of Wyresdale - Family, 267,274-276
Jane Thomas - see Haworth, Jane,
Jenner, Edward, 115
Jesper, Eleanor, 55,106,143
Jesper, Joseph, 106,158,183, 188,216,234
Jesper,Sam(uel), 105,115,125, 132,134,143,169,181,213-214
Johnson, Wm., 254
Jonathan's Business, 247
Jonathan's First Letter, 48
Jonathan's Last Letter, 236-8
Journal, George Fox's, 18,20
Journal, Timothy Cragg's, 277
Journey to Town - A Poem, 25
Kelsall Family, 267
Kelsall, Ann > Jackson, 71
Kelsall, Elizabeth > Drewry, 90,162-163
Kelsall, Ellen > Glover, 62,68, 79
Kelsall, John 1660-1685,24,281
Kelsall, Joseph, 27
Kelsall, Joseph II, 163
Kelsall, Joshua,68,159-160,163
King James II, 278
King, Rufus, 244
Kings College Cambridge, 67,149
Kitsons Iron Works, Leeds, 254
Knowsley Hall, 282
Labrey, Elizabeth later Jackson, 117,127-128,133,208,235

Labrey, Martha > Jackson, 164-5
Laithes, Janet, 17
Lamb, Hannah Mary > Abbatt, 155
Lamb, Hugh, 165
Lancashire Origin of Walns, 273
Lancaster and Preston Rly., 61
Lancaster Banking Company, 257
Lancaster Castle & prisoners, 8
Latham Street, Preston, 241
Leamington, 218
Leigh, Lancashire, 103,150,184, 232,268
Lester, T, 125
Lidbetter, Captain Thomas, 249
Little, James, 165
Liverpool, 84
London & North Western Rly., 61
London Foundling Hospital, 34
London Mdlnd. & Scottish Rly.61
Longridge, 7,8,216,218
Low Abbey, Ellel, 121,258-259
Low Temp. Lab. Cambridge, 67
Lower Moor Head, Wyresdale, 71
Lucas, Maria >Abbatt,135-6,
Lune Terrace, Lancaster, 211
Lytham, 152,175
Madagascar, 254
Manchester Guardian, 257
Manchester Photograph, 218-219
Marrying 'Out', 76,15˜
Marsden, Thomas, 235
Mary's First Letter, 50
Mary's Last Letter, 235-236
Maryport, Cumberland, 55
Mason, Thomas of Preston, 257
Middleton Hall, Goosnargh, 92
Militia, 278-280
Milner, John Philip, 155
Minister - Society of Friends, 155
Ministry and Travel, 23
Monmouth, Duke of, 278
Moone, John, 18
Morecambe Bay, 70
Morning Visits - see Calling,
Mort, D. Publisher, 120
Mulliner, Ann > Abbatt, 136
Mulliner, Susanna, 193
Mulliner, Thomas, 83,92,103, 107-110,160,193,269

INDEX

Music and Friends, 106
Names - spelling of, 2
Neshiminy, 21,22
New York Tribune 1854, 150
Newcastle-under-Lyme, 65,120,
  215-222
Nichol, Mary > Pickard, 76,95,
  98,116,120,122,126,143,148,
  186,208,259,260,261
North, Mr. Whitmore/Nwcstl,222
Oakenclough - Oaken Clough, 61,
  67,129,133,135,154,235,261,
  267
Oakenclough Paper Mill, 117
Olive Leaf League, 86,160,176,
  180,199
Orange, Prince of, 280
Ord, Boris, 148-149
Ord, Brigadier Rudolf, 148
Ord, Maria, 152
Ord, Sarah, 23,119,123,147-9,
  152,222
Ord, Thomas, 86,133,139,141,
  153,237
Ortner in Wyresdale, 27,29,30,
  31,120,210
Pales School and Mission, 155
Palmerston, Lord, 59
Park, Sarah of Skelwith, 65
Parker, Alexander, 16
Parker, Ann, 17
Parliamentary Petition 1659, 4
Parsey, I., 250
Passing the Meeting, 191-193
Pearson, Sarah - Tiffenthwaite,
  17,18
Peases of Darlington, 55
Peile, Sarah Maria > Abbatt,
  117,256-257
Pen-y-Bont, Radnor, 155
Pendle Hill, vii.,4,16
Penketh, Friends School, 178
Penn, William, 21
Pennsylvania Dilworth Family,
  270-272
Pennsylvania ffriends, 16
Philadelphia - early, 21,22
Pickard Family, 137
Pickard, Clement, 208,259
Pickard, Daniel, 194,205

Pickard, Esther > Shaw, 151,
  175,177,182,207,226-227,
Pickard, James, 208
Pickard, Jane, 161
Pickard, Mary, 236
Pickard, Samuel, 95,137,
  148,151,175,231
Pickard, Sarah, 161
Pickard, William, 231
Plague in London, 25,27,277
Pleasure Beach/Blackpool, 229
Pontefract Cake - origins, 39
Pontefract, Yorkshire, 33
Poplars, The, Fulwood, 242,245
Post Office - Faith in, 85
Potter, Beatrix, 247
Prescott, Cheshire, 84-85
Preston 'Old' F.M.H., 219
Preston - First pipe water,1,11
Preston and Wyre Railway, 152
Preston Chronicle, 65,120
Preston Court Leet 1653, 4
Preston Gas Company, 65
Preston Grammar School, 248,282
Preston Market Day Bye Laws, 65
Preston Market Place 1814, Fpce.
Preston Petticoat Alley, 11
Preston Race Weeks, 282
Preston Review, 65
Preston, 154A & B Friargate,247
Purchase of Business, Letter,
  107-108
Quaker Answer, 86
Quaker Bonnet, 217,224-227,231
Quaker Wedding Coat & Tailor,
  217
Quaker's Root & Pendle, Fpce.,xii
Queen Victoria & Albert, 152
Quernmore, 24
Quilliam, Catherine E., 54
Rabies, 190
Rawdon School, 136
Read, John of Langthwaite, 18
Red Scar, Nr. Preston, 132
Relations - Quaker, 76
Ribchester, 1
Rigby, Elizabeth > Brown, 92
Rigge, Agnes of Swarthmoor, 12
Roads - mid 19th Century, 197
Rosagreave Farm, Thornley,15,18

INDEX

Rowlandson, Janet, 208
Rowton Brook, Quernmore, 24,26
Ruabon, N. Wales, 47
Salthouse, Alice & Johnny, 134
Salthouse, T., 126,181
Samplers and Ackworth, 41,140
Sand Tray - for writing, 72
Sandlehurst, Mrs. of Preston, 133
Satterthwaite Family Tree, 64
Satterthwaite, Edward of Wray, 65
Satterthwaite, Esther, 65
Satterthwaite, George, 205
Satterthwaite, Jane > Pickard 231
Satterthwaite, Lily, 247
Satterthwaite, Michael, 148
Satterthwaite, William, 152,230
Sawrey, 247
Scotch Rebellion in 1745, 27
Seekers, 3
Sennals, Amelia, 65,74,195
Sevastopol, 248
Shaw, Robert, 151,226-227
Shorrocks, Dr., 154
Sibford, 155
Sidcot School, 93,136
Simpson, Albert of Elmhurst, 73
Skating at Penwortham, 189
Skips - Lancashire Cane, 92
Slaidburn-in-Bowland, 16
Sleep in Meeting, 158
Smallpox, 115-116
Smith, Alice of Longridge, 14
Society of Friends, 3
Southport, 233,242
Sports - Old English/Whit, 230
Spout House, Wyresdale, 30
St. Helens, 81
Stafford and Castle, 160
Staffordshire Advertiser, 120
Standing J. of Preston, 237
Stockport, 155
Stoke Friends Meeting, 122
Strike at Dolphinholme 1839, 69
Submission, to Pennsylvania, 21
Swindlehurst, Mary Kelsall, 163
Swithenbank, Thos, Wyrsdle, 173
Swithenbank, John, 81

The 'Flags' at Ackworth, 46
The Dimples, Garstang, 61
The Three Marys, 66,261
Thee & Thou - origins of:, 133
Theft of Boots, 153
Thompson, George M.P., 189
Thompson, Thomas, 24
Thown, Ann, 16
Three Jacksons/Spout House, 30
Thursfield, Rebecca, 41-45
Tower - The at Blackpool, 229
Townson, Jennet - See Cragg
Townson, John/Chapel House, 18
Townson, Margaret - Moone, 18
Townson, Mary/Chapel House, 18
Tuberculosis, 168
Tukes - William and Esther, 33
Two 'Obstinate Quakers', 5
U.S. Dilworth Family Tree, 270-272
Unlawful Quaker Meeting, 17
Vaccary, Forest of Wyresdale, 69
Vale House, Caldervale, 53-54, 67,113
Veevers, Emma, 223,237
Veevers, R., 78
Victorian Hours of Work, 222-3
Waithman, Agnes, 5
Waithman, William, 205
Wakes Weeks, 229
Walkden's Diary, 7
Walker, Joseph, 250
Walker, Mary Ann > Pickard, 231
Walker, Mary Jane > Peile, 231
Walker, Thomas, 65
Waln Family of Lancashire, 273
Waln, Ann (Dilworth), 17,18,20, 21,22,23,267
Waln, Nicholas - Newton & Penn., 20,21,22
Waln, Nicholas tertius, 22
Walne, Richard, 17
Wedding - at Woodlands, 220
Wedding and Funeral Gloves, 237
Wedding at Low Abbey 1892, 262
Wedding Witnesses, 240
Welcome - to Pennsylvania, 21
Whitmore - Coney Grove, 256
Whitmore & Station, Staffs. 221
Whittakers Frm, Thornley, 15,18

INDEX

Whooping Cough, 188-190
Wilcock, Ann, 198
Wilcockson Family, 62-63,267
Wilcockson Family Tree, 63
Wilcockson, Ann > Dilworth, 1,
   29,30,33,52,71-2,133-4,228
Wilcockson, David, 65,72,80
Wilcockson, David junr., 66,77,
   98,102,119,144-145,195-196,
   208-209,228,231-232
Wilcockson, Esther > Pickard,
   255
Wilcockson, Isaac junr., 62,77,
   126,141,189,237
Wilcockson, Isaac senr., 65,
   120,187
Wilcockson, Jane > Nichol, 98,
   134
Wilcockson, John, 140,240
Wilcockson, Mary Ann > Ord,
   86,120,138-139,141,145-146,
   148,153,175,222,260-261
Wilcockson, Mary > Harding,
   65,157,167,172-174,198
Wilcockson, Mary > Jackson,
   97,141-142
Wills - of Dilworths, 28
Wilson and Jesper, Preston,
   155,213,232,234
Wilson, Charles, 214
Winder, William/Tarnbrook, 27
Windermere, 72,143-144,
   232-233,237-238
Wither or Widders, Thomas, 6
Witnesses to Wedding, 240
Wood, William, 81,158-161,218
Woodlands, Garstang, 61,117,
   121,154
Worldliness, 180-181
Worsted 'Works', Dolphinholme,
   69
Wray Nr. Hornby, 65
Wright, Isaac of Bolton, 83
Wright, Maria - author, 25
Wyresdale - Everywhere and:
   17-28,68-72
Wythney Abbey, 70
Yellow Fever, Philadelphia, 22